God Be with the Clown

God Be With
THE CLOWN
humor in american poetry

Ronald Wallace

University of Missouri Press

Columbia, 1984

Library of Congress Cataloging in Publication Data

Wallace, Ronald.
    God be with the clown.

    Includes bibliographical references.
    1. Humorous poetry, American—History and
criticism.   2. American wit and humor—History
and criticism.   I. Title.
PS309.H85W3   1984   811'.07'09   83–17671
ISBN 0–8262–0422–8

For poetry permissions, see pp. 233–35.

for my family

Acknowledgments

I would like to thank Professors Barton Friedman, Hamlin Hill, Laurence Lieberman, Sanford Pinsker, and Walter Rideout for their generous support and encouragement. I would also like to thank the American Council of Learned Societies (in conjunction with the National Endowment for the Humanities), the Graduate School Research Committee of the University of Wisconsin-Madison, and the Wisconsin Foundation (with a grant from Norman Bassett) for financial support that enabled me to write this book.

R.W.
Madison, Wisconsin
November 1983

Contents

A little Madness in the Spring
Is wholesome even for the King,
But God be with the Clown—
Who ponders this tremendous scene—
This whole Experiment of Green—
As if it were his own!
                    —Emily Dickinson

This world is a solemn place,
with room for tennis.
                    —John Berryman

I

Introduction
Take Care to Sell Your Horse before He Dies

1

Randall Jarrell once wrote that "critics have to spend half their time reiterating whatever ridiculously obvious things their age or the critics of their age have found it necessary to forget."[1] If our age or the critics of our age have forgotten neither comedy nor poetry, they do seem to have forgotten comic poetry, or at best chosen to ignore it. While a number of critics, prompted by a new comic energy in such American novelists as Barth, Hawkes, Nabokov, Kesey, Coover, Heller, and Jong, have turned their attention to comic fiction, they have turned their backs on comic poetry. Walter Blair and Hamlin Hill, for example, refer only in passing to poetry in their otherwise excellent survey of America's humor from Poor Richard to Doonesbury.[2] And Louis D. Rubin, lamenting the exclusion of any discussion of comic poetry from his lengthy collection of papers on American humor, can only ask, "And isn't there much humor in Walt Whitman, and considerably more in Emily Dickinson? . . . Can one view Mr. Apeneck Sweeney with entire gravity, or even J. Alfred Prufrock?"[3] With the exception of Daniel Fuchs's book on Wallace Stevens, Richard Chase's suggestive study of Walt Whitman, and Constance Rourke's pioneering survey of a number of American poets, there are no extended examinations of humor in our poetry.[4]

Several reasons might be cited for this critical neglect. If our age or the critics of our age have found it necessary to forget comic poetry, it may be because often very little seems funny about our age. Given two world wars, a major depression, racial tension, nuclear proliferation, and ecological and economic crises, it isn't surprising that critics would emphasize Eliot's waste land over his practical cats, Whitman's and Dickinson's dark nights of the soul over their ebullient antics, Robert Frost's warnings over his witticisms, Wallace Stevens's solemnity over his slapstick. In the popular mind, comedy has come to be associated with comic relief—a momentary escape from the sad reality of our lives, a necessary, but ultimately minor, diversion. While the arrow through Steve Martin's head, or the almost demonic possession of his happy feet, may at some deep level

1

say something about our absurd humiliations or about our sense of powerlessness in the face of unknown and uncontrollable forces, most people would characterize his humor as daffy and zany, but ultimately frivolous or trivial.

Critics, sharing this cultural view and reluctant to downplay the importance or seriousness of poetry at a time when enough other forces are already denigrating or ignoring it, have virtually dismissed its humor. If it is permissible for the novel to be "impure," incorporating elements of comedy, somehow poetry must remain true to its high purpose, its emotional intensity, its serious exploration of our painful lives. Poetry that refuses this mantle of high seriousness, preferring to don motley, has erroneously come to be equated with light verse.

If asked to name America's best comic poet, many readers might cite Ogden Nash. "The Chipmunk" is a fairly representative example:

> My friends all know that I am shy,
> But the chipmunk is twice as shy as I.
> He moves with flickering indecision
> Like stripes across the television.
> He's like the shadow of a cloud,
> Or Emily Dickinson read aloud.[5]

There would be little disagreement about the humor of this poem or about Nash's reputation as a comic poet. In addition to being an affectionate portrait of a chipmunk, capturing that cute animal's endearing nature, the poem is a self-portrait of Nash himself—the shy, self-deprecating, literary, lovable humorist. It is also a half-serious critical commentary on the poetry of Emily Dickinson. Nash suggests that a chipmunk is like a flickering TV screen or the shadow of a cloud; that is, a little shy, a little substanceless, a little vague or confusing. If Dickinson is like a chipmunk, then she, too, is a little nervous, substanceless, vague, confusing. While Nash's light-verse poem does have a somewhat serious point to make in passing, the major thrust of the poem is just amusing and forgettable lighthearted entertainment. He certainly doesn't intend any metaphysical speculation about the nature of shyness or the relationship of the human to the natural world, nor does he mean to start a debate about the strengths and weaknesses of Emily Dickinson, topics that might be better treated in "heavy" verse.

Ogden Nash wasn't alone in his interest in light verse. Many of our best "heavy" verse poets have tried their hands at it. Emily Dickinson herself, prefiguring Nash's assessment of her, wrote a number of poems like the following:

Bee! I'm expecting you!
Was saying Yesterday
To Somebody you know
That you were due—

The Frogs got Home last Week—
Are settled, and at work—
Birds, mostly back—
The Clover warm and thick—

You'll get my Letter by
The seventeenth; Reply
Or better, be with me—
Yours, Fly.[6]

This poem is a good example of Dickinson as chipmunk—cute, clever, affectionate, and minor. And it is the kind of poem that is often trotted out as an example of Dickinson's humor. The revelation of the letter writer's identity at the end of the poem is a pleasant surprise, and it is indeed humorous to think of a correspondence between a bee and a fly about the coming of spring. Although the hint of loneliness and longing in the poem adds a slightly deeper emotional resonance, there is not much serious import here—just the shadow of a cloud.

Like Emily Dickinson, Robert Frost was given to "fooling," raising eyebrows with such occasionally stinging examples of light verse as this couplet from *In the Clearing*:

Forgive, O Lord, my little jokes on Thee
And I'll forgive Thy great big one on me.[7]

The couplet recalls Emily Dickinson's

We apologize to thee
For thine own Duplicity— (#1461)

Indeed, many of our best poets are represented in the recent *Oxford Book of American Light Verse*, proving that they, at least, have seen no antagonism between humor and poetry.

Rather than adding respectability to humorous poetry, however, the fact that these poets have all consciously written light verse has tended to rigidify the distinctions between the comic and the serious. In a paper delivered at the 1962 MLA convention, Reed Whittemore lamented the distinction between light and "heavy" verse. Whittemore speculated that the *New Yorker*, probably the most prestigious and influential magazine market for a poet during the last fifty years, must have two rooms for selecting poetry—one in which Ogden Nash, Phyllis McGinley, and John Updike were chosen, and one in which "good, high-minded Brooks-and-Warren organisms suitable for dissection in any classroom in the land" were chosen. "Two distinct rooms, one for light and one for heavy verse. . . . That this division seems rather characteristic of modern American verse in general . . . is unfortunate, for both parties." Whittemore then went on to explain the phenomenon in terms of the American psyche: "In general Americans seem to have some nasty scruples about mixing business and pleasure. Serious is serious and funny is funny, work is work and play is play; and if somebody comes along and starts to mix these neat categories, then there's trouble."[8] Whittemore is here echoing W. H. Auden's similar observation about American attitudes toward poetry: "For a 'serious' poet to write light verse is frowned on in America and if, when he is asked why he writes poetry, he replies, as any European poet would, 'for fun,' his audience will be shocked."[9]

Thus, in the popular mind, serious poetry has been equated with solemnity, humorlessness, and intellectual difficulty, while comic poetry has been equated with light verse. Recently, however, the situation for comic poets has changed. The market for light verse has virtually dried up, leaving our contemporary poets with no outlet for their comic impulses. There is only one room for poetry at the *New Yorker* now, a room that frowns on light verse. Edward Field, in his introduction to a recent anthology of contemporary American poetry, describes the altered attitude:

> It might be useful to point out some changes poetry is going through in its work of exploring language and feeling; one healthy change in the last twenty-five years is that poetry is no longer divided into "light" and "serious." It was considered daring of Oscar Williams in his postwar anthology to put a section of light verse even at the end of the volume. And humorous effects at that time put poetry into this category, though there were poets, of course, considered "lesser," like Odgen Nash, who specialized in it. If it was fun it couldn't be real poetry. Today this division has almost ceased to exist. Humor is a major element in many poets' bag of tricks, though it is not widely understood that the shock in a poem that leads to laughter is as important as the shock that leads to tears and can be equally serious.[10]

With the distinction between "light" and "serious" verse breaking down, it is perhaps easier to see clearly the pervasive presence of humor in the work of our most serious poets. In fact, humor has been one of the defining elements of American poetry from Whitman and Dickinson through Frost, Stevens, and Berryman, to David Wagoner, Maxine Kumin, and other of our best poets writing today. While these poets may not properly be labeled "comic poets," comedy has informed their style, their characteristic methods, their themes, and their general assumptions about art and modern life. This study will examine the neglected comic element in American poetry, placing it in the rich and distinctive traditions of American humor. For American poets, comedy has been not only a device; it has been a characteristic way of looking at the world. From Dickinson's witty intellectual questioning of self and society, and Whitman's humorous celebration and affirmation of America and the individual, through Stevens's heady antics, Frost's Yankee humor and dark laughter, Berryman's self-ridicule and exposure, and our contemporary surrealists' versions of an America gone pleasantly mad, comic poetry has questioned atrophied beliefs, criticized an imperfect society, and exposed the pretensions and frailties of the self and others, while also providing laughter as a weapon against chaos and despair in a world that seems increasingly indifferent and absurd.

2

If the ominousness of our social and political world, and the misleading distinction between light and serious verse, may in part explain the critical neglect of comic poetry, there are other obvious problems facing the student of comedy. Even if one accepts the premise that many of our best poets are also humorists, how does one decide when a poet is being funny and when he isn't? Since humor is often relative to a particular time and place, isn't it possible to see humor where it was never intended?

It would not be difficult, for example, to argue that the first important American comic poem was Michael Wigglesworth's "The Day of Doom," a best-seller first published in 1662.[11] The poem employs a ballad form like that used for great comic effect by Lewis Carroll in "The Walrus and the Carpenter." It boasts numerous comic rhymes like "fail'd them" and "ail'd them" reminiscent of Alexander Pope. And it draws portraits of two comic characters, the poet and his God.

Throughout the poem God is pictured as a wet blanket and a boor, the traditional comic refuser of festivity who must be expelled in order that freedom and love may flourish. Wigglesworth wants only to worship God, but God seems bent on preventing that worship at all costs, for which Wigglesworth praises him. God is a termigant, exerting all of his energy to prevent his worshippers from worshipping him. He is full of the absurd kind of reasoning that Job finds so maddening in Frost's satiric version of the biblical parable, *The Masque of Reason*.

Midway through "The Day of Doom," for example, God responds to the children who died in infancy, who argue that they are suffering for Adam's sin and not for their own:

> You sinners are, and such a share
>   as sinners may expect,
> Such you shall have; for I do save
>   none but mine own Elect.
> Yet to compare your sin with their,
>   who liv'd a longer time,
> I do confess yours is much less,
>   though every sin's a crime.
>
> A crime it is, therefore in bliss
>   you may not hope to dwell;
> But unto you I shall allow
>   the easiest room in Hell.
> The glorious King thus answering,
>   they cease, and plead no longer.[12]

This passage bears remarkable similarity to the final two stanzas of "The Walrus and the Carpenter":

> "I weep for you," the Walrus said:
>   "I deeply sympathize."
> With sobs and tears he sorted out
>   Those of the largest size,
> Holding his pocket-handkerchief
>   Before his streaming eyes.
>
> "O Oysters," said the Carpenter,
>   "You've had a pleasant run!
> Shall we be trotting home again?"
>   But answer came there none—
> And this was scarcely odd, because
>   They'd eaten every one.[13]

The walrus weeps for the little oysters, and sympathizes with them "deeply," while putting them in his stomach. God feels pity for the children who died in infancy, and sympathizes with them while putting them in hell. Thus it is scarcely odd that God's children, like the oysters, "cease" and "plead no longer." Both oysters and children are effectively silenced by the Walrus's and God's superior "reasoning." Seen from a modern, and essentially romantic, perspective, God becomes a rather malevolent comic villain—humorless, self-contradictory, petty, and mean—and only Wigglesworth, the fool and masochist, can love him for it.

That Wigglesworth's poem was neither originally intended to be funny nor perceived to be so does not detract from its comic impact today; in fact, it may even intensify it. But it does raise a central perplexing difficulty for a reader of poetry. If "The Day of Doom" were written today it would clearly be a parody or a satire of certain outmoded versions of God and human nature. Written in 1662, the poem becomes for us a curiosity, appealing for its historical value and for its unconscious humor. Indeed, the editors of a modern reprinting of the poem point to its unconscious humor as one of their justifications for reprinting.

With Wigglesworth's poem it is fairly easy, given the historical context, to determine the poet's serious intentions. Similarly, chronology prevents a possible misreading of a poem by H. C. Bunner:

POETRY AND THE POET

[A Sonnet]
(*Found on the Poet's desk*)

Weary, I open wide the antique pane
I ope to the air
I ope to
I open to the air the antique pane
　　　　　　　{ beyond?}
And gaze { across } the thrift-sown fields of
　　wheat, [commonplace?]
　A-shimmering green in breezes born of heat;
And lo!
And high
　　　　　　　　　　{ a? }
And my soul's eyes behold { the } billowy main
Whose further shore is Greece　　　　　strain
　　　　　　　　　　　　　　　　　　　again
　　　　　　　　　　　　　　　　　　　vain
[Arcadia—mythological allusion.—Mem.: Lemprière.]
　I see thee, Atalanta, vestal fleet,
　And look! with doves low-fluttering round her feet,
　Comes Venus through the golden { fields of? } grain
　　　　　　　　　　　　　　　　 { bowing }

(*Heard by the Poet's neighbor.*)
Venus be bothered—it's Virginia Dix!

(*Found on the Poet's door.*)

Out on important business—back at 6. [14]

One might suspect that this poem was intended as a parody of T. S. Eliot's "Ash Wednesday," echoing as well his "Waste Land" drafts with their classical allusions and notes by Ezra Pound.[15] Although the poem is funny in itself, since Bunner died in 1896 such parody is unlikely.

In both Wigglesworth's and Bunner's cases it is clear that the humor is in the reader and not in the poem, with historical changes adding a dimension of unintentional humor. In numerous other instances, the situation isn't so simple. Walt Whitman is an obvious case in point. Since the publication of *Leaves of Grass*, Walt Whitman's sense of humor has been in question. If portions of "Song of Myself" seem hilarious to us now, for example, can we be sure that the hilarity isn't merely our own, and not Whitman's? How we read Whitman will depend, in part, on our assumptions about comedy and comic poetry and on our knowledge of the traditions of American humor upon which Whitman was drawing. William Michael Rossetti, in his 1879 anthology *Humorous Poems*, voices the prevailing assumption about Whitman's lack of humor. "In fact, the absence of humour from the writings of Whitman—treating as he does of every possible aspect of life, work, scene, and association, in America—is a noticeable point, and may even be said to argue one limitation in his enormously capacious and sympathetic mind."[16] And Jesse Bier, in his more recent study of American humor, reiterates that "Walt Whitman . . . is the one major figure unredeemable to comedy . . . a man totally devoid of a sense of humor."[17]

Richard Chase approaches Whitman with radically different assumptions. In a book labeled "aberrant" by Willard Thorp, Chase argues not only that Whitman had a sense of humor, but that his work is fundamentally and essentially comic.[18] And Randall Jarrell insists that Whitman's comic sense is one of the "ridiculously obvious things" that critics have found it "necessary to forget." Which assumptions should govern our reading of Whitman? When Whitman practically invites us to dine on him, as the Walrus dines on oysters—"There is that lot of me and all so luscious"; "I find no sweeter fat than sticks to my own bones"—can we label him humorless?[19] When he goes about measuring gods against himself and finding them wanting,

> Magnifying and applying come I,
> Outbidding at the start the old cautious hucksters,
> Taking myself the exact dimensions of Jehovah,
> Lithographing Kronos, Zeus his son, and Hercules his grandson,
> Buying drafts of Osiris, Isis, Belus, Brahma, Buddha,
> In my portfolio placing Manito loose, Allah on a leaf, the crucifix engraved,
> With Odin and the hideous-faced Mexitli and every idol and image,
> Taking them all for what they are worth and not a cent more
> (sec. 41, p. 75),

do we keep a straight face? When he describes himself as a house—"sure as the most certain sure, plumb in the uprights, well entretied, braced in the beams" (sec. 3, p. 35)— or insists, "I find I incorporate gneiss, coal, long-threaded moss, fruits, grains, esculent roots, / And am stucco'd with quadrupeds and birds all over" (sec. 31, p. 59), can we, must we, laugh?

The problem of unconscious or unintentional humor can lead to serious misreading. Looking for humor, a reader risks becoming what Meredith called a "hypergelast," one of those "excessive laughers, ever-laughing, who are as clappers of a bell, that may be rung by a breeze, a grimace; who are so loosely put together that a wink will shake them." [20] William Bysshe Stein provides an obvious example. Most readers familiar with Emily Dickinson's "After Great Pain" would agree that it is a serious, painful poem about grief and its aftermath:

> After great pain, a formal feeling comes—
> The Nerves sit ceremonious, like Tombs—
> The stiff Heart questions was it He, that bore,
> And Yesterday, or Centuries before?
>
> The Feet, mechanical, go round—
> Of Ground, or Air, or Ought—
> A Wooden way
> Regardless grown,
> A Quartz contentment, like a stone—
>
> This is the Hour of Lead—
> Remembered, if outlived,
> As Freezing persons, recollect the Snow—
> First—Chill—then Stupor—then the letting go— (#341)

According to Stein's comic reading, the poem is not a response to grief and loss at all, but is rather a satire of nineteenth-century churchgoing. The poem recounts the "dilemma of a hypocritical churchgoer who is under constraint to maintain her mask of solemn piety," and her "great pain" results from her "studied effort to sit quietly and erectly while pretending to pay attention to a long-winded sermon." The "wooden way" and the "quartz contentment" refer to the speaker's feet having fallen asleep. At the end of the poem, forced to stand for part of the ritual on her painful feet, the speaker finally gives up the effort and sits down, but so, fortunately, does everyone else, saving her from embarrassment. According to Stein, the "deliverance by the wooden way of perfunctory faith devolves into a grotesque joke." [21]

The unfortunate equation of comic poetry with light verse, and the problems of unconscious humor and unhappy misreadings, all stem from

a single central source: the inadequacy of standard comic theory to deal
with poetry, especially lyric poetry. Dorothy Parker, herself a talented
comic poet, tried to come up with her own definition or description
of humor, but "every time I tried to, I had to go and lie down with a cold
wet cloth on my head." [22] Turning to standard comic theory would have
brought Parker little relief. Most comic theories derive from drama, and
while they may adapt fairly well to the concerns of fiction, they may seem
not especially useful for describing the lyric poetry that has characterized
American verse. Rooted in romantic melancholy, and lacking drama and
fiction's shadow connection with the "real world," the connection that
enables us to see ourselves in a comic light, lyric poetry may seem incom-
patible with humor. Further, since the lyric so relentlessly explores its creator's deepest hopes, fears, joys, sorrows, and anxieties, it is natural to
suspect occasional unconscious humor, resulting from the poet's necessary self-indulgence.

And yet, dealing as it does with the individual, his unchanging human
nature, his exalted self-consciousness, his excesses and deficiencies, his
pretensions and ignorances, his self-disgust and self-love, the lyric may be
especially amenable to comedy. Paul Claudel implies as much in his description of farce: "La farce est la forme exaspérée du lyrisme et l'expression heroique de la joie de vivre (Farce is the extreme form of lyricism and
the heroic expression of the joy of life)." [23] Similarly, Robert Frost insists
on the kinship of lyric poetry and humor:

> The style is the man. Rather say the style is the way the man takes himself;
> and to be at all charming or even bearable, the way is almost rigidly pre-
> scribed. If it is with outer seriousness, it must be with inner humor. If it is
> with outer humor, it must be with inner seriousness. Neither one alone
> without the other under it will do. [24]

Although few American poets have theorized about humor, most have,
like Frost, affirmed their need of it. Walt Whitman wrote humorous newspaper columns in response to popular taste and boasted, "I pride myself
on being a real humorist underneath everything else." [25] Emily Dickinson
enjoyed her reputation as a wit, writing humor for the Amherst paper,
crafting comical valentines to friends, and incorporating jokes into many
of her letters and poems. Wallace Stevens emulated the clown and harle-
quin. John Berryman analyzed the humor of Stephen Crane and adapted
the characters and patterns of the minstrel show to suit his own auda-
cious needs. More recently, Richard Wilbur insisted, "I don't trust anybody who isn't capable of nonsense and moments of collapse into ridiculousness." [26] And James Wright, when asked what value he placed on
humor in poetry, said, "I could not do without it." [27]

Howard Nemerov has gone so far as to suggest that structurally, at its deepest level, lyric poetry is virtually indistinguishable from the joke: "So in seeking to identify, if possible, something of the quality of expressiveness called 'poetic' you might start, not with the sublime, but down at the humble end of the scale, with such things as that, with . . . jokes."[28] Drawing liberally on Freud's study of jokes and their relationship to the unconscious, Nemerov proposes that both poetry and jokes, at bottom, seek to make "fault in this world's smooth façade." And they do so in structurally identical ways: economy of materials; a sudden reversal of the relations of the elements; an introduction of absurdity, but an absurdity that in the context of the former sense makes a new and deeper sense; a revelation of the hidden; a build-up and release of tension. Indeed, one of Nemerov's joke samples ("How do you catch the lions in the desert? Answer: you strain off the sand, and the remainder will be lions") seems structurally to resemble one of Emily Dickinson's comic recipes:

> To make a prairie it takes a clover and one bee,
> One clover, and a bee,
> And revery.
> The revery alone will do,
> If bees are few. (#1755)

Nemerov's conclusion is that many characteristics of lyric poetry are intensifications of jokes: "The compound of expectation with a fulfillment which is simultaneously exact and surprising, giving to the result that quality sometimes thought of as inevitability, or rightness."[29]

While Nemerov's argument is partly playful, and while we may not want to follow it to its extreme logical conclusion, it does usefully suggest that the lyric and the comic may derive from the same emotional burst of intensity, focusing and releasing the same exuberance. As the poets themselves have suggested, humor is an essential defining characteristic of their poetry, and no reading that ignores it can hope to approach validity.

Although the standard theories of comedy are inadequate for describing comic lyric poetry, Bergson, Meredith, Freud, Frye, and others can contribute to our understanding of the form.[30] Bergson's idea of comedy as an "élan vital," a means of keeping people human by ridiculing their mechanical tendencies and deflating their pretensions, describes one element of American comic verse, an element clearly evident, for example, in the satires of Dickinson and Frost. But Bergson's insistence on a necessary "anesthesia of the heart" fails to conform to our experience of American humor in which the profoundest clowns (and poets) always engage our sympathies and emotions. The comic lyric poem is often intensely emotional, demanding deep feeling, whether of pain or exhilaration.

Meredith's "Comic Spirit" is more charitable, demanding no anesthesia of the heart. But, like Bergson, Meredith sees comedy primarily as comedy of manners. Society is a norm of right reason and sound sense to which the aberrant individual must be made to conform. Laughter is a corrective with the goal of reforming the ridiculous person and integrating him into society by teaching him to shun what is gross. While Meredith's theory helps to explain poems like Wallace Stevens's "The Comedian as the Letter C" and some of David Wagoner's humorous pieces, and while Meredith's description of the "Comic Spirit" in some ways resembles Whitman's description of the "great poet," much American poetry refuses to shun what is gross, preferring to celebrate it and revel in it.

Thus Freud's theory of comedy as a means of overcoming repression by releasing hidden or repressed psychic energies helps to explain poets like Walt Whitman or John Berryman who celebrate the irrational, the asocial, the chaotic, in an effort to displace a repressive social order. For Freud, and for these poets, society isn't a norm at all but a potentially destructive force, a reflection of Bergson's "mechanical encrusted on the living."

If Bergson and Meredith are useful for seeing humor as a civilized tool for correcting excess and aberrance, and Freud is useful for explaining the more primitive celebration of the absurd, the irrational, and the farcical, Northrop Frye's archetypal theory is useful for seeing comedy in a religious frame as a mythic affirmation of rebirth, regeneration, harmony, and love. Frye's emphasis on the recurrent character types and plot patterns of comedy helps describe the comic personae of certain lyric poems and the dramatic movement of other more narrative poems, while focusing their essential affirmation. Selectively drawing on these and other theorists while keeping a careful eye on the poetry itself, we can begin to clarify the role humor has played in American verse.

3

According to Aristotle, tragedy is structured primarily on plot, and comedy on character. Most discussions of comic fiction and drama thus focus on characters, on their relationships with each other and with their societies. If lyric poetry seems short on characters, it always boasts at least one, the speaker of the poem, and it is with this speaker that I would like to begin. While there is, of course, a wide variety of personae in American poetry, they, like the characters of comic drama, often resemble one of two comic types, the *eiron* and the *alazon* of Old Comedy. According to Northrop Frye, the *eiron* is the witty self-deprecator and artist, the person who pretends to be less than he is, while the *alazon* is the boastful fool and impostor, the person who pretends to be more than he is. These two archetypal characters, in various shapes and guises, appear in much American comic poetry.

The first critic to analyze the function of these characters in American humor was Constance Rourke. In her brilliant pioneering study, Rourke argued that America "has produced two major patterns [of comedy], the rhapsodic and the understated," patterns reflected in two typical characters of nineteenth-century American humor, the "backwoodsman" or "Kentuckian" and the "Yankee."[31] The backwoods character, the Kentuckian, the "ring-tailed roarer," was a frontier type—boastful, adventurous, uncouth, raw—a bigger-than-life figure who claimed kin with alligators and hurricanes, drank clouds and ate whales.[32] An American version of a medieval hero, he was mighty, muscled, and godlike, living outside conventional norms and habits.

Walt Whitman clearly felt an affinity with this figure from popular humor, calling himself "a Kentuckian" and making the kind of boastful claims typical of the ring-tailed roarer:

> I inhale great draughts of space,
> The east and the west are mine, and the north and the south are mine.
>
> I am larger, better than I thought. (p. 151)

And again:

> My ties and ballasts leave me, my elbows rest in sea-gaps,
> I skirt sierras, my palms cover continents. (sec. 33, p. 61)

With his brag and swagger and bluff and blab, Whitman had, as Constance Rourke notes, "turned the native comic rhapsody, abundant in the backwoods, to broad poetic forms."[33]

Numerous passages in "Song of Myself" reflect Whitman's adaptation of this popular voice of American humor. For example, in one of the humorous Davy Crockett legends, "The airth had actually friz fast on her axes, and couldn't turn round; the sun had got jammed between two cakes o' ice under the wheels." Davy's backwoods solution to this cosmic problem is typical of the genre. He shoulders a bear and beats it against the ice until hot oil flows and frees the sun, whereupon "the sun walked up beautiful, salutin' me with sich a wind o' gratitude that it made me sneeze. I lit my pipe by the blaze o' his top-knot, shouldered my bear, an' walked home, introducin' people to the fresh daylight with a piece of sunrise in my pocket."[34] Whitman tells a similar tall tale in "Song of Myself."

Flaunt of the sunshine I need not your bask—lie over!
You light surfaces only, I force surfaces and depths also.

Earth! You seem to look for something at my hands,
Say, old top-knot, what do you want? (sec. 40, p. 73)

Crockett is big enough to free the sun from imprisonment, carrying light
from its top-knot to his friends. Whitman is so big he doesn't even need
the sun (being brighter himself), though the earth, with its top-knot,
needs Whitman. Dionysian spirit of largesse and exuberance, Whitman,
like the other comic characters in this tradition, measures himself against
the gods and finds the gods wanting.

Whitman wasn't the only poet to adapt the character of the ring-tailed
roarer to his own peculiar needs, nor was he the last. Although Wallace
Stevens, for example, might have been more refined and cultivated than
Whitman and the other backwoods characters, he nevertheless used their
characteristic devices—exaggeration, hyperbole, comic juxtaposition—
adopting the pose of the boaster. If Stevens's "Hoon" is more comfortable
having tea at his "palaz" than Whitman would have been, he no less reflects this kind of frontier comic spirit:

Out of my mind the golden ointment rained,
And my ears made the blowing hymns they heard.
I was myself the compass of that sea:

I was the world in which I walked, and what I saw
Or heard or felt came not but from myself;
And there I found myself more truly and more strange.[35]

Similarly, Allen Ginsberg's "howl," while more raw than Stevens's "hoos"
and more negative than Whitman's "yawp," reflects the same frontier
egotism. And a residue of the Kentuckian's exuberant comic claims is apparent in James Merrill's recent trilogy, which boasts such tall-tale devices
as talking atoms and communication with the dead. Finally, the tradition
retains its hold on popular comedy as well, the most obvious example
being Muhammad Ali, who in his heyday as boxer-poet laid claim to the
territory once staked out by Mike Fink and Davy Crockett, promising to
"float like a butterfly, sting like a bee."

But if the backwoods character often comically affirmed American
strength and possibility, it also served a different, more ancient purpose.
Prior to 1850 the backwoodsman was clearly a hero. The humorous tall
tales associated with him were a way of coping with a threatening and
large country, while asserting confidently that nothing was impossible for
America and Americans. After 1850, the character begins to lose power

and prestige. Mike Fink, for example, is bested by a woman, a preacher, and a Sunday School student.[36] This new role for the backwoods character, that of boastful impostor and fool whose claims are undercut and exposed, resembles that of the familiar *alazon*. It is this kind of comic character to which Meredith refers when he talks about comedy's function of reforming folly through ridicule. Rather than praising exaggeration and aberrance and deviation from socially accepted codes of behavior as Whitman and other backwoods humorists had done, literary comedians began to deflate the pretensions of such characters, either expelling them from society or reforming and reintegrating them.

This more conventional use of the *alazon* protagonist wasn't really a new development in American humor; it had been an important strain all along. John Quincy Adams, for example, sixth president of the United States and a competent versifier as well, drew on this tradition for his comic personae. In "The Wants of Man" Adams adopts an *alazon* protagonist, piling up a Whitmanesque catalogue of exaggerations designed ultimately to undercut the protagonist rather than celebrate him. While the hyperbolic speaker of the poem boasts about his wants, about how he requires so much more than ordinary mortals, Adams stands behind him deflating his absurd requirements:

> "Man wants but little here below,
>   Nor wants that little long."
> 'Tis not with me exactly so,
>   But 'tis so in the song.
>
> My wants are many, and if told
>   Would muster many a score;
> And were each wish a mint of gold,
>   I still should long for more.[37]

As the poem continues, Adams's first wish is merely for "daily bread." But almost immediately that wish is interpreted to include "all the realms of nature spread / Before me when I dine," "Four courses," and "four choice cooks from France." The incongruity of daily bread and choice French cooks ridicules the speaker's (and America's) need to have everything bigger and better. Adams then goes on to describe his preferred attire, which must be expensive, including sable furs, cashmere shawls, diamond rings, and rubies. He further wants a mansion and a thousand acres in the country, while in town, since "space is somewhat scant / And acres somewhat rare," he'll be more modest: "My house in town I only want / To occupy—a square." After seventeen stanzas of similarly exaggerated wants—art works, pianos, perfumes, pillows—when he is finally comfortable, only then will he think of others, and with mock piety submit "to the will of God / With charity to man." His final wish, however, undercuts even the pretense of piety. What he ultimately wants is merely that posterity "after ages, as they rise, / Exulting may proclaim, / In choral union to the skies, / Their blessings on my name." In President Adams's poem we find examples of the central characteristic devices of American comic poetry: a Whitmanesque exaggeration and excess, a Stevensesque dandyism and taste for the exotic, an incongruity through juxtaposition of the common and the refined, mock solemnity and piety, self-irony and satire. Whereas exaggeration is used in popular backwoods humor to elevate the protagonist, exaggeration is used here to deflate the speaker (and the America he represents).

Backwoods hyperbole is even more clearly parodied in Adams's "To Sally." [38] In this poem Adams adopts the persona of a man so righteous that he could trek from Asia's jungles to the summit of Mount Blank without fear. After three stanzas cataloguing all the possible exotic dangers he would be able to overcome, merely through virtue and righteousness, the speaker offers his one tangible proof of his powers: on his way to visit Sally he frightened a wolf away by simply raising his voice and clapping his hands. Lest it seem that this is any small feat, the speaker proceeds to explain that this beast was a more "crabbed" animal than Tangier or Tunis ever saw, "a monster," a "dry nurse of lions," the fiercest beast seen "since the days of Noah." Like the typical ring-tailed roarer, Adams's speaker claims great strength and superhuman powers. But since his many feats of daring involve no physical or mental prowess, resulting as they do merely from his supposed righteousness, his "pure and blameless" life, his boasts ring hollow. He has no need to wrestle that b'ar with Davy Crockett or face those fearful alligators with Mike Fink, or even stand up to the trippers and askers that trouble Walt Whitman. He can dismiss them all merely by his virtuous presence.

This strain of American humor, in which the *alazon* protagonist is deflated by his own exaggeration, is evident throughout our poetry. In "The Comedian as the Letter C" Wallace Stevens clearly casts Crispin as *alazon*, the boastful impostor, the "Socrates of snails," the "nincompated pedagogue," who insists egotistically that "man is the intelligence of his soil" (p. 27). Similarly, John Berryman undercuts his own pretensions to sexual, not intellectual, superiority by boasting that "his loins were & were the scene of stupendous achievement." [39]

Adams's, Stevens's, and Berryman's characteristic mode of comic exaggeration—allowing an *alazon* protagonist to expose his own excess and pretension—was a favorite of Walt Whitman as well. As a newspaper columnist, Whitman wrote sketches of backwoods characters who rendered themselves ridiculous through hyperbolic claims. One need only look at Whitman's Daggerdraw Bowieknife, Esq., for evidence of his affinity with this strain in popular humor. Thus in "Song of Myself" when Whitman recounts his stupendous feats of having intercourse with the earth— "mad naked summer night. / Smile O voluptuous cool-breath'd earth! / . . . Earth of the limpid gray of clouds brighter and clearer for my sake! . . . Smile, for your lover comes" (sec. 21, p. 49)—parodying the role of romantic lover and mistress right down to the conventional gray eyes—or with the sea—"We must have a turn together, I undress, hurry me out of sight of the land, / Cushion me soft, rock me in billowy drowse, / Dash me with amorous wet, I can repay you" (sec. 22, p. 49)—it is difficult not to see playful humor mingled with Whitman's serious intentions.

American comic poetry has thus used the figure of the *alazon*, the boaster and impostor, for two purposes. As in traditional Meredithian comedy, the *alazon* is sometimes a figure of fun whose exaggerated claims require rejection or reform. But sometimes the *alazon* transcends the convention in a peculiarly American way, celebrating an absurd but affirmative joy and strength. As long as these two purposes remain mutually exclusive, as in the light verse of John Quincy Adams and the early tall tales of Davy Crockett and Mike Fink, there is little problem of interpretation. But when, as in the case of Walt Whitman, Wallace Stevens, and John Berryman, these comic functions merge, the reader's dilemma is complicated. In much American comic poetry, the *alazon* persona is both fool and god-figure, requiring a careful balance of acceptance and rejection on the part of the reader.

The dilemma of the reader forced to hold simultaneously contradictory attitudes about the persona or character in a poem is sometimes eased by the presence in the poem of a second archetypal character, the *eiron*. The traditional *alazon* is a boastful impostor and fool; the traditional *eiron* is a witty self-deprecator and savant. In conventional Meredithian comedy of manners the conflict of *eiron* and *alazon* often forms the basis of the comic plot.

Such is the case in James T. Fields's "The Owl Critic," which provides a good introduction to the American-humor version of this archetypal figure. The two conflicting comic characters in Fields's poem are the critic himself (a young student of "owleology") and the silent barber to whom he lectures. The critic is an *alazon* who, in order to save the poor barber from the humiliation of displaying a stuffed owl that looks nothing like a real owl, verbally demonstrates its inadequacy. The critic is a learned Platonist who has studied natural history enough to know that this stuffed owl's wings are "preposterous." An owl "cannot roost / With his limbs so unloosed," and his legs are "slanted" wrong. His neck is twisted "against all bird-laws," and an owl's toe just "can't turn out so!" In short, the barber's owl is "an ignorant wreck." The glass eyes are inferior and fake, and the critic laments that he could stuff an old hat in the dark to look more like an owl than this one. When at the end of the poem the owl hops down from his perch to eye the critic, the barber, as he has silently done throughout the poem, "[keeps] on shaving."[40]

In "The Owl Critic" the two voices of American humor described by Constance Rourke are evident. The critic himself is a version of Rourke's Kentuckian, an *alazon* who claims to know more than he does. The barber, his silent foil, is a version of Rourke's Yankee, an *eiron* who pretends ignorance, seeming to know less than he does. While the pedantic, eloquent critic boasts his extensive learning and mounts a persuasive argument, the barber claims to know nothing, keeping silent about the single significant fact: the owl is alive. Without saying a word, the barber wins the debate, and the critic's elaborate argument takes an unexpected pratfall.

Although the barber is perhaps an extreme version of the *eiron*, relying on total silence as his best argument, he does reflect the characteristic self-deprecation of the type. The Yankee character, derived from the *eiron*, was usually a common-sense fellow who often appeared bumbling and ignorant, but who was in reality shrewd and cunning. Under the guise of a yokel or a peddler, a character like Jack Downing could send letters home from Washington, innocently exposing absurdity and ridiculousness more effectively than any direct satiric attack. Pretending innocence and even stupidity, the Yankee, like Socrates, contrived to come at the truth.

Walt Whitman's persona closely resembles the rhapsodic backwoods character; Emily Dickinson's closely resembles the more low-key Yankee. Constance Rourke notes, "Emily Dickinson was not only a lyric poet; she was in a profound sense a comic poet in the American tradition. . . . Her poetry is also comic in the Yankee strain, with its resilience and sudden unprepared ironical lines. Her use of an unstressed irony in a soft blank climax is the old formula grown almost fixed, yet fresh because it was used with a new depth."[41] While Dickinson is clearly more refined than the typical Yankee rustic or peddler of popular humor, she does reflect his characteristic self-deprecation and comic pretense of innocence. As an example of the Yankee *eiron*, she provides a clear contrast with Whitman's backwoods *alazon*.

While Whitman claims to be the largest figure on the road, Dickinson claims to be the smallest:

Then—look for me. Be sure you say—
Least Figure—on the Road— (#400)

If Whitman will find his personal heaven by singing loud, his voice the "barbaric yawp" of the spotted hawk, Dickinson will find her heaven by singing quietly, like a small unnamed bird:

Why—do they shut Me out of Heaven?
Did I sing—too loud?

But—I can say a little "Minor"
Timid as a Bird! (#248)

Walt Whitman is "a kosmos," "one of the roughs," "Turbulent, fleshy, sensual, eating, drinking"; Dickinson is often a small, innocent child, a delicate creature who eats and drinks like a hummingbird. Whitman claims prophetic knowledge; Dickinson claims helplessness and ignorance. Dickinson's childlike pose has disturbed some readers who find it too coy, too arch, too self-consciously quaint, too cloying. And yet when one perceives that Dickinson's pose is that of the typical Yankee of American humor, her strategy comes clear. While Whitman's and Dickinson's comic methods may seem polar opposites, their intentions are strikingly similar.

Just as Whitman uses the outrageous claims of the backwoodsman to ridicule and elevate himself, so Emily Dickinson uses the shy self-deprecation of the Yankee to ridicule and elevate herself:

I'm Nobody! Who are you?
Are you—Nobody—Too?
Then there's a pair of us!
Don't tell! they'd advertise—you know!

How dreary—to be—Somebody!
How public—like a Frog—
To tell one's name—the livelong June—
To an admiring Bog! (#288)

While on the surface Dickinson claims to be nobody, her real claim is that she is somebody, somebody who doesn't pursue trivial public approval, somebody who is strong and self-sufficient. While Whitman claims that he is enormous and limitless and no one is better than he is, Dickinson claims that she is small and limited and no one is better than she is. The typical pose of diminution and ignorance both undermines and asserts a sense of power and prestige. Dickinson herself reveals the secret of her self-deprecatory method:

I fear a Man of frugal Speech—
I fear a Silent Man—
Haranguer—I can overtake—
Or Babbler—entertain—

But He who weigheth—While the Rest—
Expend their furthest pound—
Of this Man—I am wary—
I fear that He is Grand— (#543)

Dickinson's pose of silence and frugality is as much a means of self-aggrandizement as is Whitman's more straightforward boast and blab.

Dickinson is thus a clear nineteenth-century reflection of a tradition of American humor that extends to the present. The Yankee voice of witty self-effacement and wry self-exposure is evident in Robert Frost's sly indirection and quiet good sense; in Hart Crane's "meek adjustments," "sidesteps," "evasions," and "smirks"; in Chaplin, Keaton, Woody Allen, Thurber, and Benchley, with their "little men" whose ineptitude is somehow preferable to anybody's aptitude; and it is currently evident in a whole range of young contemporary poets like Stephen Dunn, Greg Kuzma, and Larry Levis, whose awkward embarrassment at the hands of garage mechanics, insurance men, and poetry itself is ultimately a sign of special sensibility and intelligence.

Like the *alazon*, the *eiron* serves two purposes in American comic poetry. Just as the backwoods voice could both elevate and deflate characters through exaggeration, so could the Yankee voice both elevate and deflate characters through self-deprecation. The *eiron* persona is both a pose, indicating real superiority, and an existential premise, underlining a metaphysical truth: people *are* small in an absurd universe. Dickinson, Frost, Crane, Dunn, and Kuzma are all aware of the darker implications of their characteristic pose.

When the Yankee or backwoods character strays into these darker realms, the categories begin to meld into what Constance Rourke distinguishes as a third voice of American humor—the minstrel. Incorporating a note of sorrow, nonsense, and the grotesque, born out of the peculiar position of blacks in America and reflected in the early negro minstrel shows, Rourke's minstrel voice winds in and out of American poetry from the nineteenth century to the present. It is evident in Cummings's lyrics, in his Buffalo Bills and little balloon men who are alternately robust and wistful, coarse and tender, aggressive and sensitive; it is evident in Hart Crane's combination of "the everlasting eyes of Pierrot / And of Gargantua—the laughter"; it is perhaps most evident in John Berryman's *Dream*

Songs, consciously modeled on the Negro minstrel show. Rourke's prediction that the "comic trio" would continue "to merge into a single generic figure" has proved correct.[42]

But if the minstrel voice weaves in and out of American comic poetry, it seems more of a tone, an attitude, a spirit, or a music than an actual character. Although a note of nonsense, absurdity, and sadness is never far from the surface of our best humorous verse, it does not obscure the continual conflict between the two traditional comic archetypes, the *alazon* and the *eiron*, the Kentuckian and the Yankee, Falstaff and Socrates, Gargantua and Pierrot. It is to these types that one must look for the roots of the American poet's comic persona.

4

The archetypal characters, *eiron* and *alazon*, Yankee and backwoods, are evident not only in the plot patterns or personae of American comic poetry; they are evident in the very language itself. One of the few valid distinctions between prose and poetry may be, as John Hall Wheelock has suggested, that while the language of prose is usually a means to an end, the language of poetry is usually an end in itself.[43] In poetry, the language takes on its own life, and in comic poetry this life often inheres in the dramatic conflict of levels of diction. The language itself can be a boaster or a self-deprecator, a Kentuckian or a Yankee, the linguistic incongruity between the voices creating the comedy.

Walt Whitman commented on this dramatic conflict in the language of comic poetry:

> Considering Language then as some mighty potentate, into the majestic audience-hall of the monarch ever enters a personage like one of Shakspere's clowns, and takes position there, and plays a part even in the stateliest ceremonies. Such is slang, or indirection, an attempt of common humanity to escape from bald literalism, and express itself illimitably, which in highest walks produces poets and poems.[44]

Whitman's description of linguistic comedy is itself a good description of his language in *Leaves of Grass*. For Whitman, language takes on the role of one of these two characters, the "mighty potentate," an elevated or exalted figure, and the "clown," the voice of common humanity. When his language gets too high and mighty, Whitman trots in the clown to undercut it, much the way the *eiron* undercuts the *alazon* in traditional American humor. When words like *presidentiad, cartouche, imperturbe, lu-*

mine, somnambula, and *dolce affettuoso* lift their distinguished heads, *blab, chuff, drib, hap, lug, swash,* and *yawp* smack them with their slangy slapsticks.

Emily Dickinson also allowed language to take on a life of its own, with clown words intruding periodically to keep mighty potentate words from getting too haughty. In #54, a serious poem about mortality and loss, an unexpected word keeps solemnity and pain off-balance:

> If I should die,
> And you should live—
> And time should gurgle on—

"Gurgle" plays the role of clown here, disrupting any pretensions of undue solemnity.

Like Whitman and Dickinson, Wallace Stevens saw language as a living entity, capable of adopting a comic role. In a letter to Ronald Lattimore explaining the title of his "The Comedian as the Letter C," Stevens insists that the very sound of the letter C is itself a kind of comic character who takes the stage at appropriate moments in the poem:

> I ought to confess that by the letter C I meant the sound of the letter C; what was in my mind was to play on that sound throughout the poem. While the sound of that letter has more or less variety, and includes, for instance, K and S, all its shades may be said to have a comic aspect. Consequently, the letter C is a comedian. . . . Moreover, I did not mean that every time the letter C occurs in the poem it should take the stage. The reader would have to determine for himself just when that particular sound was being stressed.[45]

Throughout the poem, whenever Crispin gets too pretentious or boastful, whenever he is unduly wrongheaded or egotistical, the sounds of the letter C hiss and screech at him, warning the reader, and Crispin, not to take things too solemnly.

This sense of language having a comic life of its own is evident throughout Stevens's poetry. In "Snow and Stars," for example, a word pops in unasked, surprising Stevens, and then dominates the poem:

> The grackles sing avant the spring
> Most spiss—oh! Yes, most spissantly.
> They sing right puissantly. (133)

Grackles are rather cacophonous, unromantic birds, and when the word *spissantly* (derived from the fifteenth-century word *spissitude,* meaning thickness, compactness) slips out, Stevens is momentarily taken aback: "Oh!" Can he use such a lyrical word in this context, the interjection seems to ask? Grackles do show up in the spring, but they are black, raucous birds. Can they sing "spissantly"? Persuaded by the word itself, Stevens not only uses it but also underlines it with a companion word, *puissantly*.

Animate and headstrong language has had an appeal for most American comedians, who have seen both its usefulness and its potential difficulties. In the film *The Court Jester*, Danny Kaye is sabotaged by language that gets out of control. Hoping to determine which drink is poisoned, he strains to follow a confidante's earnest instructions: "The vessel with the pestle has the pellet with the poison, while the flagon with the dragon has the brew that is true." Or perhaps "The flagon with the dragon has the pellet with the poison, while the chalice from the palace has the brew that is true." Or perhaps . . . . Repeated numerous times and in numerous combinations, words cease to be a form of communication, becoming instead clowns doing pratfalls and throwing pies. Similarly, for Larry Levis, words can become villains, beating him up and stealing his woman:

> And the poem demanded the food,
> it drank up all the water,
>
> beat me and took my money,
> tore the faded clothes
> off my back,
>
> said Shit,
> and walked slowly away,
> slicking its hair down.
>
> Said it was going
> over to your place.[46]

According to W. H. Auden, "Verbal humor involves a violation in a particular instance of one of the following general principles of language":

> 1.) Language is a means of denoting things or thoughts by sounds. It is a law of language that any given verbal sound always means the same thing and only that thing. 2.) Words are man-made things which men use, not persons with a will and consciousness of their own. 3.) Any two or more objects or events which language seeks to describe are members, either of separate classes, or of the same class, or of overlapping classes. If they belong to separate classes, they must be described in different terms, and if they belong to the same class they must be described in the same terms.[47]

Language that acts like a character with a will of its own violates Auden's second principle of language. Auden's first principle is violated by the pun or double entendre, both favorite devices of American poets. Robert

Frost, for example, affirming his preference for formal verse, enlists God on his side: "Tell them Iamb, Jehovah said, and meant it."[48] John Berryman, whose *Dream Songs* reverberate with puns, employs a Frostian playfulness in a farewell to the recently deceased poet: "Goodbye, sir, and farewell. You're in the clear" (#39)—a possible allusion to Frost's last published collection, *In the Clearing*. In E. E. Cummings's poetry this penchant for punning can be visual as well as auditory. Cummings's typographical arrangement of words on the page can produce a kind of visual pun, as in this indirect comment on nuns:

w an d
ering

in sin

g
ular untheknowndulous s

pring[49]

The typography implies that the nuns are actually "erring" and "in sin" when they remain drab and lifeless, rejecting the joys of spring.

Like the pun, the double entendre breaks Auden's first law of language, implying two meanings where there should be just one. Double entendres, often sexual in nature, are plentiful in Berryman and Whitman. In Dream Song #350, for example, Berryman is talking about more than Ma Bell when he describes the penalty for Henry's excessive lusting after women: "There'll have to be an order / specifically to stop climbing trees, / & other people's wives: we'll cut off his telephone." A similar comic euphemism may echo in Whitman's references to "the real poem" in "Spontaneous Me": "This poem drooping shy and unseen that I always carry, and that all men carry, / (Know once for all, avow'd on purpose, wherever are men like me, are our lusty lurking masculine poems)" (p. 103). Whitman's description of the "real poem" sounds suspiciously like a covert lecture on the male anatomy, the joke both praising the grand fertility of the real poem and casting it in a comic light.

If puns and double entendres show the marks of strain (or the strain of Marx), the oxymoron, the comic catalogue, the comic metaphor, and the paradox, devices which violate Auden's third law of language (that words of one class should not be treated as belonging to another), seem a bit more sophisticated. The oxymoron, a juxtaposition of two seemingly contradictory words, is a favorite comic device of Whitman and Stevens. Whitman, for example, is "gross, mystical" (sec. 20, p. 47), while Stevens makes "oracular notations" and achieves "anecdotal bliss" (p. 13). Or, as Berryman oxymoronically remarks of Stevens, "He mutter spiffy" (#219).

The comic catalogues of Whitman, Dickinson, and Frost further place words in surprising classes where they seem not to belong. Thus Whitman juxtaposes "Peddler," "Prostitute," "President" (sec. 15, p. 43), Dickinson combines "The Fop—the Carp—the Atheist" (#1380), and Frost pairs "war and pestilence / And the loss of common sense" (p. 365), rendering the seemingly unequal as equal. Dickinson is especially fond of making abstract words concrete by breaking this law of language. Thus in "Crickets—Crows—and Retrospects" (#1271), "Retrospects" become as tangible and voluble as crickets and crows. Groucho Marx peppers his comic language with similar gems: "If you're insulted you can leave in a taxi. If that's not fast enough, you can leave in a huff. If that's *too* fast, you can leave in a minute and a huff."[50]

A more typically poetic violation of Auden's third law is the comic metaphor, and Emily Dickinson provides some of the most hilarious examples. Her poem #1388 is a masterpiece of metaphoric mockery:

> Those Cattle smaller than a Bee
> That herd upon the eye—
> Whose tillage is the passing Crumb—
> Those Cattle are the Fly—
> Of Barns for Winter—blameless—
> Extemporaneous stalls
> They found to our objection—
> On eligible walls—
> Reserving the presumption
> To suddenly descend
> And gallop on the Furniture—
> Or odiouser offend—
> Of their peculiar calling
> Unqualified to judge
> To Nature we remand them
> To justify or scourge—

Dickinson's shocked offense over the flies is comic—they've affronted her by being impolite—and the dimension of her shock and offense is comically exaggerated by the incongruity between the two halves of her metaphor, the relative sizes of cattle and fly. The discrepancy in sizes is further exaggerated by the use of *fly* as a collective noun in "Those cattle are the fly." Amassed in a "herd," the "fly" "gallop" on her furniture and make stalls of her walls, leaving her no alternative but to remand them to nature. The excessive shock is out of all proportion to its cause, as the meta-phor of cattle is out of all proportion to the flies. The comic metaphor, extended through the poem, enables Dickinson to express a real irritation with the offensive critters while laughing at herself.

Wallace Stevens uses the cow image to structure a similarly comic meta-phor. In "Depression before Spring" he describes his lovely wife: "The hair of my blonde / Is dazzling, / As the spittle of cows / Threading the wind. / Ho! Ho!" (p. 63). Unlike Dickinson, however, who uses the comic metaphor to undercut the flies, Stevens uses it to elevate his blonde. En-listing the unexpected spittle of cows and laughing at the image himself ("Ho! Ho!"), he is able to celebrate his wife romantically but without sen-timentality or affectation.

Perhaps cows are intrinsically funny, for Whitman, too, uses a cow im-age in one of his comic metaphors. In section 28 of "Song of Myself" Whitman becomes so supersensitive to touch that he must rely on lan-guage to release the tension:

> On all sides prurient provokers stiffening my limbs,
> Straining the udder of my heart for its withheld drip. (p. 57)

The comic metaphor helps alleviate an otherwise unbearably painful situation.

Linked intimately with the comic metaphor is the paradox. B. H. Fus-sell provides a lovely description of the function of paradox:

> Puns, paradoxes, and riddles do to language what pies do to faces and pratfalls to bottoms—destroy its dignity. . . . What the pun does to the word, the paradox does to the sentence. The paradox whacks the backside of syntax by imitating its structures, its pretensions to order and meaning. As an instrument of greater refinement and more delicate calibration than the pun, the paradox finds its analogue in the pie throw rather than in the bed slat. The paradox achieves its particular effects by setting up its own fall guy in the first part of the sentence to receive the pie in the second part. The greater the distance between the two parts, the more difficult the throw, but the lovelier the trajectory.[51]

Thus Josh Billings could always be assured of a laugh by attaching a para-doxical twist to the end of a potentially serious statement: "I never knew an auctioneer to lie unless it was absolutely convenient."[52] Billings's line would be mildly funny, even if he replaced the unexpected word, *convenient*, with the expected word, *necessary*. He would still be making a joke on auctioneers. But by using the paradoxical word *convenient* he doubles the humor. Walt Whitman was similarly fond of playing with paradox in an effort to make the reader reassess a fixed or rigid position. In section

24 of "Song of Myself" Whitman insists, "Copulation is no more rank to me than death is" (p. 53). The word *death* in this context renders humorous what might be a merely peculiar statement. The line as it stands introduces what seems to be a logical fallacy. If one thinks that copulation is rank, one is not likely to be persuaded that it isn't by a comparison of it with something that may seem equally rank. Whitman's argument is analogous to saying "rotten eggs are no more rank to me than fish guts are." A less comic statement might be something like "copulation is no more rank to me than love is." By comparing copulation to something many people would feel is at least as unpleasant, Whitman creates a comic conundrum, forcing the reader to attend to the paradox. The logical force of the analogy is to make copulation unpleasant. Given Whitman's attitude toward death as "lucky," he comically manages to reverse that response.

Dickinson was similarly drawn to paradox, using comic reversals to deal with loss and sadness. In #33, for example, she defines processes and emotions in terms of their opposites, providing an incremental confusion that distracts her and us from the emotional situation at hand:

> If recollecting were forgetting
> Then I remember not.
> And if forgetting, recollecting
> How near I had forgot.
> And if to miss, were merry,
> And to mourn, were gay,
> How very blithe the fingers
> That gathered this, Today! (#33)

While the initial effect of the reversals is to distract us from the emotional situation, forcing us to think through the stated paradoxes, the ultimate effect is to intensify the feeling of loss. Once we have figured out the thrust of the reversals, we are suddenly faced with the fact of loss, a fact we had put aside to play the interpretive game. Thus the comic paradox here intellectualizes the emotion and makes it bearable, but it also intensifies the emotion since the spirit of play seems incongruous with its source and object.

All of the comic stylistic devices illustrated so far are based on varieties of linguistic incongruity. Incongruity can extend to the formal level as well, setting up a conflict not between individual words or lines, but between the subject of a poem and its form. Robert Frost's "Fire and Ice" is a good example:

> Some say the world will end in fire,
> Some say in ice.

From what I've tasted of desire
I hold with those who favor fire.
But if it had to perish twice,
I think I know enough of hate
To say that for destruction ice
Is also great
And would suffice. (p. 268)

The poem clearly deals with a very serious subject—the end of the world, apocalypse. But there is a discrepancy between the solemn subject and the lilting, sing-song verse form. If one ignored the meaning of the words and listened only to the rhythm and rhyme, one would conclude that the poem was a happy one, reflecting a kind of nursery-rhyme carefreeness. This discrepancy between subject matter and verse form suggests several comic possibilities. The poem may be a satire on those doomsayers who are always preaching about the end of the world. The verse form may, that is, undercut the solemnity of the subject, putting it in a comic perspective. Or, the verse form may be a method of comically distancing the painful subject, making it available to offhand, neutral speculation. Or finally, the incongruity between subject and verse form could actually intensify the horror, in much the same way that Sylvia Plath's adoption of comical nursery-rhyme rhythms intensifies the horror of "Daddy." All three of these possibilities probably apply here, Frost's comic method giving him something to "smile at in the dust" while refusing to ignore that dust (p. 148).

The decision to emphasize the comedy of language has existential or metaphysical significance as well. By exploiting the comic mode, a poet is making a philosophical statement about himself and his world. Comic poetry ultimately reflects a fundamental discrepancy between our knowledge of language and our aesthetic theory, between our knowledge of reality and our perception of reality. We know that language is abstract, an arbitrary system of signs and symbols, yet our aesthetic theory insists that words are things, that the poem is "the thing itself," that there are "no ideas but in things." And we use elaborate strategies (image, persona, narrative, etc.) to persuade ourselves and our readers that this is true. Similarly, we know, via Heisenberg's uncertainty principle and Bergson's metaphysics, among others, that reality is constantly shifting, fluid, and unfixable, and yet we understand that reality by fixing it in place, by acting as if it were a series of immobile, discrete moments. This discrepancy between the nature of language and our assumptions about language, between the nature of reality and our perception of reality, is comic.

Fred M. Robinson, in one of the best recent books on the comedy of language, summarizes this idea:

> The thesis of *Laughter*, then, can be restated in Bergson's metaphysical terminology. The human condition itself can be seen as comic, above and beyond the exigencies and impulses of society. What is "encrusted" on us, the living, is our intellect, which perceives in fixed products a reality that is in constant process.[53]

Linguistic comedy occurs when we see the falsity of our imposition of the fixed or mechanical on language. Metaphysical comedy occurs when we see the falsity of our mechanical imposition of structure on reality.

Two analogies from comic films may make these ideas clearer. In *Bananas*, Woody Allen is alone in his small, narrow kitchen, preparing dinner. He takes a package of frozen spinach from the freezer, but the spinach is slippery and squirts out of his hand. For several seconds, in seeming defiance of gravity, the spinach squirts in and out of his hands, as he comically fails to retrieve it or engage its attention. There is both clumsiness in this scene (Allen can't hold onto the spinach), and there is consummate grace (he can keep the spinach poised in mid-air). Several central comic contradictions inform this simple scene. Allen's inability to cope with the everyday world is itself comic. Things take on a mysterious life of their own and elude him; the simple act becomes infinitely difficult and complex in a universe where things obey arbitrary laws or no laws at all. Yet the movement is also graceful; it is a spinach ballet, a union between man and thing more beautiful than any cooked spinach might be. Underlying the whole scene is our suppressed knowledge that Allen is indeed in charge of the situation, that he has practiced long and hard to make the difficult look easy, to give the illusion of being mastered by forces beyond his control while in reality having mastered them far more than the man for whom spinach is no problem. The audience is both discomfitted (he may drop the spinach and ruin his dinner; if simple spinach can cause so much trouble, worse difficulties may lurk in the future for him and for us; if normal laws break down, aren't we trapped in an absurd universe?) and comforted by the deeper knowledge that Allen is in complete control, giving the beautiful illusion of losing control.

W. C. Fields's famous bit with the pool cue is identical in effect, as the cue seems to behave with a life of its own, confounding Fields's efforts to get off even a single shot. As he readies the cue it slides off the table as if by its own volition, and, to Fields's consternation, has to be coaxed back on again. It bobs and weaves in the air, as with Allen's spinach, feinting and sparring with his fingers, eluding his attempt to grasp it. The comedy of the scene initially resides in our watching an inanimate thing take on life and seem to manipulate the human being who should be manipulating it. The scene reflects a reversal of Bergson's famous definition of the comic. Here, it isn't the mechanical encrusted on the living, but the living encrusted on the mechanical.

Our response to Woody Allen and W. C. Fields thus involves three levels. Initially, we identify with their helplessness. We, too, have had experiences of incompetence when things seemed to conspire against us. If we did not emotionally identify with them, if we did not see their plight as similar to our own experience, their performances would be just that, *performances*, and we would admire them as we admire jugglers or magicians. At a deeper level, Allen and Fields reveal that our world is not its appearances. We normally see spinach and pool cues as fixed, predictable commodities, symbolic of other certainties in our experience. When they get out of hand, disrupting our simple and neat categories, we perceive a world more mysterious and surprising than our fixed views would allow, suggesting that reality is supple and uncertain and that our pretense of knowing it at all is part of our metaphysical comedy. But the situation does not become an existential nightmare since we know that behind the illusion of ineptitude is a brilliant aptitude. The comedians control reality to show how uncontrollable it is; they manipulate experience to show it as unmanipulable.

Fields's and Allen's comic method is closely analogous to that of our comic poets. Like Allen's spinach and Fields's pool cue, language in the comic poem seems to take on a life of its own, getting out of hand and manipulating or evading its creator. Initially we identify with the situation, laughing because language has similarly manipulated or evaded us, blocking communication when it should have aided it. On a deeper level, the antics of language reflect the essential comedy of our treatment of words as things, while bringing into question our ability to see anything at all for what it is. Comic poetry points up the discrepancy between the limits of language and the limitlessness of reality, between language's need to fix reality and reality's refusal to be fixed. Comic poets, aware of these discrepancies and incongruities between fact and practice, show language misbehaving and categories breaking down.

But finally, as with Fields and Allen, we are aware that the poets are standing behind the poems, manipulating the language to look as if it were manipulating them. By adopting a comic mode, the poet is not only drawing attention to our inadequacies, pretensions, foibles, joys, and fears in an effort to expose and affirm or reform them. He is not only making a statement about the inadequacies of language to know and control reality. He is also affirming the need, ridiculously and absurdly, *to make something of it*, to make art of it. Turning defeat into triumph, defect into virtue, bumble into ballet, Fields, Allen, and our comic poets artistically shape reality to show both the ridiculousness of and the necessity of shaping reality.

One final property of comic style involves all of the characteristics discussed thus far. When asked in an interview, "Aside from your being funny, why do people laugh at you?," Woody Allen replied:

> The only thing I can surmise is that there is something about me they are responding to, above and beyond the material—something in myself that I don't see. I don't believe the performer knows what's funny about himself, or can see it . . . . They can never stand outside themselves enough to know what it is. There's something about Groucho just standing there that's comical.[54]

In another context Allen elaborates:

> Given an absolutely straight sentence, with no punch line to it whatsoever, you can have twenty people read the sentence, and Jonathan Winters reads it or W. C. Fields—it's just going to be funny without changing a word, for some intangible, built-in thing that's beyond reason . . . . It isn't the jokes that do it, and the comedian has nothing to do with the jokes. It's the individual himself.[55]

What Allen is talking about here is affect, tone, personality, *style*, partly visual, partly auditory, something in the comedian's characteristic gestures, tics, movements, and voice that distinguishes him. When Steve Martin, Groucho, W. C. Fields, or Allen himself walks on stage, they are unmistakably themselves. Similarly, when Whitman or Dickinson or Stevens or Berryman walk on stage, they could be nobody else. Allen explains, "What they [the audience] want is an intimacy with the person. They want to like the person and find the person funny as a human being."[56]

What the stage comedian achieves through physical appearance, gesture, movement, timing, and voice, the comic poet must achieve solely through language. Thus the language of a comic poem must draw attention to itself through its use of coinages, nonsense, noise, music, fractured syntax, metaphor, pun, and paradox. With its blab, yawp, hoo, gurgle, and strut, language must do tricks, perform comic dances, parade around and fall on its face, put on outlandish costumes and prance naked. Highfalutin words must bump up against the humble and meek.

Language is thus for the poet what comic features or disguises are for the clown. Bergson asks why a big nose or an unnaturally red face or a very fat person is comic, and answers that these features appear to be a disguise masking a normal person underneath. "A man in disguise," argues Bergson, "is comic." Style in comic poetry draws attention to itself as a kind of disguise, an exaggerated disguise on normal language. Thus the gaudy language of Stevens, the minstrelsy of Berryman, the panache of Whitman, and the quirkiness of Dickinson are all akin to the phony nose, the rubber thumb, the false mustache. This is not to say that style is merely ornamental. According to Bergson, "A man we *regard* as disguised is also comic." [57] Thus even the man whose nose *is* large, like W. C. Fields's, or whose mustache only *appears* pasted on, like Groucho Marx's, or who is *really* fat, like Oliver Hardy or Fatty Arbuckle, is funny. The style of an American comic poet *is* his character, yet in drawing attention to itself it becomes, like a disguise, comic. The best comic poets, like the best stage comedians, are often those with the most recognizable comic styles, or "disguises."

5

Whether the American comic poet adopts an *eiron* or an *alazon* persona or some combination of the two, whether he primarily employs stylistic devices of exaggeration or deflation, whether he dons an orange wig, a big nose, a rubber thumb, or floppy shoes, his comic method usually reflects one or more of three major modes—satire, irony, and parody. In the nineteenth and early twentieth centuries, as traditional views of the world were breaking down, as traditional values were eroding, poets turned to comedy both as a means of encouraging the destruction of atrophied ideas and beliefs and as a means of saving those ideas and beliefs that seemed indispensable.

The comic mode most often associated with attack or reform is that of satire. And as satirist, the American comic poet often adopts the role of clear-thinking common person in opposition to artificially elevated pretenders to social status. Louis D. Rubin explains, "There can be little doubt that this perspective—the vernacular perspective, set forth in opposition to the cultural, the literary—is the approved American mode of humor. The characteristic comic situation in American humorous writing is that in which cultural and social pretension are made to appear ridiculous and artificial. The bias is all on the side of the practical, the factual." [58]

Thus Emily Dickinson turns her satiric rod against the kind of artificially elevated woman she could not be. Chastizing mere social respectability and shallow thinking, Dickinson ridicules her culture's "soft, cherubic creatures" for being satisfied with a half-life:

> What Soft—Cherubic Creatures—
> These Gentlewomen are—
> One would as soon assault a Plush—
> Or violate a Star—
>
> Such Dimity Convictions—
> A Horror so refined
> Of freckled Human Nature—
> Of Deity—ashamed— (#401)

The surface of the poem masquerades as praise, describing the women in the conventional vocabulary of gentility. They are angelic and chaste, refined and ladylike. But if these women are cherubs, they are also so soft that they lack all sexual or physical appeal. They are like great stuffed dolls, soft as plush and warm as stars. The satire on their physical appearance is followed by a serious religious comment on their spiritual lives. If their bodies are so soft as to be squishy, their souls are brittle, and they have little chance for redemption. Salvation is for the common person, the humble person, not for elevated plush dolls whose convictions are "dimity"—that light, dainty cotton stuff that symbolizes the demure Victorian maiden—and whose chief horror is being human. Christ, Dickinson asserts, was a common man, a fisherman, who with his simple notion of redemption would be ashamed of them.

The superficiality of Dickinson's cherubic creatures comes under similar attack in E. E. Cummings's companion poem:

> the Cambridge ladies who live in furnished souls
> are unbeautiful and have comfortable minds
> (also, with the church's protestant blessings
> daughters, unscented shapeless spirited)
> they believe in Christ and Longfellow, both dead,
> are invariably interested in so many things— [59]

What Cummings's ladies are most interested in is gossip and meaningless charity, preferring comfortable, outmoded ideas to what is really going on all about them ("the / moon rattles like a fragment of angry candy"). Like Dickinson, Cummings satirizes triviality, conservatism, materialism, and formality here, the comic spirit keeping the poem from being merely a hostile diatribe.

Wallace Stevens is more lighthearted in his satire of a pretentious "damozel":

> She was all of her airs and, for all of her airs,
> She was all of her airs and ears and hairs,
> Her pearly ears, her jeweler's ears
> And the painted hairs that composed her hair.
>
> In spite of her airs, that's what she was. She was all
> Of her airs, as surely cologne as that she was bone
> Was what she was and flesh, sure enough, but airs;
> Rather rings than fingers, rather fingers than hands.
>
> How could you ever, how could think that you saw her,
> Knew her, how could you see the woman that wore the beads,
> The ball-like beads, the bazzling and the bangling beads,
> Or hear her step in the way she walked?
>
> This was not how she walked for she walked in a way
> And the way was more than the walk and was hard to see.
> You saw the eye-blue, sky-blue, eye-blue, and the powdered ears
> And the cheeks like flower-pots under her hair. (*OP*, p. 74)

The nonsense rhythm and rhyme here are hilarious, whimsically deflating the woman's airs.

As pretension to social respectability comes under attack, so does pretension to special knowledge. A recurrent figure of fun in American poetry is the pedagogue, the scholar, the savant, or the doctor. In "To a Historian," for example, Whitman gently ridicules the man who would "celebrate bygones," who would explore "the outward, the surfaces" in contrast to Whitman himself, who treats man "as he is in himself" and who will paradoxically "project the history of the future" (p. 4). Wallace Stevens similarly ridicules scholars in "Homunculus et la Belle Etoile" for evading the present with its potential vitality and love by shaving their heads and bodies and hiding under dark cowls and cloaks. Similarly, in "The Doctor of Geneva," Stevens rebukes his protagonist for plumbing "the multifarious heavens" while feeling "no awe / Before these visible, voluble delugings" of the real world in front of him. Finally, John Berryman continues the tradition by repeatedly satirizing assistant professors of literature who may become associates by studying his work. In a Dream Song set at the Modern Language Association convention, Berryman sympathizes with his victims while attacking them:

> Hey, out there! —assistant professors, full,
> associates,—instructors—others—any—

I have a sing to shay.
We are assembled here in the capital
city for Dull—and one professor's wife is Mary—
at Christmastide, hey!

and all of you did theses or are doing
and the moral history of what we were up to
thrives in Sir Wilson's hands—
who I don't see here—only deals go screwing
some of you out, some up—the chairmen too
are nervous, little friends—

a chairman's not a chairman, son, forever,
and hurts with his appointments; ha, but circle—
take my word for it—
though maybe Frost is dying—around Mary;
forget your footnotes on the old gentleman;
dance around Mary. (#35)

Berryman takes on the English professors here, as Whitman had taken on the historians and Stevens the doctors. If he is a bit drunk, he has "a sing to shay," and a shay is the perfect vehicle for this piece of satiric light verse. Like Whitman's and Stevens's before him, Berryman's advice to his victims is to stop pretending to status and knowledge, and instead to celebrate life, to dance around Mary. Berryman plays with multiple puns on *Mary* here—the professor's wife, the Virgin Mary, the homonym of *merry*, and perhaps (given the context of Frost) even the Mary of "The Death of the Hired Man," since by dancing around that literary figure the young hopefuls might realize their scholarly ambitions.

This satire of historians, scholars, professors, and experts of all kinds seems to be characteristic of American comic poetry. The distrust of specialization, of elevation through title alone, of intellectual snobbery, conforms with the deep American belief in equality. Whitman summarizes:

Have you outstripped the rest? Are you the President?
It is a trifle, they will more than arrive there every one,
    and still pass on. (sec. 21, p. 49)

While satire often focuses generalized antagonists—social status, intellectual pretension, the institution, false pride, and snobbery—it can also be more intensely personal. Groucho Marx once made the distinction between the amateur and the professional comedian. According to Groucho, the amateur thinks it is funny if you dress a man as an old lady, put him in a wheelchair, and push the wheelchair down a hill to a stone wall. "For

a pro," Groucho concluded, "it's got to be a real old lady." [60] Put the
scholar, the historian, the professor, the president in that wheelchair and
it is funny; he is just a type after all. Put the old woman there, and the
humor verges on tragedy. In an uncharacteristically personal attack, for
example, Emily Dickinson exposes a real old lady:

> A face devoid of love or grace,
> A hateful, hard, successful face,
> A face with which a stone
> Would feel so thoroughly at ease
> As were they old acquaintances—
> First time together thrown. (#1711)

The venom in this satiric portrait is kept in check only by the surprising
word *successful* and by the comic analogy of face and stone to old ac-
quaintances. Postwar confessional poets like Robert Lowell and Sylvia
Plath use personal satire in a similar way to attack their enemies. Lowell's
biting portrait of his father—a seagoing engineer who can't sail a boat,
drink, play golf, make money or love like a man—and Plath's black-comic
routine about her father with his vampire's heart, his Luftwaffe, and his
gobbledygoo provide vivid examples of Bergson's dictum that laughter is
"intended to humiliate . . . the person against whom it is directed." [61]

Since a favorite target of satiric poetry has been the pretenders to status, power, and special knowledge, it should not be surprising to find God
a primary victim. In his role as the infallible and omnipotent almighty
father, God represents the ultimate repressive force, the ultimate block to
human freedom. But in his apparent failure to fulfill his great claims, in
his weakness and invisibility, God comes to seem like a boastful impostor
or fool.

Thus for John Berryman "God's Henry's enemy" (#13). In *The Dream
Songs* Henry complains:

> I'm cross with god who has wrecked this generation.
> First he seized Ted, then Richard, Randall, and now Delmore.
> In between he gorged on Sylvia Plath.
> That was a first rate haul. He left alive
> fools. . . . I suppose the word would be, we must submit.
> . . . I will not be part of it. (#153)

Berryman's tendency, at least in *The Dream Songs* and before his recon-
version to the church, is to reject a god who is so mean-spirited and
clumsy. "Perhaps God is a slob." "Perhaps God ought to be curbed." God

is perhaps "Something disturbed, / ill-pleased, & with a touch of para-noia / who calls for this thud of love from his creatures-O" (#238).

Berryman's comic diatribes against God are more virulent than most poets'. Emily Dickinson, for example, is considerably more sympathetic in her comic treatment of the creator. While Dickinson attacks the institution of religion and conventional ideas about God held by the church, she teases God with numerous comic epithets. Dickinson's God is a "Mighty Merchant" (#621), a "noted Clergyman" (#324), a "distant-stately lover" (#357), and a "Burglar, Banker, Father" (#49). While these epithets make light fun of God, they also reveal warmth and love. Dickinson won't, like Berryman, rail against God, but neither will she overlook his faults. At times she can be fairly caustic:

> "Heavenly Father"—take to thee
> The supreme iniquity
> Fashioned by thy candid Hand
> In a moment contraband—
> Though to trust us—seem to us
> More respectful—"We are Dust"—
> We apologize to thee
> For thine own Duplicity— (#1461)

Dickinson's criticism of God for being all too human is echoed by Robert Frost. In *A Masque of Reason*, for example, God is a comic villain of sorts, a New England yokel who employs rather specious reasoning to argue his commitment to unreason. God thanks Job for having helped him put on a "great demonstration" to "Establish once for all the principle / There's no connection man can reason out / Between his just deserts and what he gets" (p. 589). When God isn't cast as an elevated fool in Frost's poetry, he is cast as the invisible man:

> I turned to speak to God
> About the world's despair;
> But to make bad matters worse
> I found God wasn't there. (p. 408)

And similarly:

> God once declared he was true
> And then took the veil and withdrew. (p. 342)

While the disappearance of God causes consternation for Frost, it is merely a fact for Whitman, Stevens, and many contemporary American poets. Throughout "Song of Myself" Whitman measures the various gods, "Taking myself the exact dimensions of Jehovah, / Lithographing Kronos . . ." (sec. 41, p. 75), finding none of them as large as he or any other human individual is. The disappearance of God is not a problem for Whitman, since *he* is God.

Similarly, for Stevens, God is a combination of reality and human imagination. Stevens defines God for his high-toned old Christian woman by telling her, "Poetry is the Supreme Fiction, Madame" (p. 59). And in another context he insists, "The Ruler of Reality / If more unreal than New Haven, is not / A real ruler, but rules what is unreal" (p. 485).

In a world without the traditional God, or a world in which God is seriously diminished, death becomes a more difficult problem. Indeed, religion and death have been the two most predominant themes in American comic poetry. As with religion, a comic poet has several possible methods for confronting death. Whitman and Stevens, for example, ridicule, denounce, or brazen it away. Toward the end of "Song of Myself" Whitman boasts:

> And as to you Death, and you bitter hug of mortality, it is
>   idle to try to alarm me.
> . . . .
> And as to you Corpse I think you are good manure. (sec. 49, p. 87)

Stevens even more buoyantly faces death in "Of Heaven Considered as a Tomb" when he instructs the "interpreters" to "Make hue among the dark comedians" (p. 56), that is, make color and noise to confound the icy élysée of a dead heaven. Berryman rejects death even more outrageously in *The Dream Songs* by having Henry die, and then, dissatisfied with the change, come back to life.

Whitman's, Stevens's, and Berryman's comic approach to death is to denounce it. Frost's and Dickinson's is to slide around it or to tease it into thought and friendship. If comedy is an offensive weapon, it can be defensive as well. Woody Allen remarks, "I can take care of myself. In case of danger I have this cutlass that I carry around with me . . . and in case of a real emergency, I press the handle and it turns into a cane so I can get sympathy."[62] The satirist, the man with the cutlass, himself presents a large and inviting stationary target; ridiculing others, he is himself vulnerable to ridicule. The ironist, the man with the cane, deflects attention from himself and undermines possible attack from without; ridiculing himself, he renders himself invulnerable to ridicule from others. This defensive posture of comedy is that characteristically taken by the Yankee or *eiron* of American comic poetry.

Walt Whitman brandishes his cutlass and chases death away; Emily

Dickinson displays her cane and tricks death or befriends him. In an early valentine addressed to William Howland, a tutor at Amherst College, Dickinson underlines her ironic mode. Since "mortality is fatal," she insists:

> A coward will remain, Sir,
>   Until the fight is done;
> But an *immortal hero*
>   Will take his hat, and run! (#3)

Since death will make you die, she points out, the best way to stay alive is not to get killed. One way to "run" from death is to distract him with playful jests while preparing an escape:

> Dust is the only Secret—
> Death, the only One
> You cannot find out all about
> In his "native town."
>
> Nobody knew "his Father"—
> Never was a Boy—
> Hadn't any playmates,
> Or "Early history"—
>
> Industrious! Laconic!
> Punctual! Sedate!
> Bold as a Brigand!
> Stiller than a Fleet!
>
> Builds, like a Bird, too!
> Christ robs the Nest—
> Robin after Robin
> Smuggled to Rest! (#153)

The poem is a witty combination of respectful awe (death is mysterious, secret, unplumbable), sympathy (he is a poor orphan), and mixed praise and blame (the "admirable" traits listed in the third stanza have ominous overtones), calculated to take death off guard. We can see him in the background, charmed and entertained by the smiling poet. Lulled into a sense of false security, death is not prepared for the final stanza in which his power is totally undercut and everyone escapes him. The poem is, of course, directed at the reader and not at death. In effect, Dickinson is gossiping behind death's back, getting away with it by means of a series of gentle ironies that result in death's ultimate comeuppance. While the poet talks, Christ and comedy, like little street urchins, smuggle death's trea-

sures away from him and gaily escape. Dickinson's method here, and in
other of her comic poems, reflects Meredith's definition of irony: "If, instead of falling foul of the ridiculous person with a satiric rod, to make
him writhe and shriek aloud, you prefer to sting him under a semi-caress,
by which he shall in his anguish be rendered dubious whether indeed anything has hurt him, you are an engine of Irony."[63]

Like Emily Dickinson, Robert Frost adopts evasive tactics for dealing
with potentially painful situations. Frost's characteristic pose is that of
the "drumlin woodchuck," who, with his carefully prepared "strategic retreat," "can sit forth exposed to attack / As one who shrewdly pretends /
That he and the world are friends" (p. 365). Keeping an escape route
open, retaining a low profile in the face of mortality's fatality, Frost
survives:

> If I can with confidence say
> That still for another day,
> Or even another year,
> I will be there for you, my dear,
>
> It will be because, though small
> As measured against the All,
> I have been so instinctively thorough
> About my crevice and burrow. (pp. 365–66)

Playing the role of *eiron*, aligning himself with the small and helpless,
Frost seeks to evade pain and death.

In "The Lockless Door" Frost finds occasion to use his strategic retreat:

> It went many years,
> But at last came a knock,
> And I thought of the door
> With no lock to lock.
>
> I blew out the light,
> I tip-toed the floor,
> And raised both hands
> In prayer to the door.
>
> But the knock came again
> My window was wide;
> I climbed on the sill
> And descended outside.
>
> Back over the sill
> I bade a "Come in"

> To whatever the knock
> At the door may have been.
>
> So at a knock
> I emptied my cage
> To hide in the world
> And alter with age. (p. 299)

Frost never specifies the identity of the knocker. Is it death? Sorrow? Pain? Whatever it is, if it can't be locked out of his life, it can be evaded. Frost's strategy here is to sneak out the window and call for the knocker to come in; that is, to be polite, but elusive and slippery. The call to "come in" may itself be a trap. When Frost himself later hears an unspoken, seductive call to "come in" to the darkness, he slyly slips away:

> But no, I was out for stars:
> I would not come in.
> I meant not even if asked,
> And I hadn't been. (p. 446)

The *eiron*'s evasive tactics, designed to sidestep mortality and protect the individual, are summed up in one of Frost's pieces of characteristic Yankee wisdom: "Take Care to Sell Your Horse before He Dies" (p. 570).

Evasive tactics are effective comic ploys, allowing a poet to deal with difficult emotions and situations. But such tactics do not necessarily cancel out the pain. Hart Crane, for example, poignantly evokes the mixture of humor and pathos that resonates in Dickinson and Frost as well. In "Chaplinesque," Charlie Chaplin's clown-tramp becomes symbolic of the plight of the poet, and of every modern person:

> We will sidestep, and to the final smirk
> Dally the doom of that inevitable thumb
> That slowly chafes its puckered index toward us,
> Facing the dull squint with what innocence
> And what surprise!
>
> And yet these fine collapses are not lies
> More than the pirouettes of any pliant cane;
> Our obsequies are, in a way, no enterprise.
> We can evade you, and all else but the heart:
> What blame to us if the heart live on.
>
> The game enforces smirks; but we have seen
> The moon in lonely alleys make
> A grail of laughter of an empty ash can.[64]

Just as Chaplin, leaning on his cane, will sidestep the cop's accusing finger with a combination of innocence, surprise, and smirk, so will Hart Crane sidestep death. And the heart/Hart lives on not only with a smirk, but also with the kind of innocent surprise and laughter that can see in an ash can a vision of the grail.

Crane's Chaplin, the clown or tramp sprung loose in an utterly random and yet mysteriously hostile universe in which both persons and things seem to conspire against him, has been a central comic figure in the twentieth century. James Thurber, whose own "little man" bears a close resemblance to Chaplin and other film clowns, explains: "I think humor is the best that lies closest to the familiar; to that part of the familiar which is humiliating, distressing, even tragic. Humor is a kind of emotional chaos told about calmly and quietly in retrospect." [65] Thus the Thurber man is defeated by his wife, his automobile, and other mechanical things that baffle him.

And yet, given this vision of a world gone wrong and an individual incompetent to right it, the clown or little man achieves a measure of actual heroism or success. W. C. Fields notes, "I never saw anything funny that wasn't terrible. If it causes pain, it's funny: if it doesn't, it isn't. I try to hide the pain with embarrassment, and the more I do that, the better they like it. But that doesn't mean they are unsympathetic. Oh no, they laugh often with tears in their eyes." [66] Covering pain with humiliation, the clowns expose some humorous element in themselves—poverty, helplessness, stupidity, folly, ineptness—and by laughing rise superior to it. By enlisting audience sympathy for their various hurts and humiliations, the clowns paradoxically achieve a kind of victory over the large impersonal forces that threaten them. For the clown, the grail may be an ash can, but the ash can is also a grail.

The paradox by which losers are winners and winners are losers structures much contemporary comic poetry. Stephen Dunn, for example, fairly boasts about his ignorance and ineptness in "At Every Gas Station There Are Mechanics," a poem familiar to any red-blooded American boy who feels threatened by his society's requirements for manhood:

Around them my cleanliness stinks.
I smell it. And so do they.
I always want to tell them I used to box,
and change tires, and eat heroes.
It is my hands hanging out
of my sleeves like white gloves.
It is what I've not done, and do not know.

> If they mention the differential
> I pay whatever price. When
> they tell me what's wrong beneath my hood
> I nod, and become meek.
> If they were to say I could not
> have my car back, that it was theirs,
> I would say thank you, you must be right.
> And then I would walk home,
> and create an accident.[67]

In confessing his inferiority and ignorance, Dunn marshals our support and identification, rising superior to the mechanical world that threatens him and us. Comic self-deprecation takes the place of Christian humility, promising an ultimate triumph, since the meek will inherit the earth.

The pose of the *eiron*, the belief in winning by losing, the mode of saying one thing but meaning another, leads logically to a consideration of the final major mode of American comic poetry—parody. Comedy is not only an offensive or defensive weapon, it is also a mode of belief, a method of affirmation. Although parody can refer simply to a burlesque version of another well-known piece of literature, it can have broader applications as well. Dorothy Van Ghent's definition of parody in her study of *Don Quixote* provides a good description of this mode in American poetry:

> Loosely, we tend to mean by parody a burlesque imitation of something, showing the weaknesses or falsehood of the object imitated. In this sense, the main feature of parody would be not unlike the main feature of debate, implying that one view of things was a "wrong" view and another the "right" view. . . . But it is possible for parody to be much more complex than debate. Instead of confronting two opposing views with each other, in order that a decision between them be arrived at, parody is able to intertwine many feelings and attitudes together in such a way that they do not merely grapple with each other antagonistically but act creatively on each other, establishing new syntheses of feeling and stimulating more comprehensive and more subtle perceptions. Parody . . . is a technique of presentation; it offers a field for the joyful exercise of perception and not a platform for derision.[68]

When Don Quixote sallies off after his romantic delusions, Cervantes may be making fun of the conventions of romance that foster such delusions, but he is embracing them at the same time. The virtue of parody is that it can ridicule a form or an idea while at the same time *using* that form or idea. A parody of romance uses the conventions of romance; a parody of God uses the concept of God; a parody of love and art uses the ideas of love and art. Parody has the unique capability of simultaneously ridiculing and celebrating the form and assumptions of its original, allowing a poet to affirm the seemingly unaffirmable.

The poet who embraces the modernist aesthetic is faced with many restrictions as to what he can and cannot do in a poem. While our aesthetic ostensibly claims that any subject is available to poetry, certain subjects or attitudes or styles are clearly suspect. Discursiveness, sentimentality, religious dogma, and romantic love, for example, provoke embarrassment for a poet committed to description, detachment, irony, and withheld emotion. As Robert Pinsky points out in his recent *The Situation of Poetry*, this rather cramped aesthetic has led our poets to adopt several evasive strategies, among them parody.

Whitman uses this strategy, for example, to import the rather absurd notion of "the muse" into the modern world:

> By thud of machinery and shrill steam-whistle undismay'd
> Bluff'd not a bit by drain-pipe, gasometers, artificial fertilizers,
> Smiling and pleas'd with palpable intent to stay,
> She's here, install'd amid the kitchen ware! (p. 198)

This deflating parody of the muse's traditional exalted position is Whitman's way of reaffirming her continuing power. Whitman goes to the kitchen in order to revive the old romantic notions; Stevens goes to the dump:

> Day creeps down. The moon is creeping up.
> The sun is a corbeil of flowers the moon Blanche
> Places there, a bouquet. Ho-ho . . . The dump is full
> Of images. (p. 201)

Sitting on the dump, the poet is surrounded by a litter of outworn, discarded images. Everything has been said before ("The freshness of night has been fresh a long time") and words like *dew*, with its characteristic associations, have been overused ("dew, dew dresses, stones and chains of dew, heads / Of the floweriest flowers dewed with the dewiest dew. / One grows to hate these things"). Ridiculing all the old depleted images and ideas, Stevens is able, however, to use them at the same time. By laughing at himself and his poeticizing ("Ho-ho"), by punning on the moon's color (naming her "Blanche"), he can still create a romantic, natural image of the sun as a bouquet of flowers. Exploring the dump for images, Stevens finds ways of recycling them.

Similarly, in "Sailing After Lunch," while admitting that

> . . . the romantic must never remain,
> Mon Dieu, and must never again return.
> This heavy historical sail
> Through the mustiest blue of the lake
> In a really vertiginous boat
> Is wholly the vapidest fake (p. 120)‍;

he manages to conclude with a moment of absurd romantic transcendence:

> That slight transcendence to the dirty sail,
> By light, the way one feels, sharp white,
> And then rush brightly through the summer air. (p. 121)

In this poem Stevens *uses* outmoded romantic ideas by parodying them. In "Le Monocle de Mon Oncle" he uses an outmoded romantic style similarly:

> "Mother of heaven, regina of the clouds,
> O sceptre of the sun, crown of the moon,
> There is not nothing, no, no, never nothing,
> Like the clashed edges of two words that kill."
> And so I mocked her in magnificent measure.
> Or was it that I mocked myself alone? (p. 13)

The multiple negatives and the confession of mockery permit Stevens to use the otherwise unusable majestic language. John Barth explains about his own work, "If somebody built the Chartres Cathedral now, it would be an embarrassing piece of real estate, wouldn't it? Unless he did it ironically." [69] Wallace Stevens's characteristic style is an ornate Chartres Cathedral, built parodically.

William Carlos Williams goes to Stevens's dump for material to build his own romantic monument to his love. In "Portrait of a Lady," comedy enables him to write a conventional love poem by ridiculing the very act of trying it:

> Your thighs are appletrees
> whose blossoms touch the sky.
> Which sky? The sky
> where Watteau hung a lady's
> slipper. Your knees
> are a southern breeze—or
> a gust of snow. Agh! what
> sort of a man was Fragonard?
> —as if that answered
> anything. Ah, yes—below

> the knees, since the tune
> drops that way, it is
> one of those white summer days,
> the tall grass of your ankles
> flickers upon the shore—
> Which shore?—
> the sand clings to my lips—
> Which shore?
> Agh, petals maybe. How
> should I know?
> Which shore? Which shore?
> I said petals from an appletree.[70]

Williams tries to wax poetic about his lady, using romantic nature images and references to French painters. Just when he manages to work himself into a self-consciously poetic revery, reality, or the lady, or a literary critic perhaps, breaks in and punctures him with questions, insisting on specificity. "Which sky?" "Agh! what / sort of a man was Fragonard?" (the comic slant rhyme of "agh" and "Fragonard" and "answered" further deflating him). Midway through the poem he remembers his original purpose and tries to return to the romantic comparisons of the beginning. If his paramour's thighs are appletrees, then it follows that below her knees, at her ankles to be exact, we might expect to find grass. Once again the comparison is too much for the questioner, who inquires "Which shore?," destroying the poet completely. Vainly, he tries to recover his balance, but can only repeat the beginning of the poem in exasperation as if to say to the lady, "Sit still, I'm trying to praise you." The poem is the comedy of a man stuck in old ways of seeing, unable to come up with suitable modern language of praise. But if Williams makes fun of the ineptness and blundering of his attempted love song, he is no fool. By parodying the convention, Williams is able to use it. The poem, for all its comedy, *is* a love poem, retrieving old images from the dump and giving them new life.

The difficulty Williams must overcome in this poem is not merely that of finding a way to use outdated language; it is a problem of finding a suitable way to celebrate at all. As David Wagoner points out in an interview, one of the attitudes we have come to distrust is the attitude of celebration, praise, and affirmation. Wagoner describes what he sees as three voices in contemporary poetry, the "Searching and Questioning Voices, the Warning and Accusing Voices, and the Healing and Celebrating Voices." Wagoner concludes that most poets would like to employ the healing and celebrating voice if only they could. "Yet with so many questions unanswered and so many accusations still unheeded and so much doubt and anger still plaguing us, many poets find it difficult to say Yes without feeling stupid or blind."[71]

One subject that a number of poets would like to celebrate without seeming blind or stupid is religion. Although poets like Dickinson, Frost, and Berryman poked fun at religion, they did not wish totally to reject it. While Berryman could, for example, grow angry with God, attacking him for his indifference and cruelty, he also longed for the kind of security religious faith could provide. In Dream Song #48 Berryman provides a parodic version of the promise of the resurrection:

> He yelled at me in Greek,
> my God!—It's not his language
> and I'm no good at—his is Aramaic,
> was—I am a monoglot of English
> (American version) and, say the pieces from
> a baker's dozen others: where's the bread?
>
> but rising in the Second Gospel, pal:
> The seed goes down, god dies,
> a rising happens,
> some crust, and then occurs an eating. He said so,
> a Greek idea,
> troublesome to imaginary Jews,
>
> like bitter Henry, full of the death of love,
> Cawdor-uneasy, disambitious, mourning
> the whole implausible necessary thing.

If it takes "some crust" to see the resurrection in these terms, and if the vernacular language seems on the surface a put-down of Christ's status and power, the poem nevertheless affirms it. Late in his career after Berryman had converted to Catholicism, he continued to use parody to affirm his religious beliefs. Consider, for example, his parodic and moving first prayer in "Eleven Addresses to the Lord":

> Master of beauty, craftsman of the snowflake,
> inimitable contriver,
> endower of Earth so gorgeous & different from the boring Moon,
> thank you for such as it is my gift.
>
> I have made up a morning prayer to you
> containing with precision everything that most matters.
> "According to Thy will" the thing begins.
> It took me off & on two days. It does not aim at eloquence.
> . . . .

and I believe as fixedly in the Resurrection-appearances to
   Peter & to Paul
as I believe in this blue chair.
Only that may have been a special case
to establish their initiatory faith.

Whatever your end may be, accept my amazement.
May I stand until death forever at attention
for any your least instruction or enlightenment.
I even feel sure you will assist me again, Master of insight
   & beauty.[72]

Like Emily Dickinson, mixing his own needs and desires and wants and doubts into the poem, Berryman nevertheless provides a moving confession of his faith. The comic tone, by undercutting emotion and belief, makes emotion and belief possible.

Berryman thus uses parody as did Dickinson, Stevens, Williams, and Cummings before him. Parodying romanticism, sentimentality, and religious belief, among other things, the comic poet is able to be romantic, sentimental, and religious. By making fun of outdated literary forms and ideas, the poet is able to embrace them.

6

Finally, comic poetry is able, then, to achieve a kind of balance. Whether we hold the biological view of comedy as a release of suppressed energy, the sociological view of comedy as a means to punish nonconformists, the psychological view of comedy as an outlet for frustration and aggression, or the archetypal view of comedy as a recurrent pattern of character and thought, the spirit of comedy is "a spirit of contrariness, opposing disorder to rigidity ('raising hell') but in virtually the next breath correcting disorder with regularity ('blowing the whistle')."[73] Comedy teaches us that although any order we impose on the world is fanciful and wrongheaded and subject to change without notice, impose it we must. If laughter is, as Bergson insists, "above all, a corrective,"[74] it is a corrective in the broadest sense of the term, keeping us located somewhere between the divine and the subhuman, while refusing to allow us to become either. When people or institutions get too far up, comedy pulls them down; when they get too far down, comedy pulls them up. Backwoods humor made people feel big enough to deal with a terrifying new country; Yankee humor made them feel small enough to view themselves in proper perspective. And often, paradoxically, the very humor that elevates through hyperbole and exaggeration simultaneously deflates as well, while the humor that deflates through comic irony and understatement can elevate at the same time. Comedy itself is a mode of perception in which, as Meredith puts it, you can "detect the ridicule of them you love without loving them less" and can "see yourself somewhat ridiculous in dear eyes . . . accepting the correction their image of you proposes."[75]

I began this introduction by enumerating some of the difficulties facing the critic rash enough to write about comic poetry: a general prejudice against the idea of comic poetry's seriousness, the problem of unconscious humor and pedantic misreadings, the lack of any adequate comic theory to deal with poetry. I do not claim to have solved these problems. But the description of the typical comic voices from American humor, the catalogue of comic stylistic devices of poetry, and the exploration of the three primary modes of poetry's humor should provide at least a general overview of American comic poetry and a useful starting point for a more incisive study of individual poets.

I have used the term *humor* in my title as the broadest and thus most apt description of the range and variety of American comic poetry. Incorporating wit, satire, irony, parody, farce, burlesque, and play, humor is less a form of comedy than an attitude toward life, a way of responding to experience. It is an attitude that, while embracing an awareness of people's essential foolishness and absurdity in a cosmos that seems indifferent or hostile, retains a constant commitment to the farcical, the bizarre, the incongruous, the lively, the surprising, the comic. Its characteristic method is to embrace by disclaiming and to disclaim by embracing. In Meredith's words, "If you laugh all round him, tumble him, roll him about, deal him a smack, and drop a tear on him, own his likeness to you, and yours to your neighbor, spare him as little as you shun, pity him as much as you expose, it is a spirit of Humor that is moving you."[76] Underneath it all is a spirit of affirmation, exhilaration, and celebration, of high seriousness and hilarity, of conflicting attitudes that dance in a harmonious balance until, wonderful and absurd, we feel more at home in the universe.

*   *   *

In a memorable scene from the film *Annie Hall*, Woody Allen and Diane Keaton are standing in line for a movie. In front of them a pedantic young professor, complete with tweed jacket, pipe, and elbow patches, is lecturing his date on Marshall McLuhan's philosophy. Allen begins to fidget and grimace, growing more and more impatient, until finally, unable to stand it any longer, he reaches outside the frame and pulls in Marshall McLuhan himself, who tells the young professor that his assessment is completely wrong, that he hasn't understood a word McLuhan has written, that he is an utter fool. Allen turns to the camera with an exasperated smirk of relief.

This brief scene must embody both the desires and fears of any reasonable critic. Most critics, I suppose, would prefer to play the role of Woody Allen here, confronting the wrongheadedness of other critics by pulling in the authors themselves for support. It is always possible, however, that in his enthusiasm for his own interpretations, a critic can unwittingly end up cast in the role of the tweedy professor, missing the point altogether. Both characters, however, serve their purpose. Without Woody Allen there would be no corrective, no clarification, no sharpened focus. Without the tweedy professor there would be no conflict, no dialogue, no amusement. If I have at times in this book adopted the mask of the tweedy professor, proposing some speculative or even fanciful interpretations of well-worn texts in the interests of conflict, dialogue, and amusement, I have also tried to stand near Woody Allen, encouraging him to pull in the authors themselves at every opportunity to test the validity of the interpretations. Having made a number of large generalizations about the humor of American poetry, I now propose to pull in five poets, one by one, to set the record straight.

II

Walt Whitman
Stucco'd with Quadrupeds and Birds All Over

Since the initial publication of *Leaves of Grass*, critics have accused Walt Whitman of many things, but few have accused him of having a sense of humor. James Russell Lowell, himself a noted American humorist, admitted, "I never looked into [*Leaves of Grass*] farther than to satisfy myself that it was a solemn humbug."[1] Whitman's close friend John Burroughs reluctantly agreed that humorlessness was the price Whitman paid for "strenuousness and earnestness."[2] And William Michael Rossetti, justifying his inclusion of only one Whitman poem ("A Boston Ballad") in his 1879 anthology of *Humorous Poems*, lamented that "the absence of humour from the writings of Whitman" argued an important "limitation in his enormously capacious and sympathetic mind." According to Rossetti, it was Whitman's very capacity for embracing all things equally and wholly that militated against any humorous perspective: "Accepting as he does every fact of life and of circumstance, oddity is not to him so odd as to be worth 'showing up' from that point of view, nor absurdity deserving of castigation or introspection, but simply of notice and appraisement."[3]

The assumption of Whitman's humorlessness is not confined to his earliest readers; it extends to the present. Jesse Bier, for example, in his otherwise perceptive and comprehensive study of American humor, faults Whitman for being "the one major figure unredeemable to comedy . . . a man totally devoid of a sense of humor"; "The braggadocio is without a saving jocular grace. . . . [He is] incapable of self-laughter"; "He travesties himself without the faintest suspicions that his grammar, his very words, turn ludicrous."[4] This kind of assumption leads to the criticism leveled against Whitman by D. H. Lawrence in his *Studies in Classic American Literature*. Responding to Whitman's characteristic boast, "I AM HE THAT ACHES WITH AMOROUS LOVE," Lawrence complains:

> Walter, leave off. You are not HE. You are just a limited Walter. And your ache doesn't include all Amorous Love, by any means. If you ache you only ache with a small bit of amorous love, and there's so much more stays outside the cover of your ache, that you might be a bit milder about it.

53

I AM HE THAT ACHES WITH AMOROUS LOVE.
CHUFF! CHUFF! CHUFF!
CHU-CHU-CHU-CHU-CHUFF!
Reminds one of a steam-engine. A locomotive. They're the only things that
seem to me to ache with amorous love. All that steam inside them. Forty
million foot-pounds pressure. The ache of AMOROUS LOVE. Steam-
pressure. CHUFF! . . .
   What can be more mechanical? . . . It just shows you haven't got any
self. It's a mush.[5]

If one agrees with Lawrence's assumption that Whitman is solemn about
his hyperbolic claims, then Lawrence's rather testy dismissal is valid. If
Whitman lacks a sense of humor, his braggadocio does seem mechanical,
his self a mush.

   Not all readers, however, would agree with Lawrence's assumptions.
Emerson, for example, seems to see some humor in Whitman when he
praises *Leaves of Grass* as "the most extraordinary piece of wit and
wisdom that America has yet contributed";[6] Randall Jarrell insists,
"When Whitman says 'I dote on myself, there is that lot of me and all
so luscious,' we should realize that we are not the only ones who are
amused";[7] Constance Rourke, focusing Whitman as one of her central
examples of American humor, notes, "To enter the world of Whitman is
to touch the spirit of American popular comedy";[8] and Richard Chase
describes "Song of Myself" as "the profound and lovely comic drama of
the self."[9] Such contradictory responses leave the question of Whitman's
humor unresolved. Was Whitman too serious about his work to take it
comically? Or was Whitman too serious about his work *not* to take it
comically?

   Whitman himself seemed to have contradictory feelings about the role
of humor in American literature, and his comments can be marshaled to
support either side of the continuing debate. Late in life, for example, he
disclaimed interest in humorists: "I have very little liking for deliberate
wits—for men who start out, with malice prepense, to be funny."[10] And
earlier he had made a note to himself to refrain from "puns / funny remarks / double entendres / witty remarks / ironies / sarcasms."[11]

   Whitman's notes to himself about not using deliberate wit and puns
may be directed at some of his obvious unsuccessful attempts at comedy.
In his "Autobiography of a Brooklyn Lamp" in the Brooklyn *Daily Eagle*
(a paper he edited), Whitman has his lamp say, "I always had plenty of
tin, however. Perhaps this is the reason that I became stuck up"; "And
though the people who passed were full of jibes when they looked up at
my glass house, I confidently defied them to make light of *me*."[12] In an-

other piece Whitman jokes, "Carelessly knocking a man's eye out with a broken axe, may be termed a bad axe-i-dent."[13] It may also be termed a bad pun, and it must have been efforts like these against which Whitman was warning himself in his notes to *Leaves of Grass*.

A desire to forgo the bad pun or self-consciously humorous phrase does not indicate a rejection of humor. It may even suggest an affirmation of humor. Meredith explains, "The sense of the comic is much blunted by habits of punning, and of using humoristic phrase."[14] On several occasions Whitman more directly affirmed his comic sense. In 1889, for example, he said to some Camden friends, "I pride myself on being a real humorist underneath everything else." And when he helped edit Richard Maurice Bucke's biography of him, Whitman carefully inserted the following warning in the text: "I believe that it has been assumed by the critics that he [Whitman] has no humor. There could not be a greater mistake."[15]

Although such direct comments on humor from Whitman himself are rare, his critical essays and prefaces reflect a spirit akin to the comic. Whitman's description of his aims and methods in his preface to the 1855 edition of *Leaves of Grass*, for example, bears a striking resemblance to Meredith's famous description of the comic spirit. Although Meredith's essay was written in 1877, twenty years after Whitman's preface, and although Meredith's refinement and urbanity pale before Whitman's rowdy yawp, the similarity between Whitman's definition of the poet and Meredith's definition of the comic spirit is instructive. Both Whitman and Meredith emphasize intelligence and common sense. For Whitman, the poet's "brain is the ultimate brain," and the American language is "the dialect of common sense" (pp. 713, 728). For Meredith, comedy provokes "the laughter of the mind" and is "the fountain of sound sense."[16] Both Whitman and Meredith see their respective figures of poet and comedian as correctives. Whitman notes, "If the time becomes slothful and heavy he knows how to arouse it. . . . Whatever stagnates in the flat of custom or obedience or legislation he never stagnates" (p. 713). Meredith explains that "Dulness[*sic*], insensible to the comic, has the privilege of arousing it; and the laying of a dull finger on matters of human life is the surest method of establishing electrical communications with a battery of laughter."[17]

Further, both Whitman's poet and Meredith's comic spirit embrace equality. According to Whitman, the poet evokes "that indescribable freshness and unconsciousness about an illiterate person that humbles and mocks the power of the noblest expressive genius" (p. 713). Similarly, Meredith notes that the comic spirit "enfolds them with the wretched host of the world, huddles them with us all in an ignoble assimilation, and cannot be used by any exalted variety as a scourge and a broom. Nay, to be an exalted variety is to come under the calm, curious eye of the Comic Spirit."[18] For Whitman, "the others are as good as he, only he sees it and they do not" (p. 713). For Meredith, an "insufficiency of sight in the eye looking outward has deprived them of the eye that should look inward."[19]

Both poet and comedian can be warlike: Meredith suggests, "As to this wit, it is warlike. In the neatest hands it is like the sword of the cavalier in the Mall."[20] And Whitman: "In war he is the most deadly force of the war. Who recruits him recruits horse and foot . . . he fetches parks of artillery" (p. 713). Or both poet and comic spirit can turn a calm, curious eye on grotesqueness and eccentricity. For Whitman, "Not in him but off from him things are grotesque or eccentric or fail of their sanity . . . . High up out of reach he stands turning a concentrated light" (pp. 712–13). Similarly, for Meredith, "Whenever they offend sound reason, fair justice; are false in humility or mined with conceit, individually, or in the bulk; the Spirit overhead will look humanely malign, and cast an oblique light on them, followed by volleys of silvery laughter."[21]

The parallels between Whitman's description of the "Great Poet" and Meredith's of the "Comic Spirit" are suggestive. Like Meredith, Whitman sees his poet as "up there" flashing light on people's equality; as informed by common sense, reason, and intelligence; and as a force undercutting social pretense or prestige while preaching largeness of mind and spirit. Of course, Whitman is not Meredith, and Meredith's civilized view of the comic is clearly inadequate to embody Whitman's more robust and rhapsodic rowdiness. Indeed, Bergson's idea of an *élan vital* or Freud's notion of the release of repressed emotion may more accurately define Whitman's comic spirit. But the parallels between Whitman and Meredith can direct our attention to Whitman's characteristic comedy, suggesting a context for a fresh reading of "Song of Myself."

Whitman's problem or challenge in "Song of Myself" was to persuade the reader to accept certain things that he might not normally accept. Whitman's "forbidden voices of sexes and lusts," his thoughts on the body and the soul, and on the self, democracy, and God, could be expected to outrage the typical nineteenth-century reader. Indeed, the early responses to *Leaves of Grass* reflected the prevailing moral climate. Rufus Wilmot Griswold said he would "leave this gathering of muck to the laws which . . . must have power to suppress such obscenity."[22] Even Henry David Thoreau, a humorist himself who was intrigued by Whitman, had difficulties: "He does not celebrate love at all. It is as if the beasts spoke."[23] William Michael Rossetti was clearly understating the case when he commented that Whitman "says a number of things that people consider out-of-the-way."[24] Yet it was all important to Whitman that readers assumed what he assumed, that their thoughts were his thoughts. Repeatedly in "Song of Myself" he insists that if his ideas and convictions "are not yours as much as mine they are nothing" (sec. 17, p. 45). The method Whitman adopted to enable him to say outrageous things and to disarm a reader's defensive preconceptions was the comic method. The exuberant humor of "Song of Myself," with its comic exaggerations and deflations, undercuts the reader's objections and hesitations, enabling Whitman to say things he could not otherwise have said. By exposing his own egotism, Whitman was able to be egotistical. By undercutting himself, he undermined the reader's natural tendency to want to do so.

Meredith's comic spirit hovers in the background of Whitman's comic method, but there is a stronger American source of Whitman's humor. Lawrence lamented that it was too bad that Whitman didn't know Charlie Chaplin. Although Whitman didn't know Chaplin, he did know another comic character who could serve him even better than Chaplin. Whitman wanted to make what would be considered outrageous claims about the most serious human concerns. In search of a truly American persona to espouse his comic philosophy, it is natural that he would turn to that characteristic figure of American humor famed for making outrageous claims, the popular type of the Kentuckian, the ring-tailed roarer, the backwoodsman. As I noted in the Introduction, the backwoods character of American humor was the superhuman boaster and godlike hero reflected in tall tales about Davy Crockett, Mike Fink, and others. The heroes of *Crockett's Almanac* (1852) and *The Big Bear of Arkansas, and other Tales, Illustrative of Characters and Incidents in the South and Southwest* (1845) claimed kinship with horses, alligators, bears, whales, steamboats, and tornadoes and could span the continent with a foot in either ocean while eating clouds and drinking rivers. The mighty muscled Kentuckian, roaring his frontier tall talk, appeared in newspapers, sermons, popular songs, and plays between 1800 and 1850.

Whitman's intimate familiarity with the type is suggested by his involvement with various newspapers in the years immediately preceding "Song of Myself." As a newspaper editor and writer, Whitman read many of the humorous pieces appearing in such publications as the New Orleans *Picayune* and *Delta*, two of the papers most influential in disseminating such humor. In fact, Whitman himself produced this kind of

humor for the New Orleans *Crescent*, creating characters like Daggerdraw Bowieknife, Esq., a frontier type full of bluff and swagger, who rev-
els in making "daylight shine through" his victims.[25]

Whitman's exposure to popular humor and his own attempts at it in
New Orleans apparently came at an opportune time. Before his trip to
New Orleans, Whitman had been a rather indifferent hack writer, the author of that forgettable novel *Franklin Evans: or The Inebriate*, in which
a country boy suffers degradation and torment when he falls under the
influence of alcohol in New York City, but finally reforms and lives an
honorable life. After his four months in New Orleans Whitman was the
brilliant author of "Song of Myself." Critics have enjoyed speculating
about just what happened in New Orleans to wreak such a change. Did
Whitman have an affair with an octaroon woman that expanded his capacity for love? Did he have a mystical revelation, or a homosexual encounter? Or, working at the *Crescent*, did he have an affair with the
comic spirit and a revelation of comic vision? One thing *Franklin Evans*
obviously lacks, and "Song of Myself" does not, is the comic edge that
can measure mawkishness and sentimentality.

Internal evidence of Whitman's adoption of the backwoods character
as mask in "Song of Myself" is not difficult to find. Whitman's famous
introduction of himself in section 24 of the poem clearly reflects the
swagger and brag of the humorous backwoodsman:

> Walt Whitman, a Kosmos, of Manhattan the son,
> Turbulent, fleshy, sensual, eating, drinking and breeding,
> No sentimentalist, no stander above men and women or apart from them,
> No more modest than immodest.
>
> Unscrew the locks from the doors!
> Unscrew the doors themselves from their jambs! (sec. 24, p. 52)

The arrogant self-assertion, the brash overconfidence, continues in Whitman's claims to incorporate all things: old and young, maternal and pa-
ternal, southerner and northerner, raftsman and rowdy, fancy man and
priest. He is a "teacher," a "trader," a "Nation." He is a "Kentuckian
walking the vale of the Elkhorn in my deer-skin leggings," "stuff'd with
the stuff that is coarse and stuff'd with the stuff that is fine" (sec. 16,
p. 44). Next to him, God is a mere coquette, dropping his handkerchief
for Whitman to pick up (sec. 6, p. 33). He spans continents: "My ties and
ballasts leave me, my elbows rest in sea-gaps, / I skirt sierras, my palms
cover continents, / I am afoot with my vision" (sec. 33, p. 61). Godlike
himself, he can make love to the air—"It is for my mouth forever, I am in
love with it" (sec. 2, p. 29)—the sea—"we must have a turn together";

"Dash me with amorous wet" (sec. 22, p. 49)—the wind—"Winds whose soft-tickling genitals rub against me" (sec. 24, p. 53)—and the earth— "Smile O voluptuous cool-breath'd earth! . . . Smile, for your lover comes" (sec. 21, p. 49). He can tell the sun to move over and can offer to help the earth out of her troubles. He doesn't worry about offending, because he is an elementary law and "elementary laws never apologize" (sec. 20, p. 48).

Although Whitman insists that all people share in this elevation with him, he is also able, from his position as ring-tailed roarer, to satirize and undercut those people who fail to identify with his vitality. Whitman describes some of the central objects of his satire in his own early unsigned review of *Leaves of Grass*:

> An American bard at last! One of the roughs, large, proud, affectionate, eating, drinking, and breeding, his costume manly and free, his face sunburnt and bearded, his posture strong and erect, his voice bringing hope and prophecy to the generous races of young and old. We shall cease shamming and be what we really are. We shall start an athletic and defiant literature. We realize now how it is, and what was most lacking. . . . One sees unmistakably genteel persons, travelled, college-learned, used to be served by servants, conversing without heat or vulgarity, supported on chairs, or walking through handsomely carpeted parlors, or along shelves bearing well-bound volumes . . . and china things and nick-nacks. But where in American literature is the first show of America? Where are the gristle and beards, and broad breasts, and space, and ruggedness, and nonchalance, that the souls of the people love?[26]

Gentility, social pretense, cultural and personal anemia, these are Whitman's primary satiric targets. In section 23 of "Song of Myself" he rejects "neuters and geldings" in favor of "men and women fully equipt," and goes on in section 24 to ridicule conventional polite shock or disgust by offering his own contrasting example: "I do not press my fingers across my mouth, / I keep as delicate around the bowels as around the head and heart" (p. 53).

Whitman thus satirizes those ultrarefined people who reject bodily function by displays of polite shock or fear of sexuality; he also satirizes those who elevate themselves above the body and sensory experience by clinging only to intellect. In "When I Heard the Learn'd Astronomer," faced with "proofs," "figures," "charts," and "diagrams," Whitman grows "tired and sick": "rising and gliding out I wander'd off by myself, / In the mystical moist night-air, and from time to time, / Look'd up in perfect silence at stars" (p. 271). Whitman ridicules those who prefer secondhand discourses on stars to their own firsthand experience. In "Song of Myself" he similarly ridicules those who allow learning and terminology to come between them and direct experience. Parodying the language of science, Whitman asserts:

> Having pried through the strata, analyzed to a hair,
>   counsel'd with doctors and calculated close,
> I find no sweeter fat than sticks to my own bones. (sec. 20, p. 47)

In this passage Whitman humorously deflates the experts by beating them with their own language.

Whitman satirizes people who evade life; he also exposes those who actively complain about it or pervert it. Comparing such people with the more natural animals, Whitman sputters that animals

> do not sweat and whine about their condition,
> They do not lie awake in the dark and weep for their sins,
> They do not make me sick discussing their duty to God,
> Not one is dissatisfied, not one is demented with the mania
>   of owning things,
> Not one kneels to another, nor to his kind that lived
>   thousands of years ago,
> Not one is respectable or unhappy over the whole earth. (sec. 32, p. 60)

By listing all of the things animals aren't and don't do, Whitman exposes all of the negativistic things people are and do. James Thurber offers his own version of this comic reversal. In Thurber's world animals are always happier than humans, and when animals take on human characteristics they get into bad fixes, the moral being "If you live as humans do, it will be the end of you." [27]

Whitman can be even more specific in his satiric attack, singling out the "mean man" (sec. 22, p. 51), the "skeptic" (sec. 25, p. 55), the "traitors" (sec. 28, p. 58), the "infidels" (sec. 22, p. 51), and "the swarms of cringers, suckers, doughfaces, lice of politics, planners of sly involutions for their own preferment . . . bound booby and rogue" (p. 721). In some ways "Song of Myself" can thus be seen as a grand comic corrective, Whitman pitting his own Kentuckian large-mindedness and capaciousness against all small-mindedness and exclusivity. Like Meredith's comic spirit, Whitman's comic persona deflects pretension and passivity by opposing to them diversity, vitality, and energy.

But the main thrust of Whitman's comic persona is not satiric. Rather than knocking people down, Whitman preferred to pull them up. Thus Whitman's affection for the backwoods voice seems closely to reflect the impulse behind the character's original popularity. The American frontier presented an intimidating landscape—wide open space, harsh living conditions, and threatening, unexplored wildernesses. While the backwoods character was humorous in his exaggerated prowess, he was nonetheless heroic, giving people courage in facing a large, new, and sometimes terrifying land. When Davy Crockett boasted that he could beat up a "b'ar," he wasn't lying; he *was* magnificent; he *could* beat up a "b'ar." By exaggerating the difficulties and surmounting them nonetheless, the backwoodsman gave courage to ordinary folks who would encounter lesser difficulties. If Davy Crockett could free the sun from an ice prison, then an ordinary person might be able to make it through a difficult winter. Nothing was impossible for an American. A courageous man might even aspire to Davy's heights. The tall tale was, then, a way of both reducing the opposition and elevating the self, of taming the wilderness and affirming the powers of the individual.

Whitman, too, wanted people to face unknown territories, to turn their backs on the easy, the conventional, and the secure, and to explore wildernesses of the self. By adopting the backwoods voice Whitman aimed to uplift the common person, revealing to him his own great potential. Jorge Luis Borges comments: "The task then had required a hero, a man looming larger than his fellows: Achilles, Ulysses, Aeneas, Beowulf, Roland, the Cid, and Sigurd stand out for our admiration. Clearly this tradition would run counter to the very essence of democracy; the new society demanded a new kind of hero. Whitman's response was an amazing one: he himself would be the hero of the poem."[28] As Borges realizes, the premise itself was absurd—to cast oneself as an epic hero required colossal egotism. The setting was all wrong: America with its gasometers and kitchen ware, its peddlers and prostitutes and presidents. And yet Whitman was committed to encompassing these potential inconsistencies. His central purpose in *Leaves of Grass*, he insisted, was to reveal

> "the great pride of man in himself," . . . I think this pride indispensable to an American. I think it not inconsistent with obedience, humility, deference, and self-questioning. . . . While the ambitious thought of my song is to help the forming of a great aggregate Nation, it is, perhaps, altogether through the forming of myriads of fully develop'd and enclosing individuals. . . . The ranges of heroism and loftiness with which Greek and feudal poets endow'd their god-like or lordly born characters—indeed prouder and better based and with fuller ranges than those—was to endow the democratic averages of America. It was to show that we, here and to-day, are eligible to the grandest and the best—more eligible now than any times of old were.[29]

Whitman's adoption of the backwoods persona from American humor thus serves two essential purposes. First and foremost, it represents a serious affirmation of America's limitless possibility, of her boundless energy and vitality. It is Whitman's symbolic gesture of faith in the promise of the single individual to rise as high or higher than any culture's greatest heroes and gods. And second, it represents Whitman's affirmation of American originality and uniqueness. By affirming the backwoods character's excesses and eccentricities, Whitman is affirming extreme individuality unbound by any conventional codes of behavior. By himself being gloriously aberrant, Whitman legitimized aberrancy.

But while Whitman took this backwoods voice seriously as a reflection of American uniqueness and potential, he did not take it solemnly. If Whitman laughs at his humorous society, at its shortcomings and flaws, he also laughs at himself. As I noted in the Introduction, when Whitman was writing "Song of Myself" the backwoods character had begun to lose credibility. Once a mighty, omnipotent figure, he was beginning to be bested by people presumably his inferiors. Whitman himself poked fun at the figure in his New Orleans *Crescent* sketches. Thus, if Whitman wanted to use the character seriously in his poetry, he would have to use it comically. Only by parodying the yawp and brag of the ring-tailed roarer would he be able to adopt the character as his spokesman and hero. Like Joyce, Whitman saw that the terms classically used to reflect heroism no longer applied, but the possibility of heroism still appealed. By using the diminished terms comically, Whitman and Joyce were able to restore their eroded power.

Whitman's use of a first person narrator, however, complicates the reader's response to the humor. When Wallace Stevens, for example, pokes fun at his own comic egotist in "The Comedian as the Letter C," there is little doubt about the comedy. Although Crispin is a version of Stevens, the omniscient point of view separates author from character, allowing Stevens to undercut Crispin's ignorance and egotism from without. In "Song of Myself" Whitman equates himself with his persona. But if Whitman does not, like Stevens, stand outside the action of the poem, exposing his character, he does stand inside the action of the poem, exposing himself. Whitman, as much as Stevens, laughs at the egotism and excess of his protagonist, and to take everything Whitman says at face value is to miss much of the fun of the poem.

In the "Calamus" poem, "Are You the New Person Drawn Toward Me," Whitman himself seems to warn against taking his persona too solemnly as a trustworthy ideal:

> To begin with take warning, I am surely far different from what you
> suppose;

Do you suppose you will find in me your ideal?
. . . .
Do you think I am trusty and faithful?
Do you see no further than this façade? (p. 123)

In a letter to Rudolf Schmidt, a German scholar who had written Whitman for information on American humor, Whitman compared American humor to "the old Greek" humor.[30] Thus, the "façade" Whitman adopts both to elevate and to expose himself is a combination of the backwoods ring-tailed roarer of American humor and its classical relative from "the old Greek" humor, the *alazon*, the boastful fool or impostor, the man who claimed to be more than he was. The combination of backwoodsman and *alazon* results in a parody that enables Whitman to celebrate himself by laughing at himself.

Whitman's parody of the mighty Kentuckian is evident in the *alazon* excess of his boastful exaggerations. While Whitman's backwoods boasts sometimes elevate him, they as often deflate him in their wild imposture. In section 33, for example, Whitman's claim of being a sort of mystic Paul Bunyan renders him slightly ridiculous: "my elbows rest in sea-gaps, / I skirt sierras, my palms cover continents" (p. 61). Or, in "Salut Au Monde!": "Within me latitude widens, longitude lengthens" (p. 137). Mark Twain underlines the humor of such claims in *Life on the Mississippi* when a drunken raftsman virtually quotes Walt Whitman: "Don't attempt to look at me with the naked eyes, gentlemen! When I'm playful I use the meridians of longitude and parallels of latitude for a seine, and drag the Atlantic Ocean for whales!"[31]

From the first lines of the poem, Whitman reveals his affinity with the *alazon* tradition:

I celebrate myself, and sing myself,
And what I assume you shall assume. (sec. 1, p. 28)

The lines are so well known, and so beautiful in their naive assertion, that it may now be difficult to hear their outrageous egotism, their impossible boastfulness, their eccentricity and aberrance. It is the surprising humorous exaggeration, however, that allows Whitman to make the statement at all. And in case we have missed the humor of the boast, Whitman takes it to further extremes throughout "Song of Myself." Although he modestly insists, "I am not an earth nor an adjunct of an earth" (sec. 7, p. 35), the very fact that he feels compelled to set the record straight reveals egotism. It is self-evident that a man is not an earth; by insisting that he is not an earth, Whitman in effect boasts that he is so big that he could be mis-

taken for one. If he is not an earth, he is a "world," however: "One world
is aware and by far the largest to me, and that is myself" (sec. 20, p. 48).
Whether he is an earth or a world or neither, he is large enough to be
unimpressed with what anyone else in history has had to say about the
universe. "I heard what was said of the universe, / Heard it and heard it of
several thousand years; / It is middling well as far as it goes—but is that
all?" (sec. 41, p. 75). What *Whitman* has to say about the universe is so
important, however, that he wishes "that the great masters might return
and study me" (p. 17).

In making great claims that he cannot hope to fulfill, Whitman reflects
Emerson's definition of the comic. According to Emerson, "The essence
of all jokes, of all comedy, seems to be an honest or well-intentioned half-
ness; a non-performance of what is pretended to be performed, at the
same time that one is giving loud pledges of performance."[32] Whitman
talks big in "Song of Myself" but actually does very little, a fact comically
pointed out to him by the hawk that appears in the final section. The
hawk mocks Whitman for his "gab" and for his "loitering," for talking
instead of doing, in effect urging him to practice what he preaches. For all
his big talk Whitman remains humorous to the end, his "blab" jeered at
by a bird.

Whitman thus mocks his persona by displaying his exaggeration and
ego and by exposing incongruities between his claims and capabilities.
On occasion Whitman's speaker resembles less the all-powerful backwoods roarer than the spoiled child. Notice, for example, Whitman's
mode of "helping out" in the haymow:

> I am there, I help, I came stretch'd atop of the load,
> I felt its soft jolts, one leg reclined on the other,
> I jump from the cross-beams and seize the clover and timothy,
> And roll head over heels and tangle my hair full of wisps. (sec. 9, p. 37)

The scene makes a serious point, affirming the gaiety and freedom of the
child at play. But at the same time, it evokes the incongruous picture of a
man helping whose help is no help at all. At times the healthy childlike-
ness of the haymow turns into the impish childishness of voicing taboo
subjects:

> The scent of these arm-pits aroma finer than prayer. (sec. 24, p. 53)

The line is clearly a serious statement of a belief in the holiness of the
body and in the equality of all things. But it is the impish joke that makes
the line work, the combination of "armpits" and "prayer" adding an au-

ditory paradox to the intellectual one. The line also reflects Bergson's contention that *"any incident is comic that calls our attention to the physical in a person, when it is the moral side that is concerned."*[33] So caught up in his own self-indulgent sweetness, Whitman can rhapsodize, "I dote on myself, there is that lot of me and all so luscious" (sec. 24, p. 54). Only his awareness of the humorous outrageousness of the statements enables Whitman to make them at all.

It is not only *what* Whitman says in the poem that renders him comic, it is as much *how* he says it. Throughout the poem, language gets out of hand, undercutting the speaker in ways he does not see. When the speaker brags that he is "sensual" and "breeding," for example, he doesn't seem to be aware of the contradiction between human sensuality and animalistic breeding. When he expresses a preference for men and women sexually "well-equipp'd," he seems oblivious to the mechanical implications of his preference. When he speaks of "Echoes, ripples, buzz'd whispers, love-root, silk-thread . . . the sound of the belch'd words" (sec. 2, p. 30), the comic juxtaposition of the evanescent and the gross eludes him. When his heart becomes an "udder" strained for its "withheld drip" (sec. 28, p. 57), he doesn't crack a smile. Throughout "Song of Myself" the seriousness and dignity of an image or idea is suddenly deflated by the juxtaposition of an unexpected or inappropriate word or phrase. As I noted in the Introduction, Whitman himself described this clownish aspect of his language:

> Considering Language then as some mighty potentate, into the majestic
> audience-hall of the monarch ever enters a personage like one of
> Shakspere's clowns, and takes position there, and plays a part even in the
> stateliest ceremonies.[34]

This comic play of language, going on seemingly outside the control of the protagonist, is similar to the repartee characteristic of Groucho and Chico Marx. Groucho's ceaseless talk leads the listener in circles, swallowing him up in a verbal maze, eventually depositing him back where he started without letting on where he has been or how he got there. Chico, with his homely vernacular and his misunderstanding of big words, is one of the few people who can slow Groucho down or stop him. Similarly, in Whitman, the more intellectual words clash with common slang, the elevated, poetic words clash with the humble and the vernacular, in a play of language to which the speaker seems to remain oblivious. Thus Whitman adopts the precise observational language of science to describe his sense of oneness and harmony with the universe, only to bring the elaborate airy structure tumbling down with words that turn the whole picture absurdly comic:

> I find I incorporate gneiss, coal, long-threaded moss, fruits,
>   grains, esculent roots,
>
> And am stucco'd with quadrupeds and birds all over. (sec. 31, p. 59)

The first line proposes an extreme but, if taken metaphorically, acceptable philosophic position. The second line undercuts the first's pretensions by evoking a literal picture of the speaker plastered with stucco into which random birds and animals have been lodged. If the garb is a kind of motley worn in tribute to man's infinite capacities and connections, it is nevertheless laughable.

Throughout much of "Song of Myself" Whitman expresses little awareness of his comic deflation. Donning his comic facade, he rarely acknowledges his ridiculousness directly, preferring to allow his exaggerations and incongruities to alert the reader to the comedy. Bergson notes, "A comic character is generally comic in proportion to his ignorance of himself. The comic person is unconscious." [35] Similarly, Mark Twain insists that "the humorous story is American . . . [and] is told gravely; the teller does his best to conceal the fact that he even dimly suspects that there is anything funny about it." [36] Whitman thus uses the traditional comic ploy of the comedian who doesn't get his own joke, departing from the strategy only occasionally to remind the reader, "I am of the foolish as much as the wise" (sec. 16, p. 44) and "I know perfectly well my own egotism" (sec. 42, p. 77). When D. H. Lawrence lamented that Whitman "was not able to assume one identity with Charlie Chaplin . . . because Walt didn't know Charlie. What a pity!," he was only partially right. [37] Like Charlie Chaplin, Whitman adopted the mask of the clown, not letting on that what he was doing was funny, keeping a deadpan seriousness in the face of absurd pain, humiliation, and joy. Perhaps Walt did know Charlie after all.

Although it is no doubt accurate to see Walt Whitman as a cosmic philosopher of mystic affirmations, intent on merging with the universe, it is important to remember that he also appreciated incongruities and contradictions and was capable of a comic perspective on himself and his society. In assessing Whitman's persona in "Song of Myself" we have to keep in mind simultaneously the two related comic traditions from which it was drawn—the familiar backwoods ring-tailed roarer of American humor, and the traditional *alazon* of old Greek comedy. By making his backwoods speaker an *alazon*, he could both ridicule and affirm the character and all it stood for.

Whitman's persona thus reflects Dale Underwood's definition of the comic hero:

> It is an essential of the comic hero . . . that he have this ambivalence. His attitudes and actions serve, on the one hand, to criticize his society; but they serve on the other to criticize himself. If they do only the former, the character is not comic; if they do only the latter, he is no hero. As an aspect of his ambivalence of character his wit, if he has any, will also be ambivalent. It may sometimes operate to minify his society—and then we laugh with him, or it may sometimes serve to minify him—and then we laugh at him. But it may simultaneously do both, and then the comic complexity of both character and language is at its peak.[38]

Simultaneously inflating and deflating himself and his society, Whitman used comedy not to cancel out what he was saying, but to enable him to say it. Adopting the voice of the boastful impostor and fool, he was able to affirm the energy, vitality, eccentricity, and originality that characterized America's potential and uniqueness.

The reader's response to "Song of Myself" is complicated by the balance of contradictory impulses that make up its speaker; it is further complicated by the combination of structural patterns that make up its plot. In an effort to see the poem whole, several critics have sought to describe its structure. James E. Miller, for example, suggests that "Song of Myself" is structured as an "inverted mystical experience"[39] and as an episode in a personal epic.[40] John M. Nagle sees a structure based on eight thematic "phases."[41] John Berryman speaks more generally of the self's development in the poem: "I take the work in fact to be one of Welcome, self-*wrestling*, inquiry, and wonder—conditional, open, and astonished (not exulting as over an accomplished victory, but gradually revealing, puzzling, discovering)."[42] The various descriptions are useful, wisely claiming not to define the structure of the poem (which does not readily lend itself to mechanical schema), but to provide analogues for it. If the poem is, in part, analogous to a mystical experience, an epic, a series of phases, or a gradual revealing, it is also analogous to several comic structures, and a knowledge of those structures can shed light on the poem as a whole.

Two basic plot patterns typically structure comedies. An *alazon* figure usually governs an exposure plot in which most of the action aims to undercut the protagonist, reforming him through ridicule. After a series of comic comeuppances, the *alazon* usually experiences a kind of ritual death and is either incorporated into the existing society or expelled from it. The plays of Molière and the novels of George Meredith are representative of this tradition. An *eiron* protagonist usually governs an integration plot in which two lovers, blocked from a natural union by some unnatural law, finally overcome the blocks to their happiness and marry, renewing society and promising continued vitality and life. The romance comedies of Shakespeare often reflect this pattern. Sometimes a comic work can combine these plot patterns, as in a number of contemporary American comic novels like Nabokov's *Lolita* and John Hawkes's *Second Skin*.

Since Whitman's persona in "Song of Myself" participates in the *alazon* tradition, one might expect to find the poem structured on a pattern of exposure. Indeed, the first two-thirds of the poem reflects the expected pattern, moving through Whitman's exposure of his boastful egotism to a kind of ritual death or grand comeuppance in sections 34–37 (the narration of the 1836 Mexican massacre and the defeat of John Paul Jones). Further, an exposure comedy often incorporates an *eiron* voice, a secondary character who questions and undercuts the protagonist, gradually leading him to a reformation through ridicule. In "Song of Myself" this *eiron* appears as an offstage voice to which Whitman responds throughout the poem. While this voice never actually speaks in its own right, it provokes Whitman, stimulating him to defend and explain himself. While Wallace Stevens himself takes on the role of *eiron* to undercut Crispin's *alazon*, and while John Berryman personifies the conflicting characters, putting a minstrel interlocutor in opposition to Henry, Whitman incorporates the *eiron* as an invisible presence referred to both directly and indirectly by the speaker.

The *eiron* playing to Whitman's *alazon* in "Song of Myself" takes on a variety of ghostly disguises. Sometimes it is an anonymous person of the future, sometimes a follower, a lover, or an innocent onlooker. Sometimes it is an antagonist, like death, or a doubt or conformity or convention lurking within Whitman himself. Whitman describes the voice at its most painful as something within himself reminiscent of Meredith's comic spirit:

> Withdrawn far, mocking me with mock-congratulatory signs and bows,
> With peals of distant ironical laughter at every word I have written,
> Pointing in silence to these songs, and then to the sand beneath. (p. 254)

In "Song of Myself" the figure is externalized as the "prurient provokers stiffening my limbs" (sec. 42, p. 77), the "Trippers and askers [that] surround me" (sec. 4, p. 32), "ever the vexer's *hoot! hoot!*" (sec. 42, p. 77).

When the offstage voice isn't tripping or mocking him or ironically smiling or hooting at him, it is silently judging or questioning. "Listener up there!," Whitman shouts, "Do I contradict myself? / Very well then I contradict myself, / (I am large, I contain multitudes)" (sec. 51, p. 88). Having boasted about being the poet of wickedness, Whitman responds to an apparent demur by the offstage voice, "What blurt is this about virtue and about vice?" (sec. 22, p. 50). Throughout the poem Whitman structures his comments as responses to a series of implied judgments from this invisible observer: "Why should I pray?" (sec. 20, p. 47); "Do you take it I would astonish?" (sec. 19, p. 47); "Who goes there?" (sec. 20, p. 47); "What am I?" (sec. 20, p. 47). One can hear the *eiron* voice, the voice of reason and civilized society, behind these questions commenting, "You should pray," "You are going to astonish and offend people," "Who do you think you are, anyway?" With Whitman cast in the role of *alazon* here, it is likely that the conventional reader is being cast as *eiron*. The questions Whitman answers are the kind of questions a typical nineteenth-century reader might pose in response to Whitman's blab and brag, in an effort to control or undercut him. The implied dramatic conflict between Whitman and conventional reader helps to structure the comedy.

In a typical exposure plot the *eiron*'s role is to prod the *alazon* toward self-knowledge or reform, often represented by a ritual death. Northrop Frye observes, "An extraordinary number of comic stories . . . seem to approach a potentially tragic crisis near the end, a feature that I may call the 'point of ritual death' . . . . Everyone will have noted in comic actions, even in very trivial movies and magazine stories, a point near the end at which the tone suddenly becomes serious, sentimental, or ominous of potential catastrophe."[43] The question that finally pushes Whitman into that ritual death occurs in section 35 of "Song of Myself": "Would you hear of an old-time sea-fight?" (p. 69). While the idea of an old-time sea fight with its promise of heroism and romance seems innocent at first, it is soon evident that the experience will be one of the most painful in the poem. In this section the speaker is made to see the logical consequences of his insistence that he incorporates all things and all people, all times and all places. If Whitman does incorporate everything, then he must also incorporate pain, tragedy, and despair. While his boasts of identification with suffering and humiliation have all remained rather abstract to this point, the stories of the Mexican massacre and the defeat of John Paul Jones function here like a giant slapstick, stinging Whitman into a recognition of what his bragging really means.

While these sections are vividly painful and emotionally wrenching, they are nevertheless handled the way evil or pain is often handled in comedy. John Berryman calls section 37 "this terrible, almost funny, deeply actual, final humiliation to the poet's dignity and independence."[44]

If Whitman's ritual death here is painful and terrible, it is also "almost funny," representing the kind of suffering that is permitted, even welcomed in comedy. Toward the end of section 33 (the account of the Mexican massacre) Whitman inserts a comic metaphor, "Agonies are one of my changes of garments" (sec. 33, p. 67). The metaphor is a method of distancing and controlling the horror. If agony is like a garment, then it can be put on or taken off at will. It can be changed. And several lines later Whitman notes, "My hurts turn livid upon me as I lean on a cane and observe." The line reminds us (and Whitman himself) that he is detached, an observer both in and out of the battle, who can feel for the suffering victims, but who himself will not be permanently damaged. The comic metaphor and the observer's role provide what Bergson refers to as comedy's necessary "anesthesia of the heart." Finally, the exaggerated description of the fight itself risks appearing "almost funny." As in a slapstick film comedy, like *The Return of the Pink Panther*, in which Peter Sellers remains unharmed while the entire contents of the room and the walls themselves converge on him in slow motion, so in this battle Whitman leans on his cane observing parts of structures, equipment, and people sail grotesquely in a "whizz of limbs, heads, stone, wood, iron, high in the air" (sec. 33, p. 68). While the picture is clearly terrifying and terrible, the incremental violence that does no ultimate damage to the protagonist is the kind of terror and horror characteristic of the comic form.

Up to section 38 of the poem, "Song of Myself" thus parallels the usual pattern of the traditional exposure plot. Undercut by his own exaggeration and egotism and by an implied *eiron* voice, Whitman undergoes a ritual death that might lead to reformation. That it does not lead to Whitman's reformation, that it instead leads to a new and even stronger egotism, is itself a surprising reversal of expectation, a reversal that represents a prophetic contribution to the comic form in general, foreshadowing similar reversals that were to appear in the American novel a hundred years later. Like Barth's Todd Andrews, Hawkes's Skipper, Nabokov's Humbert, and Kesey's McMurphy, for example, rather than himself being converted to society's way of thinking, Whitman converts society to his.

Whitman reaches his lowest point in "Song of Myself" at the end of section 37. Having recalled the painful Mexican massacre and the defeat of John Paul Jones, having identified intensely with the victims, he loses his vitality and almost his life:

> Askers embody themselves in me and I am embodied in them,
> I project my hat, sit shame-faced, and beg. (p. 72)

But if the askers and trippers, the vexers and provokers, almost win the victory, Whitman recovers to shout them down:

Enough! enough! enough!
Somehow I have been stunn'd. Stand back!

· ·

I discover myself on the verge of a usual mistake.

That I could forget the mockers and insults! (sec. 38, p. 72)

Whitman's "usual mistake" can be read in a number of ways. D. H. Lawrence felt that Whitman's usual mistake was his tendency to merge with
all things, rather than just empathizing with them. J. Albert Robbins suggests, "He means a false involvement in the conventionally ideal and heroic. . . . In the sudden reversal, therefore, Whitman dramatises the false
poet he might have become and indeed for a moment did become."[45]
Charles Alexander suggests that the usual mistake involves forgetting
what the classifiers and doubters have done to the ancient faith.[46] Although all of these possibilities seem valid, the "usual mistake" seems also
to include a loss of comic spirit. At the end of section 37 Whitman had
become "less the jolly one there, and more the silent one" (p. 71), aligning
himself with the quiet questioners and mockers who see life tragically
rather than comically. If experiences like the two painful ones he has just
related are typical, are in fact analogues for life in general, then he should
indeed reform and correct the aberrant notions expressed earlier in "Song
of Myself." He is on the verge of seeing life as tragic, of feeling sorry for
himself and seeing his own pain as "separate." But Whitman reasserts
himself comically, remembering that "Corpses rise, gashes heal, fastenings roll from me," and he transforms the reader, the former questioner
and asker, into his student: "Elèves, I salute you! come forward! Continue
your annotations, continue your questionings" (sec. 38, p. 72). Not only
is he not reformed by the mockers and questioners and the lessons of history and the suffering, he ends up positively exhilarated by the experience
and even more invincible. He can tell the sun to move over; he can tell
death to get lost.

The reversal of the final sections is thus a typical American joke. Whitman, the boastful impostor and egotist, himself turns out to be the hero.
While in the early sections of the poem the joke might have seemed to be
on Whitman, it is clear after section 37 that the joke was, all along, on
society and the reader. The comic figure who had exposed himself to
ridicule triumphs exuberantly over social conformity and criticism. And
what we discover is that the protagonist isn't quite what we had thought
him to be—he is loving, imaginative, alive in ways his ironic counterpart
may not be. By laughing at himself and by suffering a ritual death, Whitman takes us unaware, undercutting our potential reluctance to join him
in his wise foolishness. All along his boasts have been meant to encourage

us to be as big as he is and to leave expectation and convention behind.
Now the poem itself leaves conventional plot expectations behind and
soars into an original realm of divine comedy. I suggested earlier that the
spotted hawk of section 52 can be seen as an ironical voice, criticizing
Whitman for his gab and loitering. While that is true, it is clear that Whitman himself is also the hawk, urging the reader to stop loitering and follow him. "I too am not a bit tamed, I too am untranslatable, / I sound my
barbaric yawp over the roofs of the world" (sec. 52, p. 89).

The shape of "Song of Myself" is based in part on the comic pattern of
exposure. It is also based in part on the comic pattern of integration.
Whitman's effort to convert the reader and his society to a new world
imagined by Whitman himself is, of course, not merely evident in the final
third of the poem—it is evident from the beginning. If Whitman resembles the boastful impostor and fool of satiric comedy who must be converted or expelled, he also resembles the traditional lover of romance
comedy who must overcome the irrational laws and conventions that
block him from happiness.

While the reader functions as an *eiron* in "Song of Myself," a mocker
and tripper and asker, he also functions as Whitman's reluctant paramour. One of Whitman's methods of reforming the reader and society, as
we have seen, is to shout them down, buffet them about, laugh their negativity away, enliven them with his own boisterousness and vitality. But his
boisterous demeanor is also a disguise for another intention, that of
wooing the reader, of seducing him. "Song of Myself" is a love poem,
after all, and early in the poem Whitman provides an analogue for the
love relationship between himself and the reader when he assumes the
role of the body and invites the soul to join him. The invitation of soul by
body parallels the invitation of beloved by lover and of reader by poet.
The outcome of the invitation for the body and soul is decidedly sexual.
In section 5, soul and body waste no time in consummating their love:

> I mind how once we lay such a transparent summer morning,
> How you settled your head athwart my hips and gently turn'd
>   over upon me,
> And parted the shirt from my bosom-bone, and plunged your
>   tongue to my bare-stript heart,
> And reach'd till you felt my beard, and reach'd till you held
>   my feet. (sec. 5, p. 33)

The picture of the soul and body interacting sexually is a pleasantly comic
one. The humor of portraying the spiritual in physical terms undercuts
what moral objections a reader might foolishly bring to bear.

The union of body and soul provides a model for poet and reader, and throughout the poem Whitman woos the reader in the traditional mode of the lover. He teases the reader with confidences: "I might not tell everybody, but I will tell you" (sec. 19, p. 47). He makes romantic promises: "Stop this day and night with me and you shall possess the origin of all poems" (sec. 2, p. 85). And if he can't quite manage complete union with the reader in the poem, he does manage some rather convincing intimacy: "It is you talking just as much as myself, I act as the tongue of you, / Tied in your mouth, in mine it begins to be loosen'd" (sec. 47, p. 85). At the end of the poem, swooping with the spotted hawk, mimicking its courting ritual, Whitman makes one last humorous play for the reader, and then stops "somewhere waiting for you" (sec. 52, p. 89).

In some ways Whitman is miscast in his role as lover. In a typical romance comedy, the two lovers are opposed by an *alazon* who must be overcome so that the lovers can celebrate their union. In "Song of Myself" *Whitman* is the *alazon*. By mixing the genres Whitman foreshadows a similar mixture in contemporary American comic fiction. In Nabokov's *Lolita*, for example, Humbert Humbert is both the romance hero who envisions an idealized nymphet and the blocking figure who lusts after and violates her. In "Song of Myself" Whitman is similarly disagreeable, a man who loves everything from armpits to angels and who has exhibitionist tendencies. But by laughing at their humorous characters and by casting them as heroes of romance comedy, Nabokov and Whitman marshal reader sympathy and identification. Both Humbert and Whitman's persona aim to seduce the reader, to get their tongues into his mouth and their brains into his brain, to convince the reader that the "aberrant" is good and the "normal" is bad. Turning conventions on their heads, elevating the quirky individualist who doesn't fit into established society, Whitman, like a number of contemporary American comic novelists, aims to create a new world around his character and to entice the reader to live in it with him.

The structure of "Song of Myself" thus resembles a five-act comic drama, combining two traditional comic plots. The first act, sections 1–5, introduces the comic hero as both egotist of an exposure comedy and lover of a romance comedy. His comic concerns with the grass, the self, the body, and the soul both elevate and deflate him, as does the dramatic conflict between ego and *eiron*, poet and paramour. In the second act, sections 6–33, the comic protagonist proceeds to woo the reader by replacing the conventional unfestive and destructive society with a new world that satisfactorily solves the puzzle of being. Act 3, sections 34–37, exposes the hero to a ritual death in which reality, society, and history conspire to separate the poet from his creations, the lover from his love. In act 4, sections 38–49, the protagonist reasserts himself, overcoming the blocks to his happiness, emerging as an absurdly buoyant god. In act 5, sections 50–52, having created a world that reaches from the grass to heaven and back again to the grass, the speaker waits confidently for the reader-lover, who is purged of pretense and negativity, to catch up and join him in a harmonious union.

Combining the two archetypal comic patterns of integration and exposure, "Song of Myself" also reflects the death and rebirth of a god that is at the heart of primitive religious ritual and myth. Ultimately, it is on this religious and resurrectional side of comedy that we are to find the essential Whitman, a figure whose clownish assertiveness, backwoods boasting, and Dionysian ecstasy place him in the company of the divine fool. Throughout "Song of Myself" Whitman clearly affirms this Dionysian religious spirit, "Enclosing worship ancient and modern . . . Dancing yet through the streets in a phallic procession" (sec. 43, p. 78), a spirit which would naturally have led him to comedy. Wylie Sypher, paraphrasing Kierkegaard, notes that "the religious man must first of all be a comedian," and the "*alazon* is one of the disguises worn by the god-hero before he is sacrificed" because "God must be hated before he can be loved, denied before he is believed." [47] In "Song of Myself" Whitman becomes a comic Christ figure, crucified in sections 34–37 but self-resurrected in section 38 as a god powerful enough to make "Corpses rise, gashes heal, fastenings roll from me. / I troop forth replenish'd with supreme power" (p. 72). Whitman carries away death and triumphs over mortality by an absurd belief in his own salvational power until, in his sight, firemen become "gods of the antique wars," "the mechanic's wife" becomes the Virgin Mary "interceding for every person born," scythes become angels, and "the snag-tooth'd hostler" becomes Christ (sec. 41, p. 75).

Boy, seer, clown, fool, trickster, Kentuckian, *alazon*, Dionysus, lover, and Christ, Whitman keeps "no account with lamentation" (sec. 44, p. 80), insisting instead on the old comic virtues: "buoyancy," "gladness," "sexuality," "vitality," "Good cheer," "Hope." [48] In his combination of comic masks, Whitman thus closely corresponds to Northrop Frye's description of the central figure of Old Comedy:

> There is usually a central figure who constructs his (or her) own society in the teeth of strong opposition, driving off one after another all the people who come to prevent or exploit him, and eventually achieving a heroic triumph, complete with mistresses, in which he is sometimes assigned the honors of a reborn god. We notice that just as there is a catharsis of pity and fear in tragedy, so there is a catharsis of the corresponding comic

emotions, which are sympathy and ridicule, in Old Comedy. The comic hero will get his triumph whether what he has done is sensible or silly, honest or rascally.[49]

Whitman seeks to construct his own society (a vision of America) in the teeth of strong opposition (mockers and trippers and askers), eventually achieving a heroic triumph (the buoyant assertion of self), complete with mistresses (his soul and "you"), in which he becomes a reborn god. In the process, sympathy and ridicule are comically purged, and he gets his triumph in spite of (or because of) his silliness and rascality.

"Song of Myself" is thus a great comic poem, incorporating a persona that combines a character from early American humor with a character from Old Greek comedy in a plot that reflects patterns of exposure and integration, in a spirit of fun, nonsense, satire, self-parody, exaggeration, deflation, celebration, and surprise. It is a serious poem, but not a solemn one, presided over by a comic spirit that turns its concentrated light outward on a society threatening to grow mechanical and conventional, and inward on a self large enough both to encompass the All and be stucco'd with quadrupeds and birds all over.

III

Emily Dickinson
A Day! Help! Help! Another Day!

If Walt Whitman is often accused of lacking a sense of humor, Emily Dickinson is often accused of having one. Constance Rourke was one of the first critics to insist that Dickinson "was not only a lyric poet; she was in a profound sense a comic poet in the American tradition."[1] Following up this argument, George Whicher emphasized her humor, Richard Chase her playfulness, and Charles R. Anderson her wit. All of these critics point to the fact that as a youth Dickinson apparently gained the reputation of being a wit. She entertained her family and friends with high-spirited repartee, capricious nonsense, playful letters, and valentines filled with verbal extravagance and jokes. She was a humor columnist for the Amherst Academy publication, *Forest Leaves*, probably writing imitations of the burlesque sermons, tall tales, and mock orations that were then so popular in the local Springfield *Daily Republican*.

This tendency toward effervescence and exuberant stand-up comedy provoked her to write a number of playful light-verse poems with no ostensible purpose other than good fun. Thus it is to poems like "I like to see it lap the Miles" (#585) and "Bee! I'm expecting you" (#1035) that critics often refer when acknowledging her comic sense. But after acknowledging her comic sense, the very critics who praise her for it often apologize for its essential triviality or frivolity, labeling it "coy," "arch," or "childish." Rourke, for example, ultimately concludes, "Her poems are only poetic flashes, notes, fragments of poetry rather than a final poetry."[2] Chase finds too much "coy, childish, and awkward jollification" that makes "inspired poetic play impossible for her."[3] Even Anderson decides that the comedy is largely "scattered among the serious [poems] . . . to leaven the whole" and that Dickinson had to be careful not "to pour too much of herself into this mold."[4] While Chase and Anderson have doubts about the success of her humor, a critic like Yvor Winters has none at all. For Winters, Dickinson's attempts at humor reflect a "silly playfulness" that can render her "abominable." "Her efforts at lightness," concludes Winters, "are distressing."[5]

These critics, and others who would assure her a place in the highest ranks of American literature, prefer the dark Dickinson to the lighter one, reserving their highest praise for her tragic sense, for her poems of anguish, pain, despair, grief, agony, and death. A comic poet is, it seems, by definition a minor poet, while a tragic poet aspires, at least, to being a major poet. Thus, in her recent gloomy book on Dickinson, Inder Nath Kher insists on Dickinson's "solemn engagement with life," claiming that "living is a deadly serious business with her" and that her characteristic method of humor is "sarcasm."[6] While Kher intends her emphasis to elevate Dickinson, it in effect demeans her. Archibald MacLeish explains, "A morbid art is an imperfect art. Poets must learn Yeats's lesson that life is a tragedy but if the tragedy turns tragic for them they will be crippled poets . . . . 'Their eyes, their ancient glittering eyes' must be *gay*."[7] Karl Keller, in the best recent book on Dickinson, agrees: "Emily Dickinson's is . . . a poetry of cheer."[8] And Dickinson's niece, Martha Dickinson Bianchi, comments, "It is the element of drollery in her, the elfin, mischievous strain, that is hardest for those who never knew her to reconcile with her solemn side."[9] While Dickinson clearly had a solemn side, she also reveled in the elements of comedy, unreluctant to let her poems clown around, show off, tickle, and entertain at the same time that they went about their very serious business.

Like Walt Whitman, Emily Dickinson thus adopted a familiar character of American humor as persona to deal with the complex themes of the self, perception, social institutions, epistemology, God, immortality, death, and nature. As Whitman adapted the figure of the Kentuckian, the back-woodsman, the ring-tailed roarer, to his special purposes, Dickinson adapted the figure who seemed, in some ways, to represent its opposite— the Yankee. The backwoods voice was loud and boastful, gregarious and egotistical, full of blab and exaggeration; the Yankee voice was quiet and self-effacing, laconic and modest, full of irony and understatement. With his mode of self-deprecation, his pretense of ignorance, his ability to shine superior to an antagonist by claiming to be inferior, the Yankee was an attractive type for a poet of Dickinson's sensibility.

In an uncharacteristically direct poem, Dickinson defines her indirect method of arriving at truth:

> Tell all the Truth but tell it slant—
> Success in Circuit lies
> Too bright for our infirm Delight
> The Truth's superb surprise
>
> As Lightning to the Children eased
> With explanation kind
> The Truth must dazzle gradually
> Or every man be blind— (#1129)

Walt Whitman, wearing his backwoods mask, strove to jolt the unwary reader with his Jovian lightning bolts; Emily Dickinson, wearing her Yankee mask, preferred to dazzle the reader slyly toward the truth. But if the techniques appear diametrically opposed on the surface, they are intended to accomplish similar purposes. Both Whitman and Dickinson use their comic personae to assert themselves and gain power over experience. Whitman's characteristic method of self-mockery is exaggeration, consciously claiming to be more than he is. He knows he is not the mythic character he claims to be, and we know that he knows it. But in asserting it hyperbolically he is able to affirm things about himself and his universe that he wouldn't be able to affirm somberly. Dickinson's characteristic mode of self-mockery is deflation, claiming to be less than she is. She knows she is not the simpleminded character she poses as, and we know that she knows it. But the pose of powerlessness gives her a power she couldn't claim somberly. Both poses enable their authors to incorporate opposites: foolishness and wisdom, victim and victor, despair and ecstacy, elevation and deflation. Paradoxically, Whitman's hyperbolic self-aggrandizement becomes a kind of modesty, while Dickinson's hyperbolic self-deprecation becomes a kind of hubris. If the comic strategies are opposites, the serious results are often identical, both poets transcending convention and expectation by rendering them laughable.

A good example of how the opposing methods embrace similar purposes and results is evident in a comparison of the two poets' similar encounters with the sea. Affecting the exaggerated drollery of the tall tale, Whitman boisterously addresses the sea in section 22 of "Song of Myself":

> You sea! I resign myself to you also—I guess what you mean,
> I behold from the beach your crooked inviting fingers,
> I believe you refuse to go back without feeling of me,
> We must have a turn together, I undress, hurry me out of
>   sight of the land,
> Cushion me soft, rock me in billowy drowse,
> Dash me with amorous wet, I can repay you.
>
> Sea of stretch'd ground-swells,
> Sea breathing broad and convulsive breaths,
> Sea of the brine of life and of unshovell'd yet always-ready graves,
> Howler and scooper of storms, capricious and dainty sea,
> I am integral with you, I too am of one phase and of all phases. (p. 50)

Whitman addresses the sea aggressively from a position of confidence and power. He is the Kentuckian capable of understanding the inarticulate sea and giving it what it wants most—him. "We must have a turn together," he jests familiarly as he enters the water naked for a sexual romp, promising to dash the sea with his own "amorous wet." Elements of the tall tale are evident here, as Whitman takes on the stature of a god capable of satisfying the sea intellectually and sexually. The scene is humorous, but Whitman adopts the humorous persona, exaggerating his relationship and his ability, to make a serious comment about the necessity of embracing opposites. For Whitman, the sea represents both life and death; it is both dangerous and dainty. In showing himself to be one with the sea, he demonstrates his own capacity for incorporating opposites, for embracing life and death, body and mind, good and evil.

While the tone and mood of Dickinson's "I started Early—Took my Dog" are radically different from Whitman's, the final import of the poem is strikingly similar:

> I started Early—Took my Dog—
> And visited the Sea—
> The Mermaids in the Basement
> Came out to look at me—
>
> And Frigates—in the Upper Floor
> Extended Hempen Hands—
> Presuming Me to be a Mouse—
> Aground—upon the Sands—
>
> But no Man moved Me—till the Tide
> Went past my simple Shoe—
> And past my Apron—and my Belt
> And past my Bodice—too—
>
> And made as He would eat me up—
> As wholly as a Dew
> Upon a Dandelion's Sleeve—
> And then—I started—too—
>
> And He—He followed—close behind—
> I felt His Silver Heel
> Upon my Ankle—Then my Shoes
> Would overflow with Pearl—
>
> Until We met the Solid Town—
> No One He seemed to know—
> And bowing—with a Mighty look—
> At me—The Sea withdrew— (#520)

Like Whitman's, Dickinson's poem reflects elements of the tall tale. The sea is a huge house with mermaids in the basement and hempen-handed frigates in the upper floors, and the sea-house takes on animate form in relationship to the human. Rather than magnifying Dickinson, however, as they did Whitman, these humorous elements diminish her. Here the sea is the sexual aggressor and Dickinson is the shy, reluctant quarry, a mouse, a dew, an innocent child (though it was she, one shouldn't forget, who went to the sea in the first place). At the end of the poem Dickinson silently retreats to the safety of the town, but only *after* she has had her tryst and been "known" by the sea in a way no one in the town has. Meanwhile, the dog, her link with convention and domesticity, is long gone.

Whitman is large, aggressive, and boastful about his relationship with the sea; Dickinson is small, passive, and self-deprecating. Whereas Whitman uses humor to elevate himself, to master and incorporate the sea, to show his oneness with it and all it stands for, Dickinson uses humor to diminish herself, to be mastered by and almost incorporated into the sea, to show her separation from it. Both are comic stances, and both are ways of handling potentially destructive experience. For Whitman, the fusion of life and death, of good and evil, of the human and natural worlds, is exhilarating. For Dickinson, it is terrifying. But if their attitudes and comic stances are radically different, humor allows both to make the same shocking claim: they have had a sexual experience with the sea, they have gone beyond the narrow confines of town with its conventional morality and its security, and they have confronted elemental forces, an act that gives both a kind of special status.

Dickinson's characteristic self-deprecation and diminishment in this poem thus enable her to make a Whitmanesque boast without being offensive or indecorous: she's had sex with the sea. The absurdity and shock is defused by a persona who can "tell all the truth, but tell it slant." Treating the episode humorously, Dickinson dazzles the reader with its powerful symbolic import.

The typical Yankee's mode of approaching the truth aslant was to play the role of country bumpkin, illiterate peddler, or slow-witted downeaster, asserting his wisdom by claiming to know nothing. Emily Dickinson's characteristic mode was to play the role of child. Nowhere is this humorous child persona more evident than in her religious poems. Whereas Whitman inflates himself to the size of a god and fathers the universe, Dickinson deflates herself to the size of a child and asks to be fathered.

In this pose of the vulnerable, deprived, powerless, and naive child, she claims to be smaller than "The smallest Citizen" (#1374), "Timid as a Bird" (#248), "so shy—so ignorant" (#50), the "Least Figure on the Road" (#400). She asks humorously innocent questions, pretending to see the figurative in terms of the literal, the spiritual in terms of the physical, and the exalted in terms of the common:

> What is—"Paradise"—
> Who live there—
> Are they "Farmers"—
> Do they "hoe"—
> Do they know that this is "Amherst"—
> And that I—am coming—too—
>
> Do they wear "new shoes"—in "Eden"—
> Is it always pleasant—there— (#215)

The questions are asked in the utmost innocence by a persona who is prepared to accept affirmative answers without a second thought. The proposition of a heaven isn't something to believe or doubt, it is just a matter of childlike wonderment and curiosity. Paradise is a given for the child; she merely wants to hear more about it. The questions themselves are their own answers, embracing the affirmative premise from the outset. The tone of this poem is that of any number of humorous poems for children, poems based on questionable premises that the child won't question:

> Tell me!
> Would you rather be
> a Dog . . . or be a Cat?
> It's time for you
> to think about
> important things like that.
> Would you
>
> rather be
> a Bullfrog
> . . . or be a Butterfly?
> Which one
> would you rather be?
> Come on, now.
> Tell me why.[10]

There is no question about the realistic possibility of pursuing these choices. The playful speculation is an end in itself, a simple affirmation of unquestioning innocence and imagination.

Dickinson's child persona is not always so confident or unquestioning. Sometimes she adopts the persona in order to make a plea:

> Papa above!
> Regard a Mouse

O'erpowered by the Cat!
Reserve within thy kingdom
A "Mansion" for the Rat!

Snug in seraphic Cupboards
To nibble all the day,
While unsuspecting Cycles
Wheel solemnly away! (#61)

In this poem, the comedy is more defensive. Faced with an incomprehensible and potentially threatening universe, Dickinson diminishes herself to the size of a mouse threatened by a cat. By making herself smaller than she is and by picturing herself as already "O'erpowered" by confusion or death or sorrow, she hopes to move God to sympathy and reserve herself a place in heaven. The discrepancy between the high and the low, between mighty potentate and merciful papa, between human being and mouse or rat, between intimations of immortality and descriptions of domestic scenes, provides the incongruity necessary for comedy. The comedy here serves two primary functions: it enables Dickinson to affirm conventional truths about God, immortality, and the suffering self without sentimentality or sententiousness; it also enables her to bring God down to a manageable size. A metaphor is a proposition; if it is accepted as true, then certain conclusions necessarily follow. If Dickinson is a child, then God is literally a father. If she is a mouse, then a cupboard will suffice for her heaven. Comically turning herself into a mouse-child, she can turn God into a domestic papa, rendering him less distant and ominous by diminishing him and his heaven to an acceptable size. The humor of the poem combines demand, plea, and affirmation in an effort to assure Dickinson a niche in heaven.

Although the child persona is capable of uncritical acceptance and anxious plea, she is also capable of reluctant skepticism:

"Unto Me?" I do not know you—
Where may be your House?

"I am Jesus—Late of Judea—
Now—of Paradise"—

Wagons—have you—to convey me?
This is far from Thence—

"Arms of Mine—sufficient Phaeton—
Trust Omnipotence"—

I am spotted—"I am Pardon"—
I am small—"The Least

Is esteemed in Heaven the Chiefest—
Occupy my House"— (#964)

As in #61 and #215, Dickinson's comic method here is to adopt the *eiron*
voice and treat the exalted in common terms. If heaven is a place like
Amherst and God is a papa, then Jesus is a kind of Yankee realtor trying
to interest a wary buyer in his property. Jesus presents his business card
complete with Paradise address, offers to take her to see the property himself, and, after dismissing all her hesitations, concludes with the hard sell:
"Occupy my house." The entire poem is a parodic extension of Jesus's
biblical injunction, "Suffer the little children to come unto me." Initially,
this child isn't about to go off with a stranger. By the end of the poem one
suspects she's ready to hop in the car.

Dickinson's comic strategy in these affirmative religious poems of treating the portentous and profound in the most commonplace and familiar
terms serves several purposes. First, it enables Dickinson to indulge in
play, an activity frowned upon by her adult peers. After reading a Dickinson poem aloud before an audience once, Robert Frost remarked, "Poetry
is play . . . and that is one of its chief importances. You shouldn't be too
sincere to play or you'll be a fraud."[11] Dickinson could play by adopting
the persona of the innocent child, for whom play comes naturally. Second,
by diminishing herself she is able to bring ideas of God and religion in
general down to a realm where she can embrace them. Humorously treating God, Jesus, and immortality in everyday human terms, she can give
the abstract concepts the palpable form and meaning that they lack.
Third, humor enables her to assert some important truths aslant that she
could not have asserted directly. Dickinson could no more express her
deepest beliefs in conventionally acceptable terms than could Walt Whitman. But both poets saw in conventional notions a residue of necessary
human truth. Whitman's comic strategy for affirming his religious convictions is to set himself up as a kosmos, one of the roughs, a somebody, and
brag his way into heaven. Dickinson's comic strategy is to claim ignorance
as a duller scholar, a little girl, a nobody, and sneak her way into heaven.
By treating conventional religious practices, sentiments, and beliefs comically, she is able to use them.

Dickinson's comic affirmative religious poems are not always her best,
leaving her vulnerable to complaints of coyness, whimsicality, and childishness. As Walt Whitman's persona reflects the brash swagger and fast
talk of Groucho Marx, Dickinson's reflects Harpo, with his mellifluous
harp, his sweet and lovable childlike innocence, his deep, if antic, affec-
tions, and his humorous and profound silences. But if Dickinson shares
with Harpo his harp (his sweetness and light), she also shares his horn

(his deviltry and impishness). Harpo's innocent pose enables him to embrace women, put frogs in his hat, sleep with horses, and use the staid and refined Margaret Dumont's arm as a skyhook from which to elevate his leg, effectively shattering all social pretense and affectation. In both Harpo and Dickinson, the naive exuberance, the shy smile, and the angelic pixie can give way to the Lord of Misrule, permitting unconventional or indecorous behavior that would not be tolerated if it were not comic. Dickinson insists in a letter, "Unless we become as Rogues, we cannot enter the Kingdom of Heaven."[12]

Sometimes Dickinson's comic deflation of pretense and fraud can be so gentle that it scarcely looks like an attack:

> Will there really be a "Morning"?
> Is there such a thing as "Day"?
> Could I see it from the mountains
> If I were as tall as they?
>
> Has it feet like Water lilies?
> Has it feathers like a Bird?
> Is it brought from famous countries
> Of which I have never heard?
>
> Oh some Scholar! Oh some Sailor!
> Oh some Wise Man from the skies!
> Please to tell a little Pilgrim
> Where the place called "Morning" lies! (#101)

Dickinson's satiric exposure of the supposed experts whose "knowledge" can't begin to answer her simple questions is so innocently framed here that one could easily miss the sly smirk underlying the humorous pose. The exposure of science and analytic intelligence, of savants and experts, is more directly evident elsewhere:

> "Arcturus" is his other name—
> I'd rather call him "Star."
> It's very mean of Science
> To go and interfere!
>
> I slew a worm the other day—
> A "Savant" passing by
> Murmured "Resurgam"—"Centipede"!
> "Oh Lord—how frail are we"!
>
> I pull a flower from the woods—
> A monster with a glass

Computes the stamens in a breath—
And has her in a "class"!

Whereas I took the Butterfly
Aforetime in my hat—
He sits erect in "Cabinets"—
The Clover bells forgot.

What once was "Heaven"
Is "Zenith" now—
Where I proposed to go
When Time's brief masquerade was done
Is mapped and charted too.

What if the poles should frisk about
And stand upon their heads!
I hope I'm ready for "the worst"—
Whatever prank betides!

Perhaps the "Kingdom of Heaven's" changed—
I hope the "Children" there
Won't be "new fashioned" when I come—
And laugh at me—and stare—

I hope the Father in the skies
Will lift his little girl—
Old fashioned—naughty—everything—
Over the stile of "Pearl." (#70)

The persona here is the petulant, smart-alecky, spoiled, "naughty" little girl who is really good at heart. She will hold onto her old-fashioned values no matter what mean old science tries to do to them. The satire isn't so much an attack on science as it is an attack on technicians who substitute learned jargon for true observation, who explain things away rather than explaining them. Honking her horn and slapping the experts with her slapstick, Dickinson is able to affirm imagination, miracle, and play. Like Walt Whitman's "When I Heard the Learn'd Astronomer," this poem contrasts the individual's superior sensual appreciation of the skies with the experts' inferior intellectualism.

If Dickinson could use her childlike pose of innocence to undercut science, she could also use the tools of science to undercut religion:

"Faith" is a fine invention
When Gentlemen can *see*—
But *Microscopes* are prudent
In an Emergency. (#185)

According to Emerson, "The oldest gibe of literature is the ridicule of false religion. This is the joke of jokes. In religion, the sentiment is all; the ritual or ceremony indifferent. But the inertia of men inclines them, when the sentiment sleeps, to imitate that thing it did; it goes through the ceremony omitting only the will, makes the mistake of the wig for the head, the clothes for the man."[13] A number of critics, apparently sharing Emerson's sentiments, have argued that Dickinson's "satire is aimed not at God, but at Man's imperfect view of him." "It was the very intimacy which she felt for the person of God that enabled her to engage in such banter. She was impatient with sacrosanct piety."[14] Indeed, many Dickinson poems show her keeping the sabbath by staying at home, or rejecting the "antique volume" for a more contemporary version of the real truths it contains.

But in a number of poems, Dickinson seems impatient not only with the wig, but with the head itself. Dickinson sometimes uses humor to bring God down to a level where she can embrace him; she also uses humor to bring God down to a level where she can question or expose him as a fraud. Using her prudent microscope on God, she discovers blemishes and flaws:

> I meant to have but modest needs—
> Such as Content—and Heaven—
> Within my income—these could lie
> And Life and I—keep even—
>
> But since the last—included both—
> It would suffice my Prayer
> But just for One—to stipulate—
> And Grace would grant the Pair—
>
> And so—upon this wise—I prayed—
> Great Spirit—Give to me
> A Heaven not so large as Yours,
> But large enough—for me—
>
> A Smile suffused Jehovah's face—
> The Cherubim—withdrew—
> Grave Saints stole out to look at me—
> And showed their dimples—too—
>
> I left the Place, with all my might—
> I threw my Prayer away—
> The Quiet Ages picked it up—
> And Judgment—twinkled—too—

That one so honest—be extant—
It take the Tale for true—
That "Whatsoever Ye shall ask—
Itself be given You"—

But I, grown shrewder—scan the Skies
With a suspicious Air—
As Children—swindled for the first
All Swindlers—be—infer— (#476)

In some ways, the poem is a joke on the speaker, much like the joke Huck
Finn unconsciously plays on himself. In Twain's novel, having been directed by the Widow Watson to "pray every day, and whatsoever I asked
for I would get," Huck prays "three or four times" for fishhooks, but
when none are forthcoming, decides "there ain't nothing in it."[15] Taking
the biblical promise literally rather than figuratively, Huck exposes himself to ridicule, while at the same time reflecting Mark Twain's own bitter
amusement and disillusionment with religion. In Dickinson's poem, the
speaker also begins with an innocent belief in the literalness of the promise. She confides that she has modest needs and will only ask God for one
thing—Heaven—and not a very large heaven at that, just one big enough
for someone her size. The unconsciously egotistical request amuses God
and the heavenly host, whose smiles seem like leers to the speaker, and
she immediately sees her mistake and gives it up. But the humor directed
against the speaker in no way cancels the sense of disillusionment, of broken promises, of the loss of childlike faith brought on by God's all too
human, insensitive response to her error. In the end, Dickinson grows
shrewder, somberly suspicious, ready to see God and her fellow humans
as swindlers. The humor in the poem is directed partly against human
misinterpretation of divine will; it is also directed against a God so detached that he could allow such misunderstandings and callously laugh at
the victims. God's cosmic laughter may be intended to effect a reformation through ridicule, but it ultimately embitters the potential worshiper,
exposing a failed promise of scripture.

In a number of poems God's laugh turns sneering or indifferent:

I asked no other thing—
No other—was denied—
I offered Being—for it—
The Mighty Merchant sneered—

Brazil? He twirled a Button—
Without a glance my way—

> But—Madam—is there nothing else—
> That We can show—Today? (#621)

Dickinson is ready to pay everything for her draught of heaven, but God, the sneering, mighty merchant taken with his own importance, merely chides her. God won't come up with Heaven or Brazil; neither will he offer consolation in time of grief:

> Of Course—I prayed—
> And did God Care?
> He cared as much as on the Air
> A Bird—had stamped her foot—
> And cried "Give Me"—
> My Reason—Life—
> I had not had—but for Yourself—
> 'Twere better Charity
> To leave me in the Atom's Tomb—
> Merry, and Nought, and gay, and numb—
> Than this smart Misery. (#376)

Why did God bother breathing life into clay? Why did he bother sending Christ to redeem Adam's sin if sentience and salvation meant such suffering? Dickinson would rather be with the atom, or with Adam, than enmeshed in this smart misery, alone, without "You." God is a "thrifty Deity" who thinks in big terms, his "Perturbless Plan" taking precedence over the separate individual, prompting him to "Proceed—inserting Here—a Sun—There—leaving out a Man—" (#724). He is a "disappointing God" whose line is busy most of the time, a recorded message droning "Disciple, call again" (#1751).

Although the "Sun" that God inserts in place of a man in #724 may be a Son, and although this son carries on a vicarious courtship, wooing us in the name of the "distant-stately Lover," Jesus comes in for his own share of Dickinson's humorous deflation and attack:

> I shall know why—when Time is over—
> And I have ceased to wonder why—
> Christ will explain each separate anguish
> In the fair schoolroom of the sky—
>
> He will tell me what "Peter" promised—
> And I—for wonder at his woe—
> I shall forget the drop of Anguish
> That scalds me now—that scalds me now! (#193)

Ostensibly about celestial reconciliation, this poem is structured on the terrible discrepancy between the pain of the moment and the explanation to come. The image of Christ as schoolteacher in a schoolroom heaven, lecturing in minute detail on material that is of no interest to his pupils, is grotesquely comic. Dickinson will get the answers when she doesn't want them; she gets the anguish now.

Ultimately, though, even direct attacks on God acknowledge his power and necessity. No matter how outraged she can be with God's "supreme iniquity" and "Duplicity," her comic perspective keeps her from rejecting him altogether:

> Those—dying then,
> Knew where they went—
> They went to God's Right Hand—
> That Hand is amputated now
> And God cannot be found—
>
> The abdication of Belief
> Makes the Behavior small—
> Better an ignis fatuus
> Than no illume at all— (#1551)

Comedy enables Dickinson to ridicule and affirm religious ideas simultaneously. As Robert Frost puts it, "For, dear me, why abandon a belief / Merely because it ceases to be true" (p. 77). "Better to go down dignified / With boughten friendship at your side / Than none at all. Provide, provide!" (p. 404).

I have argued that Dickinson's Yankee perspective—her child-persona and her *eiron* voice—provides a means of achieving elevation through self-deprecation. Pretending to be small, she shows that she is large. Pretending to know nothing, she shows that she knows everything. While this explanation defines the humor of many of Dickinson's poems, the pose of ignorance can function differently as well. The method of Socrates can be a way of demonstrating real knowledge in contrast to false claims and pretensions; it can also function literally, as a symbolic reflection of a profound and inescapable human unknowing. The theme of unknowing characteristically takes one of two forms in Dickinson's poetry—that of buoyant light verse, and that of painful black humor.

Poem #500 is a good example of Dickinson's use of light verse to explore this serious theme:

> Within my Garden, rides a Bird
> Upon a single Wheel—

Whose spokes a dizzy Music make
As 'twere a travelling Mill—

He never stops, but slackens
Above the Ripest Rose—
Partakes without alighting
And praises as he goes,

Till every spice is tasted—
And then his Fairy Gig
Reels in remoter atmospheres—
And I rejoin my Dog.

And He and I, perplex us
If positive, 'twere we—
Or bore the Garden in the Brain
This Curiosity—

But He, the best Logician,
Refers my clumsy eye—
To just vibrating Blossoms!
An Exquisite Reply!

The poet and her dog are out for a walk and see a hummingbird. The poet is delighted by the vision, and after the bird disappears she speculates philosophically on whether reality is created by the perceiving mind or whether it actually exists apart from the perceiver. Is reality internal, a product of imagination and perception? Or is it external, an objective fact? The classicist dog suggests that reality is objective, and he points to the blossoms as proof.

Charles R. Anderson, embracing the fashionable modernist assumption that "a structure of images" is preferable to "logic," compares this hummingbird poem unfavorably with the later one (#1463). In #500, "The rape of the rose was too long drawn out, the speed of flight blurred by conflicting images, and for the bird's magical disappearance she fell back on a fanciful cliché from fairy tales." The earlier poem is, for Anderson, but a clumsy version of the later, because "the discursive method she employed . . . broke down the poem as a poem" in an "unexpected shift to exposition."[16] Anderson fails to see the comic method of #500, a method that makes it different in kind from #1463. In the later poem Dickinson means to capture as best she can the evanescence of the hummingbird: "a route of evanescence," "a resonance of emerald," "a rush of cochineal." In the earlier poem she aims instead to explore the comedy of perception.

The comic fulcrum of #500 is the very moment Anderson faults as inept:

> Till every spice is tasted—
> And then his Fairy Gig
> Reels in remoter atmospheres—
> And I rejoin my Dog.

In this third stanza, Dickinson has given us one of the great comic tonal shifts in poetry. The first three stanzas dealing with the hummingbird purport to be light and airy, using sensory images, images of speed and exotic places, and short vowel sounds. But the last line of stanza three brings the whole airy vision back down to the real world of dogs. The slant rhyme of "Gig" and "Dog" is a kind of auditory joke, a shift from the bright and airy to the earthbound and commonplace. The last line of the stanza slows the whole poem down like a record player suddenly shifted from 78 to 33⅓ when the appropriate speed is 45. The comic shift sends us back to the beginning stanzas of the poem. Indeed, Anderson is right in a sense. The description of the hummingbird in those stanzas does seem strained and unconvincing; Dickinson's efforts at evocation seem ponderous or clichéd. But that is the very point of the poem. The poet has not captured the bird in words: her words are not the bird and cannot be the bird. The philosophical dog has won the debate about where reality resides from the very first lines in the poem—it is out there in the world, an objective fact that a human being can only distort by perceiving. Dickinson notes in another context, "Perception of an object costs / Precise the Object's loss" (#1071). In the early hummingbird poem Dickinson explores the uncertainty principle and finds that as a limited human perceiver she can't determine both the speed and direction of a hummingbird at the same instant. The first four stanzas of the poem, with their intentional clumsiness and tentativeness, merely verify the final philosophical position comically advanced by the professorial dog. The cumbersome image of the traveling mill, the strained effort at attributing sacramental significance to the bird, the incongruous juxtaposition of word and sound combine to show the limits of perception. Reality may be "out there," but in the act of trying to capture it, we necessarily distort it. We can't know reality, and our small efforts to fix it in words are absurd, producing clumsy approximations. And yet the dog has given her some good advice about how she might create the illusion of capturing the bird in words. His "exquisite reply" of pointing to the blossoms becomes the focus of her second hummingbird poem, in which she abandons the theme of the comedy of perception, and instead merely evokes the excitement of the experience. This does not make the second poem a better poem; it merely makes it a different one.

Poem #500 uses the mode of light verse to explore the serious theme of human unknowing. Poem #128 also poses as light verse, but threatens to turn dark as well:

> Bring me the sunset in a cup,
> Reckon the morning's flagons up
> And say how many Dew,
> Tell me how far the morning leaps—
> Tell me what time the weaver sleeps
> Who spun the breadths of blue!
>
> Write me how many notes there be
> In the new Robin's ecstasy
> Among astonished boughs—
> How many trips the Tortoise makes—
> How many cups the Bee partakes,
> The Debauchee of Dews!
>
> Also, who laid the Rainbow's piers,
> Also, who leads the docile spheres
> By withes of supple blue?
> Whose fingers string the stalactite—
> Who counts the wampum of the night
> To see that none is due?
>
> Who built this little Alban House
> And shut the windows down so close
> My spirit cannot see?
> Who'll let me out some gala day
> With implements to fly away,
> Passing Pomposity?

The poem is structured as a series of comic questions about who is responsible for the world's wonders. The tone ranges from shy innocence to arrogant demand as the speaker asks questions of the natural world that apply only to the human, turning God by implication into a bridge builder, architect, and workman. The absurd analogies and preposterous demands turn quite serious in the final stanza. The persona's inability to answer her own questions becomes an emblem of spiritual blindness. The humorous attempt to know the unknowable, to explain the inexplicable, leads to an ominous moment of existential doubt. The dangerous moment passes, however, answered by the innocent hope of the final lines. Perhaps her questions are merely the pompous demands of a spiritually blind person, and she will be able to fly beyond them one day with the help of some unseen answerer.

The theme of human unknowing takes its darkest, but nonetheless comic, form in poem #465:

> I heard a Fly buzz—when I died—
> The Stillness in the Room
> Was like the Stillness in the Air—
> Between the Heaves of Storm—
>
> The Eyes around—had wrung them dry—
> And Breaths were gathering firm
> For that last Onset—when the King
> Be witnessed—in the Room—
>
> I willed my Keepsakes—Signed away
> What portion of me be
> Assignable—and then it was
> There interposed a Fly—
>
> With Blue—uncertain stumbling Buzz
> Between the light—and me—
> And then the Windows failed—and then
> I could not see to see—

For all its meditative solemnity, the poem adopts a deliberately funny point of view: a woman sitting somewhere hereafter is telling someone (us? other dead people?) how she died. Thus, in some ways the poem can be seen as a kind of satire on nineteenth-century death watches. In the nineteenth century people often gathered around the deathbed, partly in sympathy, partly in hope of seeing God or hearing the dying person describe heaven. It was believed that at the moment of death the dying person might have a vision of God and the heavenly light that could be communicated to the onlookers. The onlookers in this poem have cried all their tears, and now their eyes are dry. They anxiously wait for the King, God, to show up and assure them of his existence. The dying person herself looks on at the scene. What appears, however, is not God at all, but a fly, undercutting the onlookers' foolish hopes. Perhaps the poem is insisting that the deathbed is the wrong place to look for God; all that will be found there is the mundane world of flies.

The meter of the poem provides a comic incongruity with the subject matter. The poem is written in the typical hymn meter, quatrains of alternating four beat and three beat lines. The poem can be sung, for example, to a hymn like "O God Our Help in Ages Past." But the subject matter is not what one would expect in an ordinary hymn. In "O God Our Help in Ages Past," God is a "help" one can rely on for salvation and support in time of need. In Dickinson's parodic hymn, we find merely a dead person and a fly. The hymn rhythm is simple and religious; the subject matter is unconventional and heretical. The comic incongruity adds to the thematic tension.

But the poem is more than just a dark satire of conventional death watches or conventional religious belief. It is also a disturbing comic inquiry into human limitation, focusing the discrepancy between our desire to know and our capacity for knowledge. As a dying person, Dickinson wonders what is going to happen to her. She is caught in a "Stillness . . . Between the Heaves of Storm," suggesting a moment between the storm of daily life and another storm in heaven or hell. Like the onlookers, she is looking for God. In her last moments she "willed my Keepsakes—Signed away / What portion of me be / Assignable." She can will away her material belongings; they are "Assignable." Is her soul also assignable? Can she will it to God? Between her and the answer comes the curious fly. Is it God? If so, the poem is very bleak, suggesting that God is a fly. Is it the devil? Possibly. The devil is sometimes called the lord of the flies. Its sky-blue color makes it seem good, but its intrusion between the poet and the light makes it seem bad. In other Dickinson poems the fly is variously a delightful correspondent ("yours, Fly") and an obnoxious cattle that herd upon the eye.

The function of the fly in this poem might be clearer in the context of one of stand-up comedian George Carlin's humorous anecdotes. Carlin relates an experience we have all, in one form or another, presumably had: You finally get up the courage to ask someone for a date, someone you've long admired from afar. The person accepts, to your delight and surprise, and the evening is heavenly. Everything goes perfectly. As you say goodnight at the door, turning to kiss your new beloved, you notice a small piece of spinach between his or her teeth. For all its sophomoric humor, the analogy graphically describes the function of the fly in Dickinson's poem. The fly is the piece of spinach in the teeth of the beloved, the mundane world that constantly obscures one's vision of spiritual things. At the end of the poem the doors of perception close, blank with the buzzing fly of uncertainty. Whitman was capable of embracing everything; the aroma of armpits and prayer were equal means of attaining a

visionary truth. Dickinson was stumped by the unknowable and inexplicable, by the flies that herded on the eye restricting vision to brief and
passing ecstatic moments, moments ultimately called into question by
death and God's possible duplicity.

All of the poems discussed thus far are good examples of Bergson's assertion that *"a comic effect is always attainable by transposing the natural
expression of an idea into another key."* [17] Treating the profound and portentous in everyday terms or the commonplace and trivial in elevated language, seeing God as a merchant or papa and herself as a rat or gnat, allowing her dog to win a philosophical argument or a fly to disrupt a death
watch, these are evidence of the kinds of transposition to which Bergson
refers. Many of Dickinson's characteristic stylistic devices also reflect a
kind of transposition from natural expression to some surprising other
key. Her comic metaphors, definitions, and catalogues, like the larger
structures of her poems, often deflate the grand or elevated. Thus a "Retrospect" becomes something very like a "Cricket" or a "Crow" (#1271).
The soul becomes a "Poltroon" (#292). Hope is a "strange invention"
(#1392) or "the thing with feathers" (#254). The use of metaphor, definition, or catalogue to deflate profundity on the stylistic level is a device
used by many contemporary comedians. It would not be difficult to argue
that Woody Allen, for example, was influenced by Dickinson. It was no
accident that he titled one of his funniest books, *Without Feathers*, after
Dickinson's poem #254, a line of which he quotes on the acknowledg-
ments page. Much of his own humor reflects Dickinson's terseness, economy, surprise, and deflation. In the film *Love and Death*, for example,
when Allen confesses that he "feels a void inside" him and is asked "What
kind of a void?," he replies, "An empty void," a joke that rivals Dickinson's "fatal mortality."

As Dickinson's comic metaphors, definitions, and catalogues reflect a
stylistic equivalent of her self-deflating comic persona, her oxymorons
and paradoxes reflect a stylistic equivalent of her characteristic theme of
balancing opposites. Thus she speaks of a "woe of ecstasy" or a "Burglar!
Banker." [18] The oxymoron, linking two contradictory ideas in a single entity, is a characteristic linguistic structure for Dickinson's sense of contra-
dicton and ambiguity. The paradox functions similarly, often drawing
contradictions out to absurd lengths.

> A Death blow is a Life blow to Some
> Who till they died, did not alive become—
> Who had they lived, had died but when
> They did, Vitality begun. (#816)

The playful repetition of opposites leads almost to nonsense, ridiculing the Christian notion of afterlife while asserting it at the same time. The incremental repetition of opposites renders #898 similarly comic: "How happy I was if I could forget / To remember how sad I am."

Sometimes, a stylistic joke will both deflate the inflated and inflate the deflated while balancing opposites at the same time. Thus in #526, "To hear an Oriole sing / May be a common thing— / Or only a divine." And in #290 the "unconcern" of the Northern Lights "infects my simple spirit / with Taints of Majesty." In these examples, the words *only*, *infects*, and *Taints* conflict with *divine* and *Majesty*, comically transposing the natural expression into Bergson's "other key."

Paradox is, for Dickinson, a means of balancing opposites. It can also be a defensive weapon or shield against loss and death. In a world where God is not necessarily trustworthy, other means must be found to handle extreme, painful situations. Two of Dickinson's paradoxical comic shields against loss and its attendant suffering are her theory of compensation and her domestication of death.

Although none of Dickinson's several poems based on the theme of compensation—that every evil confers some balancing good—could be called particularly funny, the theme itself is deeply comic:

> Success is counted sweetest
> By those who ne'er succeed.
> To comprehend a nectar
> Requires sorest need.
>
> Not one of all the purple Host
> Who took the Flag today
> Can tell the definition
> So clear of Victory
>
> As he defeated—dying—
> On whose forbidden ear
> The distant strains of triumph
> Burst agonized and clear! (#67)

The familiar poem embraces a comic paradox as a sure defense against loss. If you cannot have what you want, you theorize that not having what you want is better than having what you want. But then what you *really* want is not to have what you want. Thus you end up getting what you want. Failure and success, frustration and satisfaction, defeat and victory are comically inverted. In #801 Dickinson defines the wry perspective:

And novel Comforting

My Poverty and I derive—
We question if the Man—
Who own—Esteem the Opulence—
As We—Who never Can—

Desire is preferable to possession; poverty richer than riches. It is a "novel Comforting" indeed.

As the theory of compensation tricks loss into being a benefactor, the domestication of death tricks death into being a friend:

Afraid! Of whom am I afraid?
Not Death—for who is He?
The Porter of my Father's Lodge
As much abasheth me! (#608)

Dickinson relates to death much as she did to God in the poems discussed earlier: she brings him down to her level. He is a porter, an orphan, a pickpocket, a supple suitor, an Amherst gentleman, a friend:

Because I could not stop for Death
He kindly stopped for me
The Carriage held but just Ourselves
And Immortality. (#712)

Like Whitman, who sees in death the cycle of eternal recurrence that connects animal and vegetable and mineral, so Dickinson can see in death a kind of marriage to immortality, since death provides the only way into heaven (if there is one). Seen from the proper comic perspective, the perspective of compensation, death could be a friend rather than an enemy, paradoxically giving life while taking it away. At best you might end up in heaven. At least when you are dead no one can kill you since "Dying— annuls the power to kill" (#358).

Dickinson's theory of compensation and her domestication of death are defensive shields against a world that seems confusing or hostile. While Dickinson is ultimately quite serious about the need for these defensive postures, she can laugh at her attitudes and strategies as well. If defeat is preferable to victory, and if death is itself a victory, one can logically come to fear victory:

A Day! Help! Help! Another Day!
Your prayers, oh Passer by!
From such a common ball as this
Might date a Victory!
From marshallings as simple

The flags of nations swang.
Steady—my soul: What issues
Upon thine arrow hang! (#42)

The poem begins as a kind of joke on the theory of compensation. Since
success is counted sweetest by those who ne'er succeed, the persona here
is terrified of victory. "Oh no," she laments. "I may have a victory today!"
To endure a victory she would need all the help she could get, and so she
begs the nearest passerby for his prayers. The poem could be read as the
humorous self-criticism of a person who is so supersensitive that even vic-
tories present terrors for her. In the first stanza, Dickinson is clearly
laughing at herself, the exaggerated fervor of her response incongruous
with its stimulus.

In the second stanza, however, the joke shows its serious side. The
comic cry for help becomes a serious call for attendance to the great possibilities present in a day. On days just such as this the common earth has
provided ammunition for nations to rise and fall. The final two lines are a
warning or an encouragement to her soul to recognize its tremendous responsibility in facing what could be the start of something vital, magnificent, or terrible. In a way the poem is a kind of pep talk to her self to face
experience head-on and not shirk responsibility for her own life. It is also
a comic defense against real terrors. By laughing at her fears, by exaggerating her helplessness, she hopes to control the uncontrollable.

The theme of laughter as both a defensive posture and a strategy for
embracing life in all its pain and ecstasy is further developed in #165:

A *Wounded* Deer—leaps highest—
I've heard the Hunter tell—
'Tis but the Ecstasy of *death*
And then the Brake is still!

The *Smitten* Rock that gushes!
The *trampled* Steel that springs!
A Cheek is always redder
Just where the Hectic stings!

Mirth is the Mail of Anguish—
In which it Cautious Arm,
Lest anybody spy the blood
And "you're hurt" exclaim!

In this poem Dickinson defines "Mirth" as a kind of armor, a defense
against further vulnerability. Laughter confines a hurt to the individual
involved, preventing others from compounding it by remarking upon it.

But there is a pun on the word *mail* here. If laughter is a kind of armor, it is also a kind of postal message. The three stanzas are grammatically and structurally parallel. A "wound" makes a deer leap the "highest" into an "Ecstasy of *death*." Violence makes rocks "gush" and steel "spring" and cheeks turn "red." The leap, the gush, the spring, and the red are, in effect, messages ("Mail") from the deer, the rock, the steel, and the cheek, just as mirth is the "Mail" of anguish. "Mail" here thus becomes news of an ecstatic sort. In the first two stanzas, affliction sends out ecstatic messages. The wounded deer leaps, the smitten rock gushes, the trampled steel springs, and the stung cheek reddens, just as the anguished person laughs. Mirth is structurally connected to ecstasy, gush, spring, and flush, all images of vitality and energy. Mirth is thus a protective covering, but it is also a kind of news of the highest sort, news of a compensating ecstasy, gush, spring, and flush, provoked by anguish.

Mirth can be a compensation and a means of masking one's hurts from others; it can also be a means of deflecting one's hurts from oneself. An effort to achieve a kind of Bergsonian anesthesia of the heart is evident in the structure of a number of Dickinson's poems on loss and death. In poems #412, 415, and 587, for example, what begins as a serious and potentially unbearable experience is capped off with a joke. Poem #412 uses a legal metaphor to explore the moment of death. Dickinson finds herself judged guilty of some "shame" by a jury, and sets about to make her soul "familiar—with her extremity— / That at the last, it should not be a novel Agony." The poem begins with foreboding and fear, the poet preparing herself for the horror of death. But the final meeting of soul and death turns out to be rather pleasant, not terrible, the meeting itself defused with a pun:

> But she, and Death, acquainted—
> Meet tranquilly, as friends—
> Salute, and pass, without a Hint—
> And there, the Matter ends—   (#412)

Both the legal matter (the case under consideration) and the physical matter (the poet's body) end in the tranquil and amiable pun. The little joke comes as a surprise, undercutting the ominous tone with which the poem began.

Poem #415 uses a closing joke similarly, if less tranquilly, to put the death of someone else in perspective:

> Sunset at Night—is natural—
> But Sunset on the Dawn

Reverses Nature—Master—
So Midnight's—due—at Noon.

Eclipses be—predicted—
And Science bows them in—
But do one face us suddenly—
Jehovah's watch—is wrong.

In this poem an unexpected death threatens to eclipse the poet's own life. It is as unnatural for someone to die before their time as it is for sunset to occur at dawn. Thus if an unpredicted eclipse or death occurs, it must be a mistake; God's watch must be wrong. The final unexpected joke is a shock, both protecting against and expressing the anguish in the poem.

Poem #587 functions similarly:

Empty my Heart, of Thee—
Its single Artery—
Begin, and leave Thee out—
Simply Extinction's Date—

Much Billow hath the Sea—
One Baltic—They—
Subtract Thyself, in play,
And not enough of me
Is left—to put away—
"Myself" meant Thee—

Erase the Root—no Tree—
Thee—then—no me—
The Heavens stripped—
Eternity's vast pocket, picked—

The poem is even more personal than #415, which deals with unexpected loss in the abstract. Here, the speaker laments the loss of one who was so important to her that he seemed part of her. The tone is anguished and grief-stricken until the final line, which, as in the preceding two poems, functions as a kind of joke. The picture of eternity's vast pocket, and death as its petty thief, is comic. The shift to the unexpected joke here is an effort to anesthetize the heart and to avoid self-pity, but it also functions to intensify the sorrow and pain. The intrusion of humor into this intensely painful, personal poem is an incongruity that twists the true sentiment grotesquely out of shape, focusing the suffering as much as deflecting it. Dickinson explains her strategy in #1715: "The truth I do not dare to know / I muffle with a jest."

In a number of poems Dickinson uses the reverse of this structural pattern. The preceding poems begin with serious situations and emotions and then relieve the tension with a concluding joke that can intensify the pain as well. In other poems Dickinson employs the reverse of this method, beginning with the humorous and concluding with the intensely serious. The initial humor disarms the reader, leaving him vulnerable to the shocking pain of the close. The little quatrain #688 is a paradigm of this strategy:

> "*Speech*"—is a prank of Parliament—
> "*Tears*"—a trick of the *nerve*—
> But the Heart with the heaviest freight on—
> Doesn't—always—move—

The poem starts with a joke that would seem more appropriate to a satire of Parliament than to a serious poem about grief beyond words. The second line seems more serious but is still a humorous definition, deflating tears to the kind tricked up by the nervy King and Duke in *Huckleberry Finn*, who deceive the gulled populace by lathering themselves with tears and flapdoodle. The third line is more serious still, but it is nevertheless witty, equating the heart with a freight train. All three lines are entertaining diversions from the real center of the poem—the unspeakable grief that stops the heart cold. The final line, with its three detached words sitting on the page like stalled train cars, falls heavily on the reader's own (and to this point, unmoved) heart.

Dickinson's well-known poem #435 uses the residue of humor in a similar way:

> Much madness is divinest Sense—
> To a discerning Eye—
> Much Sense—the starkest Madness—
> 'Tis the Majority
> In this, as All, prevail—
> Assent—and you are sane—
> Demure—you're straightway dangerous—
> And handled with a Chain—

Again the poem begins with a kind of joke, a humorous paradox that in other poems deflects pain by providing a comic perspective. The idea that madness is sense and sense is madness is a wry one to which we easily assent. The ominousness of our assent becomes apparent only toward the end of the poem, and especially in the final violent image. The incongruity between the tone of the first and last lines produces a comedy that refines to agony.

Poem #33 provides a final example of Dickinson's use of comic paradox to intensify seriousness:

> If recollecting were forgetting,
> Then I remember not.
> And if forgetting, recollecting,
> How near I had forgot.
> And if to miss, were merry,
> And to mourn, were gay,
> How very blithe the fingers
> That gathered this, Today!

The series of paradoxes on which the poem is structured makes it sound curiously like a nonsense poem or puzzle. The seemingly playful linguistic embroideries effectively cloak the situation, inviting the reader to play the game of figuring out the literal meaning hidden in the confusion of comic reversals. Only after the reader has taken the time to untangle the logic does the impact of the poem's true subject hit home. The realization that poet (and reader) have been making a language game of such pain intensifies that pain. Since recollecting is not forgetting, then she does remember. Since missing is not merry and mourning is not gay, her fingers must be anything but blithe. The effort to conceal the hurt, to make it don the mail of mirth, ultimately mails the news of its true pain to the reader, who not only has had to wait for the delivery, but has had to tear open the envelope as well.

This poem and the similar #898 ("How happy I was if I could forget / To remember how sad I am") verge on linguistic nonsense, suggesting a flirtation with madness on the part of the persona. If laughter can reflect a comic perspective, it can, at its extreme, reflect total loss of perspective, recalling the horror of Meredith's hypergelast, the person who laughs incessantly and inappropriately:

> The first Day's Night had come—
> And grateful that a thing
> So terrible—had been endured—
> I told my Soul to sing—
>
> She said her Strings were snapt—
> Her Bow—to Atoms blown—
> And so to mend her—gave me work
> Until another Morn—

And then—a Day as huge
As Yesterdays in pairs,
Unrolled its horror in my face—
Until it blocked my eyes—

My Brain—begun to laugh—
I mumbled—like a fool—
And tho' 'tis Years ago—that Day—
My Brain keeps giggling—still.

And Something's odd—within—
That person that I was—
And this One—do not feel the same—
Could it be Madness—this? (#410)

This poem can be taken as a companion piece to #42. In that poem the poet asks help in facing a "Day" and gets that help from her soul, whose bow (a weapon, not a musical instrument) is equipped with a quiver of arrows and a saving defensive laughter. Soul and laughter combine to enable the poet to handle a day that threatens to envelop her. In #410, the dreaded day is over and night is upon her. The soul's "Bow" (the musical instrument) is blown to atoms, and laughter provides no defense. Instead, laughter itself seems an indication of madness and horror. The laughter of the mind here takes on a terrible life of its own, locking the poet in an asylum of despair. Dickinson's poems thus reflect the whole range of laughter, from the self-deprecative defensive laughter of the ironist, through the offensive laughter of the satirist and the affirmative laughter of the parodist and humorist, to the insane laughter of the hypergelast.

It would not be fair to end this chapter on so horrifying and unsettling a poem as #410. Dickinson, like Archibald MacLeish, knew that a morbid art was an imperfect art, and her comic sense continually militated against despair and madness. If life was a tragedy, Dickinson characteristically chose to view the tragedy comically. Given the choice of "Heaven— / Or only Heaven to come / With that old Codicil of Doubt" (#1012), she opted to "look a little more / At such a curious Earth!" (#79), where "the most important population / Unnoticed dwell, / They have a heaven each instant / Not any hell" (#1746). If she sometimes seemed coy or priggish, more often than not she would "resign the prig" and "taste a liquor never brewed" (#214) until "ten of my once stately toes / Are marshalled for a jig!" (#36). Drunk on God or grace or nature or the muse, she would "repeat the Summer day" (#307) or produce a sunset, which if less ample than the sun's was "more convenient / To Carry in the Hand" (#308). And if her ecstasy smacked of madness,

A little Madness in the Spring
Is wholesome even for the King,
But God be with the Clown—[both an assertion and a prayer]
Who ponders this tremendous scene—
This whole Experiment of Green—
As if it were his own! (#1333)

For all her modesty and self-effacement, Dickinson thus finally claimed as large a comic role for herself as did Walt Whitman. With the smallest of materials she was able to make a world anew:

To make a prairie it takes a clover and one bee,
One clover, and a bee,
And revery.
The revery alone will do,
If bees are few. (#1755)

IV

Robert Frost
Fighting on Both Sides at Once

In his humorous short story "The Next Time," Henry James recounts the difficulties of two novelists, each of whom aspires to, but fails to achieve, the capabilities of the other. Ralph Limbert is eternally doomed to write literary masterpieces acclaimed by the critics but which no one buys or reads, while Mrs. Highmore is doomed to write popular best sellers ignored or attacked by the critics. No matter how hard Limbert tries to write a trashy popular success, he manages only to produce a masterpiece. No matter how hard Mrs. Highmore tries to write a masterpiece, she manages only to produce, in "sets of triplets," trashy popular successes. At one point in the story, Limbert goes so far as to beg a reviewer to pan or ignore his new novel so that it will have a chance of success, while Mrs. Highmore hopes that no one will buy her work so that the critics will praise it.

The strange and humorous paradox that structures James's story provides a good analogue for the plight of the poet in America. In other countries poets often enjoy both popular and critical success. And in America it is not uncommon for novelists to enjoy similar status, achieving both a wide readership and the respect of the academy. The poet in America, however, is usually doomed either to a large audience but scorn from the serious reader (Edgar Guest, Rod McKuen, Nikki Giovanni) or to critical acclaim but indifference and neglect from the popular audience (Wallace Stevens, John Berryman, Maxine Kumin).

Robert Frost is one of the few American poets who managed to be both popular and critically acclaimed in his lifetime. Given the relatively low priority of poetry in this country, Frost's achievement is especially surprising when one considers the personal factors that might further have worked against him. The very characteristics of Frost's verse that would have appealed to a popular audience might have been expected to put off the critics, while those characteristics that would have appealed to the critics might have been expected to put off the popular reader. Frost's sentimentality, his affirmation of old pieties, his conservative politics, and his conventional verse form should have appealed to the popular reader who preferred a comfortable familiarity, but drawn scorn from the serious reader who embraced emotional toughness, novelty, liberalism, and stylis-

107

tic experimentation. Conversely, Frost's essential skepticism about God and religion, his conviction of human isolation, limitation, and ignorance, and his perception of the difficulties of human communication should have appealed to serious readers, but offended a popular audience.

While a complex combination of factors probably accounts for Frost's achievement of both critical acclaim and broad popularity despite the factors working against him, one central explanation lies in his sense of humor. Assuming the familiar mask of the Yankee from nineteenth-century American humor, Frost was able to embrace contradictory feelings and beliefs, affirming and questioning them at the same time. From behind the Yankee mask, Frost was able continually to qualify and complicate his themes, undercutting any potentially antagonistic reader. That the humorous pose was an intentional strategy to defuse criticism and marshal reader support is evidenced in a statement Frost made about the purposes of humor in his work:

> I own any form of humor shows fear and inferiority. Irony is simply a kind of guardedness. So is a twinkle. It keeps the reader from criticism. . . . At bottom the world isn't a joke. We only joke about it to avoid an issue with someone. . . . Humor is the most engaging cowardice. With it myself I have been able to hold some of my enemy in play far out of gunshot.[1]

Frost would agree with Emily Dickinson that "an *immortal hero* / Will take his hat, and run!" (#3). But for both Dickinson and Frost, evasion, self-deprecation, and the pretense of ignorance and smallness are not merely means of avoiding confrontation; they are strategies for winning confrontations.

Dickinson's version of the Yankee character is often that of the child whose innocence and naiveté enable her to question both death and God without reprisal; Frost's characteristic version of the Yankee is that of the bemused, amiable, good-hearted, slow New England farmer. Like the familiar peddler or rustic of nineteenth-century American humor whose pretense of ignorance was the guarantee of knowledge, Frost's persona achieves victory through evasion. Behind a mask of self-deprecation, understatement, whimsy, and joke, Frost is able to boast while seeming modest, remain detached while seeming friendly, embrace sentimentality while seeming tough-minded, question old pieties while affirming them, and give the impression of simple dependability and honesty while remaining elusive, evasive, and skeptical. Frost himself explains: "You get more credit for thinking if you restate formulae or cite cases that fall in easily under formulae, but all the fun is outside saying things that suggest formulae that won't formulate—that almost but don't quite formulate. I should like to be so subtle at this game as to seem to the casual person altogether obvious."² For the popular reader, Frost did seem simple and altogether obvious. For the more serious reader, Frost presented intriguing complexities and enigmas.

One of Frost's formulas that doesn't quite formulate is his persona itself. On the surface Frost seems to be the unassuming country farmer, the affable and amiable friend who defers graciously to the reader's needs and wishes, the demure Dickinsonian innocent. But underneath he is also the boastful self-promoter, the detached and self-sufficient loner who gets what he wants, the waggish Whitmanian poseur. Frost established his characteristic persona in his first book, *A Boy's Will*. Two poems from that book, "Into My Own" and "The Vantage Point," are representative of his strategy, revealing how Frost can boast under the guise of modesty and remain detached under the guise of friendship.

"Into My Own" is structured as a journey the poet would like to take someday to a "vastness" somewhere near "the edge of doom" where there is neither open land nor highway, a place where others could find him unchanged, still holding them dear. Although the poem teases the reader to speculate on the actual destination (death? heaven? the great unknown?), that destination is irrelevant to the central focus slyly introduced by the title:

> One of my wishes is that those dark trees,
> So old and firm they scarcely show the breeze,
> Were not, as 'twere, the merest mask of gloom,
> But stretched away unto the edge of doom.
>
> I should not be withheld but that some day
> Into their vastness I should steal away,
> Fearless of ever finding open land,
> Or highway where the slow wheel pours the sand.
>
> I do not see why I should e'er turn back,
> Or those should not set forth upon my track
> To overtake me, who should miss me here
> And long to know if still I held them dear.
>
> They would not find me changed from him they knew—
> Only more sure of all I thought was true. (p. 5)

The actual journey on which the poem takes us is into Frost's "own"; that is, into the self-confident, even boastful assurance of the final line: "Only more sure of all I thought was true." The line by itself would seem arrogant, smug, and self-satisfied. Frost's challenge in the poem is to make the reader not only accept the boastful final line, but affirm it as strongly as Frost would. Deflecting the reader's attention to some place that does not exist is one strategy for overcoming rejection, but that is only part of Frost's elaborate comic evasion. The first thirteen lines of the poem are structured on a series of denials and negations calculated to undermine reader rejection of the final line. The discrepancy between the firm assurance and boast of that line and the careful qualification and timid hesitation of the first thirteen is incongruous. Frost doesn't really want to enter these dark woods any more than he does in his later poems like "Stopping by Woods" and "Come In." What he wants to do is "come into his own"; that is, to succeed as a poet and have all his many readers accept his wisdom.

To trick the reader into acceptance, Frost employs a series of evasions and denials. He "wishes" that the trees "were not" the "merest mask of gloom." Unfortunately, they are. But if they were not, then he would "not be withheld" from "stealing away" into them. And if they were not but a mask, and if he were not withheld, then he does "not see why" he should turn back or why others should "not set forth" after him to find him "not . . . changed." The multiple negatives are comic, incremental repetition being a common comic device, entrapping the reader in a crafty Socratic monologue. Accepting each modest step along the way commits one to accepting the final immodest conclusion. Caught up in the intricate whimsical speculation, caught up in the slowly unwinding joke, the reader is surprised (and delighted) by the punchline. If double negatives make a positive, the poem seems to suggest, then quadruple negatives must make an even larger positive. Adopting the pose of the cautious and modest Yankee, Frost persuades the reader to follow him on the road to himself just as effectively as does Walt Whitman with his immodest bluff and cajolery. Like Whitman at the end of "Song of Myself," Frost is there at the end of this poem, "in his own," smiling and waiting for the reader to catch up.

The humorous strategy of boasting under the guise of modesty enables Frost to reaffirm old truths and pieties as counters to diminishment and limitation. "On a Tree Fallen Across the Road" is a good example:

> The tree the tempest with a crash of wood
> Throws down in front of us is not to bar
> Our passage to our journey's end for good,
> But just to ask us who we think we are
>
> Insisting always on our own way so.
> She likes to halt us in our runner tracks,

And make us get down in a foot of snow
Debating what to do without an ax.

And yet she knows obstruction is in vain:
We will not be put off the final goal
We have it hidden in us to attain,
Not though we have to seize earth by the pole

And, tired of aimless circling in one place,
Steer straight off after something into space. (p. 296)

The sonnet both mocks and celebrates people's ego and determination. The parenthesis in the title, "(To Hear Us Talk)," sets the tone, suggesting a put-down both for those who talk as if their lives are impossibly difficult and for those who talk as if they can overcome anything. Within the sonnet itself, Frost insists on people's capacity to prevail but at the same time has nature mock them for their pretension ("to ask us who we think we are / Insisting always on our own way so"). Having thus mocked himself, Frost ends with an absurd affirmation of his capabilities. Hyperbolically exaggerating his strengths in a Whitmanesque tall-tale manner, the speaker both laughs at his pretensions and asserts his powers. A tree in the road might stop us, but moving the earth on its axis is nothing—an "old top knot," "an easy morning's ride." Combining deflation and exaggeration, the poem laughs at both pessimists and optimists, enabling Frost to affirm people's real strengths without seeming Pollyannaish or blind.

"Into My Own" and "On a Tree Fallen Across the Road" introduce one aspect of Frost's Yankee strategy, allowing him to boast while seeming modest. "The Vantage Point" introduces another, enabling him to be detached while seeming friendly:

If tired of trees I seek again mankind,
    Well I know where to hie me—in the dawn,
    To a slope where cattle keep the lawn.
There amid lolling juniper reclined,
Myself unseen, I see in white defined
    Far off the homes of men, and farther still,
    The graves of men on an opposing hill,
Living or dead, whichever are to mind.

And if by noon I have too much of these,
    I have but to turn on my arm, and lo,
    The sun-burned hillside sets my face aglow,
My breathing shakes the bluet like a breeze,
    I smell the earth, I smell the bruisèd plant,
    I look into the crater of the ant. (p. 24)

The speaker of this poem is isolated from mankind on a hill where he can see both town and country, the abodes of the living and the dead. The theme of the isolated individual is one that Frost was to return to in subsequent poems. His very persona, with its characteristic self-sufficiency, coolness, and detachment, reflects the theme of people's essential isolation and alienation, a theme that figures so hauntingly in poems like "An Old Man's Winter Night," "The Witch of Coös," and "Thatch." But here, as in other poems, humor works against the potentially tragic perception. "The Vantage Point" is based on a comic paradox or joke: the best way to get close to people is to get far away from them. When the speaker tires of trees and wishes to "seek again mankind," he goes not to the town where mankind lives, but to a distant hill from which, unobserved himself, he can observe mankind. If he tires of mankind he has merely to turn over and "look into the crater of the ant" (though in "Departmental" he will find there, too, an analogue for the human comedy). Frost's "vantage point" enables him to accomplish contradictory things. By detaching himself from people in order to observe them, he achieves the sort of "anesthesia of the heart" that Bergson prescribed as necessary for comedy. And the detachment itself suggests the larger theme of human isolation and lack of communication. But, paradoxically, the joke also breaks down the barrier of distance and separation, intimately involving the reader with the speaker. A joke establishes a communion, a sharing of the joke. By "getting" the joke, the reader participates in a symbolic act of solidarity, creating a friendly conspiracy of insiders.

Frost's jokes can be on the reader, as in "Into My Own," or they can be on Frost himself, as in "The Vantage Point." Although the humor is subtle and understated in both poems, it is finally what prevents Frost from seeming boastful and smug or detached and cold. It is what engenders the necessary relationship between poet and reader.

Because jokes on oneself are more apt to win the identification and sympathy of others, Frost often presents himself in a humorous light. If it begins to seem like Frost is trying to do too much in his poetry (or in his life)—reconciling opposites, holding contradictory ideas, being boastful and modest or intelligent and stupid at the same time—he can find fun even in that. In "The Armful," for example, Frost poses as a comical nerd, a Jerry Lewis clown who has stacked up so many bundles that he can do nothing but collapse under them, the parcels comically controlling him rather than him controlling them:

> For every parcel I stoop down to seize,
> I lose some other off my arms and knees,
> And the whole pile is slipping, bottles, buns,

Extremes too hard to comprehend at once,
. . . .
I crouch down to prevent them as they fall;
Then sit down in the middle of them all. (p. 343)

The poem is a serious one about treasuring all experience, about being in
Henry James's words "one on whom nothing is lost," but Frost's method
of stating the theme is to adopt a humorous persona and laugh at himself.

In "The Armful" Frost laughs at himself for trying to grasp and hold
too much. In "New Hampshire"—a long, whimsical poem that employs
satire, parody, and irony in a kind of good-natured Will Rogers monologue—Frost laughs at his Yankee pose of claiming to need very little:

I choose to be a plain New Hampshire farmer
With an income in cash of say a thousand
(From say a publisher in New York City).
It's restful to arrive at a decision,
And restful just to think about New Hampshire. (p. 212)

The discrepancy between the "plain New Hampshire farmer" and the
man with a cash income from a New York City publisher is comic, undercutting Frost's deceptive, if congenial, pretense. In the same poem he en-
larges his laughter to include other writers, similarly well off, who must
fabricate despair and suffering in order to write great literature:

How are we to write
The Russian novel in America
As long as life goes so unterribly?
There is the pinch from which our only outcry
In literature to date is heard to come.
We get what little misery we can
Out of not having cause for misery. (p. 207)

How can we writers "be Dostoievskis," Frost asks, "On nothing worse
than too much luck and comfort?" Lionel Trilling and Frost's "terrifying
poetry" notwithstanding, Frost's characteristic attitude to the human
condition is a comic one.

The Yankee strategy of telling truth aslant by laughing at oneself can
present difficulties. If the speaker is mocking himself in a poem, how can
we be sure that he isn't mocking the "truths" he utters as well? In "The
Black Cottage," for example, the speaker is a minister who may or may
not be reliable. Conventionally, a minister is an honest, trustworthy, good
man, a leader on whom one can count for advice and insight. Frost's minister seems good-humored enough, but he also has his faults and flaws.

He is a garrulous, gossipy man who talks interminably until he is suddenly cut off in the middle of a rather bizarre fantasy about a desert land populated by all the old truths that have been abandoned. The minister longs to keep the old truths alive, but there is some question about which truths he supports. Earlier in the poem he had expressed humorous skepticism about Jefferson's notions of equality. Referring to the old woman whose abandoned cottage he is visiting, the minister says:

> Her giving somehow touched the principle
> That all men are created free and equal.
> And to hear her quaint phrases—so removed
> From the world's view today of all those things.
> That's a hard mystery of Jefferson's.
> . . . .
> . . . . The Welshman got it planted
> Where it will trouble us a thousand years. (pp. 75–76)

The minister seems exasperated by Jefferson's notions and skeptical of racial equality at all. When the minister notes that the old woman believed that the Civil War answered such questions, he concludes, "What are you going to do with such a person?" (p. 76). While the minister thus ridicules the old woman for her beliefs, doubting whether they are true at all and doubting whether after all the years she could have any real feelings about her husband's sacrifice in the war, he uses her for his own ends. When the younger parishioners ask for some slight modernization of the traditional creed, the minister uses the old woman as an excuse not to make changes he doesn't want to make. Thus the minister in this poem seems rigid, racially biased, gossipy, and insensitive, making his reliability as a narrator doubtful. When he voices his central truth, it is thus difficult to know how Frost views it:

> For, dear me, why abandon a belief
> Merely because it ceases to be true. (p. 77)

At first gasp, the statement seems absurd. If a belief isn't true, it would be foolish, perhaps even dangerous, to cling to it. Is Frost satirizing prejudice and rigidity? Perhaps. But the minister's explanation of his statement also seems valid, clarifying the comic paradox:

> Cling to it long enough, and not a doubt
> It will turn true again, for so it goes.
> Most of the change we think we see in life
> Is due to truths being in and out of favor. (p. 77)

Where does Frost stand? Should one abandon a belief merely because it ceases to be true? The minister argues no. Frost's satiric exposure of the minister argues yes. Humor allows Frost to have it both ways at once. Like Emily Dickinson, Frost laughs at old truths and asserts them simultaneously. He defines his strategy in "To a Young Wretch":

> The war god [is] no special dunce
> For always fighting on both sides at once. (p. 470)

Fighting on both sides at once, Frost forces the reader to reexamine the truth and decide on its validity himself.

Frost uses a similar strategy in one of his most admired poems, "Mending Wall." It is in some ways a paradigmatic Frost poem, using the familiar Yankee persona with his wry understatement and whimsy both to question and to embrace a truth about human experience. On the surface it seems simple enough:

> Something there is that doesn't love a wall,
> That sends the frozen-ground-swell under it,
> And spills the upper boulders in the sun;
> And makes gaps even two can pass abreast. (p. 47)

Frost/frost is the something that doesn't love a wall; just as the spring thaw will topple the literal stone wall, the speaker (motivated by spring's mischief) will topple metaphoric walls between people. The literal wall comes to stand for all barriers to communion and communication. Frost aligns himself with nature in wanting those barriers down, suggesting that the natural human impulse is to confront life not singly, but "two abreast." Nature doesn't love literal walls; the speaker doesn't love metaphoric walls.

The speaker's antagonist in the poem is a neighbor who does love walls, who believes that "Good fences make good neighbors." The speaker represents the fluid, flexible, vital, and civilized; the neighbor represents the immovable, rigid, mechanical, and primitive. The comedy of the poem is partly the narrator's satire of this man so ruled by convention and conformity that he can't see through an old cliché. Rather than adjusting his ideas to fit a new situation (a speaker who desires relationship and communication), the neighbor adjusts the situation to fit his old ideas (other people are enemies to guard oneself against). The cliché "Good fences make good neighbors" is thus a kind of fence or wall itself, an example of Bergson's mechanical encrusted on the face of the living. According to the speaker, it is no longer valid or necessary:

> There where it is we do not need the wall:
> He is all pine and I am apple orchard.
> My apple trees will never get across
> And eat the cones under his pines, I tell him.
> . . . .
> "Why do they make good neighbors? Isn't it
> Where there are cows? But here there are no cows." (p. 47)

The idea of apple trees eating pine cones is an absurd one, effectively ridiculing the neighbor's archaic rigidity. In stolidly asserting the cliché, the neighbor becomes comically dangerous, "like an old-stone savage armed" to prevent any real relationship or communication.

The conflict between the two characters recalls the familiar one of Old Comedy between the *eiron* and the *alazon*, the witty self-deprecator and the deluded impostor who claims to know more than he does. The speaker views the neighbor with amused detachment, refusing to be brought down by his solemnity. Although the speaker has superior knowledge, he will not impose it on the neighbor, preferring to proceed by self-deprecation, understatement, and indirection, the usual method of the *eiron* or Yankee:

> "Something there is that doesn't love a wall,
> That wants it down." I could say "Elves" to him,
> But it's not elves exactly, and I'd rather
> He said it for himself. (p. 48)

While the neighbor states his cliché with an infuriating self-assurance, the speaker moves by hesitation, circumlocution, speculation, and teasing. The speaker's role is, like the spring thaw, to seep inside the wall and bring it down by expanding it. The neighbor's role is, like an old savage, to haul heavy stones to the wall, securing it by weighting it down. The speaker is whimsical and wise; the neighbor is dull and deluded.

But even on the surface the comic conflict is not so simple. There are others in addition to Frost and frost who want walls down—hunters:

> The work of hunters is another thing:
> I have come after them and made repair
> Where they have left not one stone on a stone,
> But they would have the rabbit out of hiding,
> To please the yelping dogs. (p. 47)

The speaker is all in favor of spring bringing down walls, but hunters are another matter. Hunters tear down walls to destroy life, and the speaker is quick to fill up the gaps they make. Spring tears down walls to affirm life, and the speaker prefers to leave open the gaps it makes. Thus, although the speaker claims that he wants walls down, there are instances when he wants them up. The contradiction between his words and his actions complicates his character and the theme of the poem. Perhaps the narrator isn't as reliable as he at first appeared to be.

Despite the speaker's insistence that he only loves walls when there are cows or hunters, it is he, and not the neighbor, who initiates the wall repair each spring: "I let my neighbor know beyond the hill." And if, as he claims, what he really wants is a closer relationship, he does little to bring it about; indeed, he does much himself to prevent it. While the speaker is attractively witty and playful in his attitude and the neighbor is humorless, the speaker's wit has an edge of attack and sarcasm that seems less than friendly. It is the speaker's sarcastic remark about the likelihood of his apples eating pine cones and his summary dismissal of the neighbor's adage (which could easily be taken as a pleasantry rather than a defense) that lead the speaker to turn the neighbor into an almost inhuman savage. We identify with the speaker's imagination and wit, but when it leads him to exaggerations that dehumanize the neighbor we must begin to wonder about the speaker's true intentions. Does he really have any interest in bringing down *any* walls, literal or figurative? Indeed, he clings to his own adage, "Something there is that doesn't love a wall," as fiercely as he faults the neighbor for doing. Perhaps the speaker himself is self-deceived, deluded by his imaginative embroideries into creating a huge human barrier out of a simple literal fence. Perhaps the speaker has tried to ride his metaphor too far and it has broken down. Frost, if not his narrator, was well aware of this danger:

> Unless you are at home in the metaphor, unless you have had your proper poetical education in the metaphor, you are not safe anywhere. Because you are not at ease with figurative values: you don't know the metaphor in its strength and its weakness. You don't know how far you may expect to ride it and when it may break down with you.[3]

So caught up in his metaphor, so taken with his witty perceptions, perhaps the speaker is incapable of seeing the thing itself. In painting his comic picture of the intractable neighbor, the speaker himself begins to seem the more intractable of the two.

Since we see the neighbor only through the unreliable speaker's eyes, we may be getting a false or imperfect image. Perhaps the neighbor's motives are open and friendly, and the speaker is more like a suspicious stone-savage in not being able to see them. Perhaps the neighbor's concern about apple trees and pines is not for himself but for the speaker, since the acidity of the pine trees might more likely harm the speaker's apples than vice versa. We cannot, of course, know the neighbor's true character or intentions. But the speaker's sarcasm, his imaginative embroideries, and the contradictions between his words and his actions make his speculations as suspect as our own.

Further, the speaker's avowed position on wall dismantling puts him in direct contradiction with many of Frost's other poems about walls. In "The Vantage Point" Frost reveals that when he tires of trees and seeks mankind, he doesn't do it by seeking out his neighbors. Instead he goes to a hill and observes them invisibly, the distance itself being a kind of wall that permits both detachment and involvement. In "Triple Bronze" he affirms the necessity of protection against "the infinite": first "my hide," then "a wall," then a "national boundary." "And that defense makes three / Between too much and me" (p. 468). But the poem that seems to have most bearing on "Mending Wall" is "The Cow in Apple Time":

> Something inspires the only cow of late
> To make no more of a wall than an open gate,
> And think no more of wall-builders than fools.
> Her face is flecked with pomace and she drools
> A cider syrup. Having tasted fruit,
> She scorns a pasture withering to the root.
> She runs from tree to tree where lie and sweeten
> The windfalls spiked with stubble and worm-eaten.
> She leaves them bitten when she has to fly.
> She bellows on a knoll against the sky.
> Her udder shrivels and the milk goes dry. (p. 157)

The cow here, like the speaker in "Mending Wall," wants walls down and ridicules those who would build them up. At the beginning of the poem the cow could seem heroic in her rejection of rigid rules and barriers. But ignoring walls and human folly, the cow turns silly, "drooling," running "from tree to tree," even "flying." The cow's size and function make her behavior ridiculous, and the poem shifts to a kind of light-verse buoyancy. But in the last line the dark consequences of the cow's behavior are clear. She becomes barren and worthless, her udder shriveled and dry. In "The Cow in Apple Time" walls clearly serve a positive purpose—they keep death out. Death would like walls down, would like differences erased, would like everything to merge in a great facelessness. Thus walls hold back chaos and confusion, and the neighbor's adage still reflects a truth. In primitive times walls kept people from killing each other. In our more civilized times walls serve a similar function, preserving the identity and privacy that death would like to destroy. Walls for Frost are both a metaphor for an inescapable human isolation and a necessary means of preserving life and identity.

The two conflicting characters in "Mending Wall" thus resemble the *eiron* and the *alazon* of Old Comedy, and the narrator himself seems to incorporate elements of both characters. Further, the structure of the poem recalls the two typical comic patterns we saw in our discussion of "Song of Myself," integration and expulsion. In Shakespearean romance comedy, for example, the pattern is usually one of integration, with two lovers uniting after overcoming the barriers that society or custom or some irrational law has placed between them. In "Mending Wall" the speaker's avowed desire to bring down the wall is an impulse reminiscent of such comedy, though the actual building of the wall serves a similar function. The fact that some of the wall has come down is an excuse for the two to come together in at least a brief moment of cooperation and communion, participating in a mutual human activity. In Meredithian satiric comedy the pattern is usually one of exposure; a character is either reformed through ridicule or expelled from the society. In "Mending Wall" the speaker's action of rebuilding the wall is a metaphoric reflection of such exclusion. If neither speaker nor neighbor is reformed by the satiric exposure, both exclude the other from their world by completing the wall. The romance-comedy elements in the poem prompt us to reject walls for keeping people apart; the satiric elements in the poem prompt us to affirm walls as a method of keeping our distance from the aberrant individual.

The combination of characters and plot patterns is a central cause of critical confusion over the poem. Swinging back and forth between *eiron* and *alazon*, between integration and exposure, between wall dismantling and wall building, "Mending Wall" embraces opposite positions. One cannot choose between them, for the balance of opposites is what is important. Each spring moves toward recovery, reform, integration, and harmony; each fall moves toward exclusion and isolation. To have the wall down forever would be to blur human identity and individuality, to stop the game that brings people together. To have the wall up forever is to separate people permanently. It is the rhythm of pulling down and building up, a comic rhythm, that ensures continued human relationship. Good fences do paradoxically make good neighbors as the two men come together each year for the purpose of shutting each other out.

Frost finally wants it both ways. The speaker and neighbor are two halves of a single character. If the stones in the wall are like "loaves," sug-

gesting communion and togetherness, they are also like "balls," suggesting masculinity and war. Neither character is right or wrong; neither
adage is true or false. Both represent ways of seeing the world that are
limited and flawed without the other. Frost himself said as much in an
interview with *The Harvard Service News*. The interviewer summarizes:

> Clarifying the meaning of "Mending Wall," Frost denied that he had any
> . . . allegory in mind other than the impossibility of drawing sharp lines
> and making exact distinctions between good and bad or between almost
> any two abstractions. There is no rigid separation between right and
> wrong. "Mending Wall" simply contrasts two types of people. One says,
> "Something there is that doesn't love a wall." And the other replies, "Good
> fences make good neighbors."[4]

"Mending Wall" is a paradigmatic Frost poem, an example of Frost at his
frustrating best. Donning the Yankee mask, pretending to be one thing
while really being another, holding opposites in mind at the same time,
evading and embracing simultaneously, Frost tricks readers into looking
for the right and wrong side of an issue while himself taking both sides at
once. The title of "Mending Wall" itself seems to encompass the whole
poem. *Mending* may be a gerund, since the action of the poem involves
the mending of a wall. But the word may also be a participle modifying
wall. The wall is no ordinary wall, it is a *mending* wall, a wall that can
heal, a place where people can go "at spring mending-time" to mend the
gaps in their lives. Separation and union, disharmony and healing, these
are the opposites Frost means to reconcile in his richly comic poem.

Personal walls provide a momentary stay against confusion and chaos
in human relationships. Stylistic walls help contain and control the pull
toward poetic formlessness. One of the old truths, currently out of favor,
that Frost held determinedly throughout his life was the power of conventional formal verse. At a time of great stylistic and technical experimentation, Frost insisted on using meter and rhyme. He criticized Emily Dickinson for sloppiness; he insisted that when God said "Iamb" he meant it;
and he complained that writing free verse was like playing tennis without
a net. Although a number of contemporary American poets are once
again writing sonnets, sestinas, villanelles, and even couplets (suggesting
that the old truth may be coming back into fashion), during Frost's lifetime few poets so successfully evaded technical experimentation.

Frost believed passionately in traditional forms, feeling that rhyme and
meter carried with them an evocative power accrued over generations.
And he saw forms as necessary barriers to play over, or work with and
against. He also saw in them a great comic potential. In numerous poems,
Frost delights in the comic dimension of his chosen form. In "Blueber-

ries," for example, Frost draws attention to the comic potential of his meter while recounting a playful narrative as well. "Blueberries" is full of good-natured fun, focusing the narrator's mixed admiration and antagonism for Loren and his large family, the champion berry pickers of the region. The narrator blooms with exuberance over his discovery of some berries that the usually "thrifty" Loren has somehow overlooked, giving the narrator a rare opportunity to beat him to the punch. The poem concludes with the narrator savoring a vision of the berries he and his friend will pick the next day even though Loren thinks they have "no right":

> "They'll be there tomorrow, or even tonight.
> They won't be too friendly—they may be polite—
> To people they look on as having no right
> To pick where they're picking. But we won't complain.
> You ought to have seen how it looked in the rain,
> The fruit mixed with water in layers of leaves,
> Like two kinds of jewels, a vision for thieves." (p. 81)

The sensory imagery accounts in part for the poem's exuberance, but the metrical pattern itself conveys the speaker's enthusiasm and buoyancy. The anapestic tetrameter line moves the narration on breathlessly, conveying the excitement of the discovery and the urgency of getting to the blueberries before Loren does. The situation is basically a comic one to begin with: grown people competing over wild blueberries with all the secrecy and precaution of rival executives involved in corporate espionage. The excitement of the speaker is incongruous with the triviality of the situation. But the anapestic tetrameter line, used by Cowper and Landor and Swinburne and Dr. Seuss for comic effect, serves a similar purpose here, marshaling the humor that has been associated with it over the centuries. Frost draws on this tradition to capture the whimsy, playfulness, and silliness of the narrative and the speaker's childish excitement. Indeed, passages of the poem could easily have been conceived by Dr. Seuss:

> "Do you know,
> I was just getting through what the field had to show
> And over the wall and into the road,
> When who should come by, with a democrat-load
> Of all the young chattering Lorens alive,
> But Loren, the fatherly, out for a drive."

> "He saw you, then? What did he do? Did he frown?"

> "He just kept nodding his head up and down.
> You know how politely he always goes by.

But he thought a big thought—I could tell by his eye—
. . . .
He has brought them all up on wild berries, they say,
Like birds. They store a great many away.
They eat them the year round, and those they don't eat
They sell in the store and buy shoes for their feet." (p. 79)

The Lorens here begin to sound like some strange Dr. Seussian creatures who live on berries. *The Lorax*, for example, plays on the same metrical pattern:

He snapped, "I'm the Lorax who speaks for the trees
which you seem to be chopping as fast as you please.
But I'm also in charge of the Brown Bar-ba-loots
who played in the shade of their Bar-ba-loot suits
and happily lived, eating Truffula Fruits.

"Now . . . thanks to your hacking my trees to the ground,
there's not enough Truffula Fruit to go 'round.
And my poor Bar-ba-loots are all getting the crummies
because they have gas, and no food, in their tummies!" 5

The relentless rhythm, commonly used for similar children's and nonsense verses, often necessitates filler lines and phrases. Rather than worrying about filler, Frost, like Dr. Seuss, seems to revel in it, playing it for the kind of jokes George Carlin uses in his stand-up comedy routines. "A hot water heater!" Carlin exclaims. "Who would want to heat hot water?" Similarly, we might ask Frost, "Shoes for their feet! What else would they want shoes for, their ears?" The meter encourages such humorous filler phrases, adding to the whimsy of the whole.

"Blueberries" is essentially a light-verse poem. But Frost could use the anapestic tetrameter line for ultimately serious poems as well, the incongruity between the usually comic meter and the serious theme providing an edge against lugubriousness. "Good-by and Keep Cold," for example, a poem about preparing against winter and all it stands for, boasts the same metrical pattern as "Blueberries." The poem begins by ostensibly focusing a crisis ("This saying good-by on the edge of the dark") that suggests death or some permanent leave-taking. And it ends with the ultimate helplessness of the speaker to make things stay ("But something has to be left to God"). But the surprising narrative—the poet is saying good-bye not to a person or to life itself but to an orchard—and the unexpected metrical line militates against chaos or despair:

> Reminds me of all that can happen to harm
> An orchard away at the end of the farm
> All winter, cut off by a hill from the house.
> I don't want it girdled by rabbit and mouse,
> I don't want it dreamily nibbled for browse
> By deer, and I don't want it budded by grouse.
> (If certain it wouldn't be idle to call
> I'd summon grouse, rabbit, and deer to the wall
> And warn them away with a stick for a gun.) (p. 281)

The metrical scheme, the surprising shift in tone, and the joke about summoning predators just to warn them away with a stick do not deflate the seriousness of the poem, but they provide a momentary stay against its ultimate implications.

Frost draws attention to his meter for comic purposes; he plays similarly with his rhymes. After reading a poem of Emily Dickinson's, Frost is reported to have said, "Rime reminds you that poetry is play . . . and that is one of its chief importances. You shouldn't be too sincere to play or you'll be a fraud."[6] Couplets are funny; quadruplets are funnier. In "Goodby and Keep Cold" Frost plays with his rhymes, passing off *house, mouse, browse,* and *grouse* as exact rhymes, encouraging the reader to mispronounce them. Frost was unhappy enough with Dickinson's use of slant rhyme to make it likely that this lapse was intentional, the humor buffering the solemnity of the theme. Comic rhymes recur throughout Frost as a kind of signature. Parodying Isaiah 2:4, Frost banters:

> The first tool I step on
> Turned into a weapon.[7]

The rhyme of *step on* and *weapon* adds to the comedy. In "The Last Mowing" the rhyme draws attention to a hidden pun:

> Then now is the chance for the flowers
> That can't stand mowers and plowers.
> It must be now, though, in season
> Before the not mowing brings trees on. (p. 338)

The "not mowing" could allow flowers to reestablish themselves, as Frost would wish, or it could result in "treason," the trees usurping the flowers' rightful place.

By playing with the comic potential of his rhyme and meter, Frost acknowledges the artificiality of form. But his style is never the extravagant delight in itself that characterizes Whitman, Dickinson, Stevens, Berryman, and others. In most cases Frost's art is the art that conceals art, the makeup that makes the actor appear natural under the stage lights. Frost shares with Emily Dickinson her preference for Yankee self-deprecation and humor, but he never approximates her fractured syntax, metrical deviations, or ecstatic condensation of experience into intense lyrical bursts. He shares with Whitman, Stevens, Berryman, and Cummings a fondness for punning and wordplay, but he avoids their noisier and more ostentatious ribaldry. It is thus easy for us, attuned as we are to the stylistic novelty of blab and brag and strut, to miss Frost's quieter fooling.

All of Frost's careful artifice is directed toward establishing the Yankee plain style, the illusion of unpretentious straight talk that characterizes the Yankee farmer. I suggested earlier that Frost's persona reflects a sense of isolation and detachment as well as a commitment to communion and communication. Frost's language itself reflects this conflict. Just as the characters in many of Frost's poems seem isolated, victims of collision rather than communication, so his language often quietly contradicts or works against itself. In "The Mountain," for example, when the narrator, an ignorant outsider, tries to get some information about a mountain from a friendly local, the very language that should aid him partially thwarts him. The local tells the narrator about a stream on the mountain-top that is "cold in the summer," "warm in the winter." When the narrator asks the man for proof of the stream's existence, the man replies, as if his answer had any logic,

> "I guess there's no doubt
> About its being there. I never saw it." (p. 58)

The juxtaposition of the two statements implies some logical connection between them: there is no doubt about its being there *because* I never saw it. The two statements bump against each other, colliding in a sort of false logic that humorously confuses. The man continues:

> "One time I asked a fellow climbing it
> To look and tell me later how it was."

> "What did he say?"
> "He said there was a lake
> Somewhere in Ireland on a mountain top." (p. 58)

Again, the reply has no logical connection to the question, but is juxtaposed as if it does. The syntax itself shares the penchant for collision that the characters experience in their lives.

The sense of isolation and miscommunication is further reflected in the typically abrupt closure of many of Frost's verse narratives. "The Mountain" ends as the ox cart suddenly lurches off, swallowing the man's final words. "The Black Cottage" ends in the middle of the minister's odd revery as he smacks the clapboards with his hand and bees peer out.

But if Frost's characteristic style reflects the isolation of his Yankee characters and persona, it also reflects the sense of community inherent in jokes. The joke requires an audience; laughter implies a shared perception between speaker and hearer. Verbal collisions in Frost's poems can signify isolation and miscommunication, but they can also provide jokes that assure companionship or domesticate terror and loneliness. Thus death itself becomes merely a time to "settle down" (p. 246) with the "mute folk," "the tireless folk," "As sweet companions as might be had" (pp. 6–7). To transform the dead into mute and tireless folk is a joke that undercuts death's terrors.

Frost's best jokes are often embedded in metaphors to provide what he called "the pleasure of ulteriority."[8] Metaphor is at base related to the joke: both bring unlike things together in some surprising way, providing an insight or release of tension. Frost often uses his metaphors to joke the natural world down to a controllable human size. Thus he is sure the world and its people will go on forever if only the sun stays true; that is, "if nothing goes wrong with the lighting" (p. 555). If the sun is merely stage lighting we don't have to worry too much; stage lights are fixable. In other poems wildflowers are personified so that Frost can get the birch branches "off the wild flowers' backs" (p. 154). Venus is a light bulb screwed in by Edison (p. 512), trees are "educated into boards" (p. 211), and flowers are a pair of telephones through which lovers can communicate (p. 147). The comic metaphors bring the large and alien into the human realm, making connections possible.

The humorous revival of a "dead" metaphor can also enable Frost to embrace an old truth that has shriveled into a cliché:

> The rose is a rose,
> And was always a rose.
> But the theory now goes
> That the apple's a rose,
> And the pear is, and so's
> The plum, I suppose.
> The dear only knows
> What will next prove a rose.
> You, of course, are a rose—
> But were always a rose. (p. 305)

The comparison of woman to rose is an impossibility for a modern poet. A rose by any other name may smell as sweet, but a rose by its own name smells musty and archaic. To do the impossible, to compare his lover to a rose, Frost makes a joke of it. The repetition of the word *rose* itself, the incrementally repeated rhyme on the word, and the strained analogies laugh at the central metaphor and allow Frost to use it one more time. The final lines regain the lost power of the metaphor, affirming its historical validity. Frost's mock consternation with the misuse of the image enables him to use it gently and evocatively.

Similarly, he can compare fireflies to stars by joking "of course, they can't sustain the part" (p. 306). And he can use stars symbolically by undercutting their symbolism, replacing the star itself with "something like a star" (p. 575). The poem ends with a telling pun: "To stay our minds on and be staid." Old images, old verities, old metaphors can provide a momentary stay against confusion, even if it means that we have to risk being "staid" (archaic, stodgy) in order to use them.

Frost's poems often end like this, with a joke that almost pulls the rug from under the reader, forcing him to go back through the poem to see whether it has been serious or not, whether he has been fooled into assenting to something he wouldn't ordinarily assent to. As in a joke, the punch lines of some of Frost's poems send solemnity tumbling, teasing the reader into thought. Frost insists:

> The style is the man. Rather say the style is the way the man takes himself; and to be at all charming or even bearable, the way is almost rigidly prescribed. If it is with outer seriousness, it must be with inner humor. If it is with outer humor, it must be with inner seriousness. Neither one alone without the other under it will do.[9]

Frost uses his Yankee humor and formal foolery to trick the reader into accepting the old pieties and affirming even the most diminished of lives, but he also uses his humor to trick the reader into questioning certain old verities, notably conventional views of God and religion. Although Frost was basically a religious man, his jests with God, like Emily Dickinson's, served both as protection and interrogation.

Frost exposes his poetic mask and indirectly criticizes God in the early poem "Revelation":

> We make ourselves a place apart
>   Behind light words that tease and flout,
> But oh, the agitated heart
>   Till someone really find us out.
>
> 'Tis pity if the case require
>   (Or so we say) that in the end
> We speak the literal to inspire
>   The understanding of a friend.

> But so with all, from babes that play
>   At hide-and-seek to God afar,
> So all who hide too well away
>   Must speak and tell us where they are. (p. 27)

The poem begins as a definition of Frost's Yankee manner, with instructions to the reader for playing the game. Frost suggests that all his teasing and flouting is really intended to make the reader look closely behind the comic mask. The purpose of "hiding" behind the mask is to be found out, just as the purpose of hide-and-seek is to be caught eventually. Without the catching, the hiding ceases to be any fun. Frost's original note on the poem in *A Boy's Will* indicates that "the poet . . . resolves to become intelligible." Just as in hide-and-seek it is sometimes necessary to make a noise to help the finder find you, so in a poem it is sometimes necessary to "become intelligible" to make one's needs and loves known. Until the third stanza the poem is a witty account of Frost's comic method and of the game playing that occurs in any relationship. But in the final stanza the poem shifts to another level, focusing on "God afar." Indeed, the whole poem can be read as a kind of challenge to God, who is too well hidden, who plays the role of Yankee/*eiron* so flawlessly that no one can find him. The poem that begins as an amiable explanation of one aspect of the human comedy almost casually leaps to a more profound and serious comedy in the third stanza, implicating God in the subterfuge and sneaking him a kind of ultimatum.

The indirect criticism of God becomes more direct later in Frost's canon:

> I turned to speak to God
> About the world's despair;
> But to make bad matters worse
> I found God wasn't there. (p. 408)

When Frost finally does rout God out of his hiding place, he finds an all-too-human figure. The God of "A Masque of Reason" is a teaser and mocker and practical joker, a limited figure full of corny wisecracks and folk drollery. God explains his ludicrous reasons for making Job suffer. His plan was "a great demonstration" to

> Establish once for all the principle
> There's no connection man can reason out
> Between his just deserts and what he gets. (p. 589)

The lesson of Job is for man "to learn his submission to unreason" (p. 596). Job's ordeal, it turns out, was God's attempt to restore his own sadly sagging prestige.

"A Masque of Reason" is by no means Frost's best work. Like some of the other verse satires, it tends to be glib, superficial, and jokey, employing the kind of easy humor that led critic and poet Radcliffe Squires to wish "that Frost had cut out some of that arch kidding around." [10] It is not in these satires but in his best-known "serious" poems that we find the Frost behind the mask using humor to permit encounters with God and death. In the satires Frost blames God for being evasive and elusive, for keeping himself hidden. But in poems like "After Apple-Picking," "Birches," and "Stopping by Woods," Frost shows himself to be evasive and elusive, keeping a low profile to avoid God's or death's attentions.

"After Apple-Picking" could be read as a comedy of surfeit and excess. After a season of apple growing and picking, after a life of trying to cherish each experience, holding them all in an armful that must eventually tumble, the poet looks back on his labor. In part, the poem seems to put overweening ambitions and desires into a comic frame, with the poet not rejecting his past but seeing it for what it was. The world now looks strange to him, seen through the pane of ice he skimmed off the drinking trough. From the perspective of age and winter, the ambitions of his youth look fondly humorous. Read as a kind of comic allegory for an individual's life, the poem thus represents a moment of peaceful leave taking and quiet acceptance. The speaker concludes by wondering whether his sleep, well deserved after a day (a life) of labor, will be troubled with the kind of dreams he imagines in the poem, or whether it will be long and dreamless, like the woodchuck's hibernation.

But if the poem can be taken as a comic allegory of a life, it also clearly suggests a comic religious allegory. "After Apple-Picking" seems to be a kind of joke on the fall of Adam and Eve in the garden, who also found themselves facing troubled dreams after picking the apple. Adam and Eve's apple picking condemned everyone to the kind of labor that has so exhausted the poem's speaker. It is a labor he wouldn't trade away, but now he is tired and his ladder points "toward heaven still," suggesting a possible final destination and reward.

The question of destination and reward is implied in the poem's final lines:

> One can see what will trouble
> This sleep of mine, whatever sleep it is.
> Were he not gone,
> The woodchuck could say whether it's like his
> Long sleep, as I describe its coming on,
> Or just some human sleep. (p. 89)

There are several ways to read these lines. Literally, the contrast is between two kinds of sleep. The speaker wonders whether his sleep will be long and dreamless like the woodchuck's hibernation or brief and dream ridden like a human's nightly rest. But the allusion to the Fall, the rather bizarre nightmare described by the poet, and the symbolic resonance of the close suggest that the sleep referred to at the end may not be a literal sleep at all, but a metaphor for death. Thus the implied question may contrast life and death. Will the sleep coming on be death, or just literal sleep? It is also possible, however, that the woodchuck's sleep and the human's sleep reflect not a contrast of two kinds of sleep or a contrast of sleep and death but a contrast between two kinds of death. If the woodchuck's sleep is taken to be hibernation (a kind of death and resurrection), then the human sleep by contrast becomes an ultimate sleep, a final death, and the "just" is a tragic irony. If the woodchuck's sleep, however, refers to its animal death (a finality, since animals aren't redeemed by Christ), then the human sleep becomes by contrast a death and resurrection, and the "just" provides a comic irony. Frost has phrased the contrast in such a way as to permit multiple complication. Is the sleep coming on just sleep? Or is it death? If it is sleep, then what kind of sleep is it? Dreamless woodchuck sleep? Or troubled human sleep? If it is death, then what kind of death is it? An ultimate death? Or rest and resurrection? Frost refuses to answer the question, preferring to leave the reader with a quiet smile. The sleep coming on may be just an ordinary night's sleep; it may be "just" a final and irrevocable death; or it may be "just" eternal life. The woodchuck, comically elevated to the level of omniscient sage, could tell us, but he is gone. The potentially visionary poem is thus undercut comically at the end by an ironic "just," by an ambiguous and unresolvable question, and by a superior talking woodchuck.

The humorous ending is a way of teasing the reader into thought. It is also one of Frost's characteristic Yankee evasions. As Frost uses comedy to protect himself from critics, he also uses comedy to protect himself from the most dangerous critic of all—death. Frost is the woodchuck who has so cleverly absented himself at the end of the poem. Having exposed himself to attack, he retreats at the moment of crisis to his burrow under the farm. Frost rarely confronts death head-on as do Whitman and Dickinson, preferring instead to sidle around it, to keep a low profile in hopes of not being noticed, to sneak through customs without declaring any more than he has to (p. 447). Rather than use humor to berate death as Whitman does or to befriend him as Dickinson does, Frost uses his humor as "the most engaging cowardice," to slip by or trick or disarm death into complacency. He is careful not to make the wrong move or say the wrong thing that might send him from an April that seems like May back into the middle of March (p. 357).

Frost's comic evasions are thus defensive. Referring to a new biography of Jesus, Frost faulted the author for trying "to make out that Jesus had a sense of humor. . . . Jesus was a man of sorrows, not a good fellow or a humorist. Humor is the beginning of doubt. It's defensive: you're not going to let them get you, let them know where you are sensitive." [11] But if humorous evasions and deflections are a mode of protection, they are also a mode of perception. In "A Passing Glimpse" Frost insists:

> Heaven gives its glimpses only to those
> Not in position to look too close. (p. 311)

Frost is probably referring to the fact that looking slightly aslant of a star enables one to see it more clearly than one could straight on. Using humor as an evasive tactic, Frost is able to avoid dangerous confrontations while seeing truths more clearly. Like Emily Dickinson, he tells the truth by telling it slant.

The humorous evasions that provide both protection and perception are further evident in those Frost poems that more clearly focus potential encounters with death and oblivion. In "Mending Wall" Frost explores the human impulse to wall death out, to form relationships that are really exclusions. "Stopping by Woods" explores the opposite impulse, to surrender oneself to oblivion, to ignore all walls and barriers. "Stopping by Woods" is a more solemnly beautiful poem than "After Apple-Picking" but uses, in a very understated way, some of the same humorous devices for evading direct confrontation with death. In "After Apple-Picking" Frost introduces the talking woodchuck at the end of the poem to defuse the tragic implications of the final lines, restoring a comic balance. In "Stopping by Woods" the thinking horse, who fortunately asks Frost if there is "some mistake," provides a similar whimsical release of tension, breaking the seductive spell of the dark woods and reminding the poet that he's got business elsewhere:

> My little horse must think it queer
> To stop without a farmhouse near
> Between the woods and frozen lake
> The darkest evening of the year.
>
> He gives his harness bells a shake
> To ask if there is some mistake. (p. 275)

The thinking horse is a quiet joke with serious implications—it both underlines the poet's loneliness at this moment and undercuts the poet's drift toward dissolution.

The thinking horse is not the only humorous participant in the poem.

The opening line introduces an indirect joke that similarly underlines and undercuts the seriousness of the experience:

> Whose woods these are I think I know.
> His house is in the village though;
> He will not see me stopping here
> To watch his woods fill up with snow. (p. 275)

The owner of the literal woods is an absentee landlord who lives in town. The owner of the figurative woods is also an absentee landlord with a "house" in town—the church or funeral home. The implied joke does not deflate the hypnotic pull toward darkness, but it does help to put the experience in perspective and to enable Frost to recover his balance at the end. Indeed, the final lines, in all their lovely solemnity and with their implied promises between man and village and between man and his soul, also resonate with humor. There is a quiet Frostian smile under the polite refusal to be seduced. "Thank you for the invitation," Frost seems to say, "but I'm a bit busy today. Perhaps another time." The incongruity between the polite refusal and the dark compelling woods is profoundly comic. The penultimate line contains the joke; the final line is more serious in tone, as the poet recognizes the full implications of his narrow escape. He will return to his social promises changed, with a new recognition of the deeper spiritual promises he keeps. "Stopping by Woods" could not be called a comic poem, but the humor of the house in the village, the thinking horse, and the initial promises provides a means of retaining balance and perspective in the face of the absolute.

"Birches" uses humor similarly to deflect death, providing a defense for the poet while enabling him to see more clearly by seeing aslant. As in "Stopping by Woods" and "After Apple-Picking," Frost feels the pull of the "straighter darker trees" and entertains the urge to move toward them. Even in death the birches are beautiful:

> They click upon themselves
> As the breeze rises, and turn many-colored
> As the stir cracks and crazes their enamel.
> Soon the sun's warmth makes them shed crystal shells
> Shattering and avalanching on the snow-crust—
> Such heaps of broken glass to sweep away
> You'd think the inner dome of heaven had fallen.
> They are dragged to the withered bracken by the load,
> And they seem not to break; though once they are bowed
> So low for long, they never right themselves. (p. 152)

The description of the ice-covered trees is so lovely that it is easy to forget that the loveliness is short-lived, that ice storms break even resilient
birches, killing them. The broken glass of heaven is also beautiful, but
dangerous, needing to be swept away. Frost knows when he looks at the
birches that ice storms have caused the damage. Preferring, however, not
to give death its due, Frost manages to evade Truth by humorously posing
his own more affirmative truth in its stead. The transition from ice storms
with all their sterile destructiveness to boys with all their fertile creativity
is made with the help of an image as humorous in its own right as the
woodchuck or the horse were in the previous poems:

> You may see their trunks arching in the woods
> Years afterwards, trailing their leaves on the ground
> Like girls on hands and knees that throw their hair
> Before them over their heads to dry in the sun. (p. 152)

Radcliffe Squires remarks that these lines represent "one of the most absurd comparisons in all poetry."[12] The image may be absurd, but it is
nevertheless persuasively lovely and sexual, providing a joke on the ice
storm and a distraction for the reader. When the ice storm tries to wedge
its unpleasant deathly truth between Frost and his imagination, Frost's response is not to accept or reject it but to transform it into something
other. For all the ice storm's efforts to destroy the trees and dishearten the
man, all it can manage to do is to change the birches into girls. The image
is a joke on the ice storm's presumptuousness, a joke that distracts the
reader from the destructive Truth and enables him to accept Frost's more
affirmative truth about the boys. Having tricked the ice storm in this
manner and established his friendly relationship with the reader, Frost is
able to dismiss death even more directly with a humorous jibe:

> But I was going to say when Truth broke in
> With all her matter-of-fact about the ice-storm
> I should prefer to have some boy bend them. (p. 152)

If the reader can accept the impossible, absurd, and beautiful image of the
girls, how much easier it is to accept the more likely (if untrue) explanation of the boy's swinging. The reader's attention is thus deflected from
death to life, from other world to this world, from nature to man. The
grammar itself begins to believe Frost's fiction as the conditional tense
verbs subtly shift to the simple declarative past tense. Grammatically, the
wish becomes a fact:

> One by one he subdued his father's trees
> By riding them down over and over again

Until he took the stiffness out of them,
And not one but hung limp, not one was left
For him to conquer. He learned all there was
To learn about not launching out too soon
And so not carrying the tree away
Clear to the ground. He always kept his poise
To the top branches, climbing carefully
With the same pains you use to fill a cup
Up to the brim, and even above the brim. (p. 153)

Since the birches are girls drying their hair in the sun and the boy bends them to the earth which is "the right place for love," it is reasonable to suspect a kind of sexual allegory here, evoking a humorous euphemism for intercourse and an affirmation of human continuity. The poem is thus not so much a contrast between Truth and fiction as between two kinds of fictions—the ice storm's fiction about the broken glass and withered bracken of death, and Frost's fiction about the long-haired girls and adventuresome boys of love.

"Birches" is a Dickinsonian poem in its preference of earth over heaven, its belief that not having is sometimes better than having, its dismissal of death by deflation, its identification with boyhood, its jests and transformations. Yet a sadness also infuses the poem, a sadness locked in the central metaphor. Even if we accept the fiction, the boy, as effectively as any ice storm, will eventually bend the birches to the ground so that they can no longer be climbed. The "stay" of the poem may be exhilarating, but it is also momentary. The poem ends in Frost's characteristically understated Yankee way with a return to the conditional and a line that includes both smile and sigh: "One could do worse than be a swinger of birches" (p. 153).

Frost uses humor as a tactic of evasion and avowal. He can pause by the dark woods and return to town; he can climb the birches and return to earth. In some of his darker poems, those Lionel Trilling praised as "terrifying," the humor is strained but not abandoned. "Once by the Pacific" provides a good example:

The shattered water made a misty din.
Great waves looked over others coming in,
And thought of doing something to the shore
That water never did to land before.
The clouds were low and hairy in the skies,
Like locks blown forward in the gleam of eyes.
You could not tell, and yet it looked as if

> The shore was lucky in being backed by cliff,
> The cliff in being backed by continent;
> It looked as if a night of dark intent
> Was coming, and not only a night, an age.
> Someone had better be prepared for rage.
> There would be more than ocean-water broken
> Before God's last *Put out the Light* was spoken. (p. 314)

The poem is a serious apocalyptic vision, suggesting that we had better be prepared for a violent end and an angry judgment. The threatening picture of a storm blowing in off the Pacific gives the poet a premonition of an ominous future. And yet, without canceling its seriousness, the poem is peppered with comic strategies intended to control and distance the vision, robbing it not of its destructive power but of its terror for us and the poet. Indeed, the whole poem resembles a parody of a gothic novel or grade B horror film. The storm itself becomes a kind of scary monster who "thinks of doing something to the shore / That water never did to land before." We can see the mad scientist rubbing his hands with glee or the villain dreaming up some improbably horrible torture for the hero. "The clouds were low and hairy in the skies / Like locks blown forward in the gleam of eyes." The metaphor is frightening in the same way that any movie monster is, but the incongruous comparison of clouds to hair keeps us safely distanced, reminding us that this storm is just a storm and not the apocalypse after all. The biblical parody of the last line, a reversal of God's words in Genesis, caps off the humor. Humor thus serves two purposes in this poem. On the one hand, it enables Frost to make a statement about the apocalypse. The poem delivers a serious warning that, if stated solemnly, would be dismissed as religious fanaticism. Humorously exaggerating the storm into an apocalyptic vision, Frost is able to have the vision. On the other hand, the comedy helps control the potential terror of the vision, providing a distance that stays the confusion.

Humor functions similarly, if more subtly, in "Desert Places." The first three stanzas of this poem build a troubled, disturbing picture of a world being effaced and a person being silenced by a loneliness and blankness and pure expressionlessness that insidiously overtakes everything. The repetition of "falling" and "loneliness" sets up a hypnotic rhythm that begins to blur distinctions under a monotonous, spiritless pulse. The jokes in the final stanza are a kind of whistling in the dark, both asserting human will and spirit and intensifying the terror of the experience:

> They cannot scare me with their empty spaces
> Between stars—on stars where no human race is.

> I have it in me so much nearer home
> To scare myself with my own desert places. (p. 386)

The word *scare* is comically incongruous with the seriousness of the situation, and the comic rhyme of "spaces" and "race is" helps establish a tone of bluff overconfidence in the face of the void. But if the humor distances the void out there, it intensifies and magnifies the void "in here." Frost's own internal abysses exceed the terror of any merely external threats. Yet the joke is a saving joke, reflecting sanity and strength, a refusal to give in to *any* desert places. Frost may be, like the snow, "benighted" (covered by night and darkness), but he is not "benighted" (ignorant). In eyeing his terrors and expressing them, he stays them, if only for the moment.

Laughter in a poem like "Desert Places" borders on desperation. In a number of Frost poems laughter is not a sign of health at all, but a sign of the kind of madness Emily Dickinson expresses in #410, "The first Day's Night had come." In "Home Burial," for example, the speaker boasts, "I shall laugh the worst laugh I ever laughed. / I'm cursed" (p. 72). In "Out, Out," after his hand is severed by the power saw, "The boy's first outcry was a rueful laugh" (p. 171). In "The Vanishing Red" the miller who murders the Red Man "laughed / If you like to call such a sound a laugh" (p. 179). Poems like these prompted Lionel Trilling to insist that Frost was a "terrifying poet. Call him, if it makes things any easier, a tragic poet, but it might be useful every now and then to come out from under the shelter of that literary word. The universe that he conceives is a terrifying universe."[13] Trilling's intentions were good—to redeem Frost from the status of minor poet by making him out to be a tragedian and to insist that he wasn't after all a throwback to the nineteenth century but one of "us moderns." But Frost never cared much for Trilling's assessment, preferring to think of himself not as a terrifying and tragic poet, but as a reassuring and comic poet.

Frost might have directed Trilling to a poem written years earlier, "The Lesson for Today," in which Frost answers those who would see our age as dark. The ministerial parody of the title sets the mock-heroic tone of the poem, in which Frost imagines a debate with some medieval scholar about whose age was the darkest:

> You and I
> As schoolmen of repute should qualify
> To wage a fine scholastical contention
> As to whose age deserves the lower mark,
> Or should I say the higher one, for dark. (p. 472)

The contest turns out to be something of a draw. If we feel small in the face of a vast indifferent cosmos, if "space ails us," the people of the dark ages also felt small in the face of God. Frost learns that what he thought was the modern age's "more profound disgrace" was "doubtless only my conceit" (p. 473). The complaint is the same in every age:

> We all are doomed to broken-off careers,
> And so's the nation, so's the total race.
> The earth itself is liable to the fate
> Of meaninglessly being broken off.
> (And hence so many literary tears
> At which my inclination is to scoff.) (p. 475)

The parenthetic joke reflects Frost's characteristic choice of attitudes with which to face such painful truths:

> There's nothing but injustice to be had,
> No choice is left a poet, you might add,
> But how to take the curse, tragic or comic. (p. 472)

Frost chose to take the curse comically, maintaining a "lover's quarrel with the world," practicing an affectionate resistance that enabled him not only to evade death and deflect terror but affirmatively to embrace life. As I suggested at the outset, Frost's Yankee persona of self-deprecation and wry understatement enabled him to assert himself and his imaginative vitality as buoyantly and absurdly as could Walt Whitman. Frost could conceive a terrifying universe, but he preferred to face that universe from a comic perspective that enabled him not merely to evade but to enjoy.

In "A Hillside Thaw," one of the great neglected comic masterpieces of American poetry, Frost uses his Yankee persona, his version of the Thurberesque "little man," to make claims worthy of a Whitmaniac:

> To think to know the country and not know
> The hillside on the day the sun lets go
> Ten million silver lizards out of snow!
> As often as I've seen it done before
> I can't pretend to tell the way it's done.
> It looks as if some magic of the sun
> Lifted the rug that bred them on the floor
> And the light breaking on them made them run.
> But if I thought to stop the wet stampede,
> And caught one silver lizard by the tail,
> And put my foot on one without avail,
> And threw myself wet-elbowed and wet-kneed

In front of twenty others' wriggling speed,—
In the confusion of them all aglitter,
And birds that joined in the excited fun
By doubling and redoubling song and twitter,
I have no doubt I'd end by holding none.

It takes the moon for this. The sun's a wizard
By all I tell; but so's the moon a witch.
From the high west she makes a gentle cast
And suddenly, without a jerk or twitch,
She has her spell on every single lizard.
I fancied when I looked at six o'clock
The swarm still ran and scuttled just as fast.
The moon was waiting for her chill effect.
I looked at nine: the swarm was turned to rock
In every lifelike posture of the swarm,
Transfixed on mountain slopes almost erect.
Across each other and side by side they lay.
The spell that so could hold them as they were
Was wrought through trees without a breath of storm
To make a leaf, if there had been one, stir.
It was the moon's: she held them until day,
One lizard at the end of every ray.
The thought of my attempting such a stay! (pp. 293–94)

The poem begins with a comic tall-tale metaphor: the rivulets released by
a spring thaw down a hillside are ten million silver lizards. If you accept
the improbable metaphor you are caught in the exuberant joke of the
poem. Frost marvels that the wizard sun has changed the snow into lizards by some sleight-of-hand that the ignorant poet can't understand. The
poet is a gullible fool, the dull-witted individual who can't explain or control the simplest facts of daily life. Before he knows it, the lizards change
again into cattle, the change brought about subtly by the word *stampede*,
which effectively mixes the metaphor. With silver snow lizards stamped-
ing, Frost turns helplessly silly, picturing himself leaping and diving in an
effort to catch the speedy and elusive creatures while getting only "wet-
elbowed" and "wet-kneed." Frost's innocent pose is comic here, turning
the simple phenomenon of snowmelt into an unfathomable magic act. He
misperceives the thaw itself, and he misunderstands the response of the
birds. According to the speaker, the birds double and redouble their song
not because that is what naturally happens in spring as the birds return,
and not because they are naturally disturbed by his noisy flailing, but because they are so amused by the befuddled anticking of poet and silver

lizard-cows and want to join the fun. The discrepancy between Frost's innocent, straight-faced misinterpretations of the scene and our knowledge
of the simple reality is comic.

But if the pretense makes him appear foolish, it also makes us see the
simple phenomenon anew. We see the lizards and cattle, we see the magic
of nature, and are reminded of how little we really do understand such
miracles. We laugh at the speaker here but share his excitement and
amazement. We, too, get wet chasing after the lizardy rivulets, surprised
by the stampede of unlikely images. Frost's sly pretense of accepting the
drama as literal enables him to joke us into "knowing" the country in the
same childlike and joyful way that he does.

In the second stanza Frost's tone shifts from the exuberant to the con-
fidential. The sun's performance over, and the participatory fantasy past,
Frost turns to the reader to describe another strange phenomenon. Although he wasn't able to hold those lizards down with his foot he knows
someone who can—the moon, the witching moon. Again Frost ignores
the simple fact—that at night it gets cold again and refreezes the melted
snow—and instead postulates an absurd explanation: the moon casts her
spell on the lizards (which have now metaphorically changed into bees, a
"swarm"), turning them into rock. The silver lizard-cattle-bee-rocks remain frozen in place, one "at the end of every ray." Frost ends the poem
with a characteristically self-deprecatory innocence: "The thought of my
attempting such a stay!"

In part the poem is a playful celebration of spring, tricking the reader
into seeing it anew. In part, the poem is a whimsical admission of people's
limitations and ignorance of the simplest phenomena. But in part the
poem is also a buoyant affirmation of the poet's own great powers. Pretending to be baffled by the wizard sun and the witching moon, pretending to laugh at himself for even thinking about attempting such a "stay,"
the poet himself ultimately outperforms the moon and sun. *He* freezes
those lizards into words. *He* invents the metaphor that turns snowmelt
into lizards in the first place. Ultimately the poem is not about spring at
all. It is about poetry, about the powers of poetry to transform and fix,
to examine and exult, to provide the necessary stay. Pretending to be an
inept, powerless, and foolish clown in the poem, Frost is able to be a
godlike mage. Laughing at his attempt to make such a stay, he craftily
makes it.

In "A Hillside Thaw" Frost couches exuberant boasting in his characteristic understatement and self-deprecation. Refusing to be pinned down
to that neat formula, however, in other poems he is even more Whitmanesque in his celebration of himself and his great capabilities:

I've tried the new moon tilted in the air
Above a hazy tree-and-farmhouse cluster
As you might try a jewel in your hair.
I've tried it fine with little breadth of luster,
Alone, or in one ornament combining
With one first-water star almost as shining.

I put it shining anywhere I please.
By walking slowly on some evening later,
I've pulled it from a crate of crooked trees
And brought it over glossy water, greater,
And dropped it in, and seen the image wallow,
The color run, all sorts of wonder follow. (p. 304)

So what if it is the speaker who is moving and not the moon? The effect is the same. If by walking he can make the actual moon "move," by writing poetry he can make his imaginative moon, or anything else, do exactly what he wants. With his "mischievous, vagrant, seraphic look" (p. 23), he can turn dust to gold (p. 312), convert north wind to south (p. 274), and "sing the wildflowers up from root and seed" (p. 298). He can "seize earth by the pole" (p. 296) and "romp through the dark" (p. 331). And if the dark doesn't please him? No problem:

I may return
If dissatisfied
With what I learn
From having died.[14]

If he does return, both his popular and his scholarly audiences will be waiting.

V

Wallace Stevens
The Revenge of Music on Bassoons

Wallace Stevens disliked "explanations" of poetry, believing that an element of obscurity or mystery was necessary to keep a reader's interest. In a letter to Ronald Lattimore, Stevens insisted, "I have the greatest dislike for explanations. As soon as people are perfectly sure of a poem they are just as likely as not to have no further interest in it; it loses whatever potency it had."[1] Indeed, many of Stevens's best poems seem to reflect the pronouncement he made in "Man Carrying Thing": "The poem must resist the intelligence / Almost successfully" (p. 350). There is little likelihood that Stevens is in danger of being understood in the near future. His work is full of enough contradictions, coinages, archaic usages, intellectual complexity, exuberant playfulness, and willful obscurity to keep any diligent critic happy for a lifetime.

If critics have understood one general thing about Stevens, it is that he is often a comic poet. While critics have resisted Walt Whitman's comedy almost successfully and apologized for Dickinson's and Frost's, they have consistently insisted on Stevens's profound use of comedy, particularly in *Harmonium*, his first book. As early as 1926 Harriet Monroe, one of Stevens's first supporters and publishers, noted that Stevens "is of the race of the great humorists, using the word in its most profound sense."[2] Since then, Daniel Fuchs and Robert Pack have written full-length studies of Stevens's comedy, while Samuel French Morse and Fred M. Robinson have traced the connections between Stevens and Bergson.[3]

Stevens himself rarely mentioned comedy or humor in his prose, but the word and its colleagues probably appear more often in Stevens's poetry than in that of any other American poet. Some of Stevens's favorite character types are those of comedy: comedian, buffo, fop, princox, scaramouche, sophomore, egotist, poltroon. And his favorite images are images of comedy: bananas, buttocks, spring, paramour, motley.

An almost universal recognition of Stevens's humor has not, however, resulted in any universal agreement about the meaning, even the literal meaning, of many of Stevens's poems. Explications of individual Stevens poems are often directly contradictory. Abbie F. Willard goes so far as to charge that studies of Stevens's comedy have suffered from "diluted half-truths and misreadings."[4] An examination of the tradition of American

141

humor to which many of Stevens's poems belong may help them to resist the intelligence somewhat less successfully.

While Frost and Dickinson adopt a pose of self-deprecation and ignorance, pretending to be smaller than they are, Whitman and Stevens characteristically adopt a pose of self-aggrandizement, pretending to be larger than they are. Dickinson's "Business is Circumference," enclosing experience within limited and therefore controllable boundaries. Stevens's business is what he calls the "central man," imagining largely enough to incorporate all of reality. Dickinson's and Frost's comedy works largely by deflation, irony, and understatement; Stevens's and Whitman's comedy works by exaggeration, hyperbole, and overstatement. Thus Frost and Dickinson participate in the Yankee tradition of American humor, while Stevens and Whitman participate in the rhapsodic backwoods tradition. Theodore Roethke evokes this tradition in a poem praising Stevens's legacy to contemporary poets:

> Roar 'em, whore 'em, cockalorum
> The Muses, they must all adore him,
> Wallace Stevens—are we *for* him?
> Brother, he's our father![5]

It may seem strange at first to think of Stevens, one of our most civilized poets—the urbane and witty offspring of the French symbolists, the elegant gentleman and dandy—as a close relative of Whitman, the Kentuckian, the ring-tailed roarer. Yet in the guise of the dandy, Stevens uses the very devices of the Kentuckian—exaggeration, hyperbole, boast, and blab. Stevens's confident and cocky gaudiness, his joy in babble and noise, and his exuberant exaggerations are a more civilized version of Whitman's barbaric yawp. As R. W. B. Lewis has pointed out, Stevens is "the most cultivated of Whitman's literary grand-nephews,"[6] and a strain of Whitmanesque high spirits and revelry, boasts and egotism, runs throughout Stevens's early poetry especially.

Like Whitman's, Stevens's central subject is the self caught between the conflicting demands of reality and the imagination. All of the masks and voices and anecdotes of *Harmonium* are the various faces of that self, as are the varied catalogues of Americans in Whitman's "Song of Myself." If Whitman finally lets his imagination run wild, however, breaking conventions and creating a new reality around himself, Stevens is usually more skeptical, keeping a careful balance. But rather than expressing his skepticism toward Whitman's transcendental beliefs in the Yankee manner of self-deprecation, Stevens employs Whitman's own manner of deflation by exaggeration. As in Whitman, Stevens's boast and brag and strut can both elevate him and his vision of the power of the poet and at the same time undercut him comically. In Whitman this comic strategy ultimately produces a comic god or backwoods kosmos. In Stevens it produces more often an aspiring clown or backwoods dandy. Stevens differs from Whitman in his more detached vision of people's realistic limitations, but he is nevertheless committed, like Whitman, to an affirmation of people's imaginative possibilities. While Whitman uses comedy to help him transcend these limits, fusing opposites and contradictions, Stevens uses comedy to help him achieve a balance, or, like Frost, to fight on both sides at once.

Although Stevens often qualifies the Whitmanesque assertions of his personae, he sometimes affirms them without a trace of irony. In a number of poems a Whitmanesque figure appears as hero or heroine, making great claims for the powers of the individual self, the muse, and the imagination. Whitman himself appears briefly at the beginning of "Like Decorations in a Nigger Cemetery":

> In the far South the sun of autumn is passing
> Like Walt Whitman walking along a ruddy shore.
> He is singing and chanting the things that are part of him,
> The worlds that were and will be, death and day.
> Nothing is final, he chants. No man shall see the end.
> His beard is of fire and his staff is a leaping flame. (p. 150)

This is Whitman the Kosmos, projecting the future out of himself, rejecting any end to things, pursuing (as Stevens puts it later in the poem) "the search for a tranquil belief," a search that will itself keep "the future . . . emerging out of the past, / Out of what is full of us . . . the search / And the future emerging out of us seems to be one" (p. 151). Stevens was apparently ambivalent about Whitman, claiming on one occasion that although he had read *Leaves of Grass*, as a "figure" Whitman meant nothing to him.[7] But this Whitmanesque figure appears more than once in Stevens's poetry. In *Harmonium* the figure appears as a bard having "Tea at the Palaz of Hoon" and as a harmonious singer of "The Idea of Order."

Although it may be a bit difficult to picture Whitman having a polite cup of tea at the Palaz, his spirit is evident in the calm strength of Hoon:

> Out of my mind the golden ointment rained,
> And my ears made the blowing hymns they heard.
> I was myself the compass of that sea:
>
> I was the world in which I walked, and what I saw
> Or heard or felt came not but from myself;
> And there I found myself more truly and more strange. (p. 65)

When asked the identity of "Hoon," Stevens said he couldn't recall the name's origin. He thought it meant "everybody, or rather, anybody" or "Who knows?"[8] Maybe only "Hoon knows," but the universal figure in the poem who sees himself as the very world in which he walks, as the *source* of "the ointment sprinkled on my beard," "the hymns that buzzed beside my ears," and "the sea whose tide swept through me," recalls Walt Whitman in his profound egotism and power. In this poem, Hoon, like Whitman, creates the world by perceiving it. He claims, with no apparent irony from Stevens, to be the "intelligence of his soil."

In "The Idea of Order at Key West" this Whitmanesque figure takes on female form:

> She was the single artificer of the world
> In which she sang. And when she sang, the sea,
> Whatever self it had, became the self
> That was her song, for she was the maker. Then we,
> As we beheld her striding there alone,
> Knew that there never was a world for her
> Except the one she sang and, singing, made. (pp. 129–30)

In other poems, like "Bantams in Pine-Woods" and "The Comedian as the Letter C," Stevens deflates this Whitmanesque figure of godlike imaginative power, turning the poet into a strutting "universal cock" or a pretentious "clerk of experience." But here Stevens affirms the tall-tale capabilities of the character, reflecting Stevens's own avowed desire "to be that in nature which constitutes nature's very self. I want to be nature in the form of a man, with all the resources of nature."[9] Or, as he explains in "The Man with the Blue Guitar," he wants the self to be "A substitute for all the gods: / This self . . . One's self and the mountains of one's land, . . . The flesh, the bone, the dirt, the stone" (p. 176). Stevens won't, with Whitman, have people become God. But he will have them become *like gods*, imagining greatly while "striding among the cigar stores, Ryan's Lunch, hatters, insurance and medicines" (p. 185). For both Whitman and Stevens the poet is a person among people, at home with both the trivia of everyday life and the potential for divinity within him. If Stevens won't assert people's holiness as wholeheartedly as will Whitman, he will embrace Whitman's concomitant notion of happiness:

> the cloak
> And speech of Virgil dropped, that's where he walks,
> That's where his hymns come crowding, hero-hymns,
> Chorals for mountain voices and the moral chant,
> Happy rather than holy but happy-high. (p. 185)

The poet must be "Son only of man and sun of men," "no god but man /
Of men whose heaven is in themselves" (pp. 185–86).

Stevens shares Whitman's belief in the power of poetry to create supreme fictions, to endow people with an almost godlike responsibility. He
also shares Whitman's comic method of expressing and exploring these
ideas, adopting comic masks as a means of exaggerating and deflating
such pretensions. Language itself becomes a kind of comic mask for Stevens, taking on a life of its own in the same way it did for Whitman.
Whitman explained his comic style by describing language as a "mighty
potentate" continually being undercut by "a personage like one of Shak-
speare's clowns." The comic conflict of high and low styles enables "common humanity to . . . express itself illimitably" producing "poets and
poems." [10] Stevens describes the poet's language similarly in "Notes Toward a Supreme Fiction":

> [The poet] tries by a peculiar speech to speak
>
> The peculiar potency of the general,
> To compound the imagination's Latin with
> The lingua franca et jocundissima. (p. 397)

The "imagination's Latin" is Whitman's "mighty potentate"; the "lingua
franca et jocundissima" is Whitman's "clown" disrupting the solemn cer-
emonies of the exalted with its slang, coinages, borrowings, and nonsense. Section 9 of "Notes Toward a Supreme Fiction" (from which Stevens's definition is taken) combines high and low style for comic effect in
just the manner he describes. The poet's "gibberish" can be "luminous"
or merely "flittering"; it can be a "meditation" or merely "chaffer the
time away" (p. 396). *Luminous* and *meditation* are mighty potentates,
the imagination's Latin, while *flittering*, *chaffers*, and *gibberish* are the
corresponding clowns, jocundissimally undercutting their masters.

Language in Stevens, as in Whitman, struts and brags and wears outlandish costumes and funny noses as well as elegant ruffled shirts and diamond
stickpins. Stevens's language can circle meditatively around philosophical
subjects while dancing in a ring of childlike nonsense. The important
thing for both poets is movement:

> There must be no cessation
> Of motion, or of the noise of motion,
> The renewal of noise
> And manifold continuation. (p. 60)

When language (and life) gets too debonair, too exalted, or too inert, the
comic drama described by Whitman and Stevens ensues:

Under the eglantine
The fretful concubine
Said, "Phooey! Phoo!"
She whispered, "Pfui!"

The demi-monde
On the mezzanine
Said, "Phooey!" too,
And a "Hey-dei-do!" (p. 211)

Unlike "Johannisberger, Hans," who appears at the end of this poem, and who is able to see beauty in the raw reality of his surroundings—the metal grapes, the rusty, battered shapes of pears and cheese, the crack across the pane, the dirt along the sill—the concubine and the demi-monde are trapped in a conventionally beautiful scene of false elegance and cliché. Buoyed by history and the imagination's Latin, the mighty potentate holds thrall over them. Words like *eglantine, concubine, whispered, mezzanine,* and *demi-monde* evoke remote, romantic, literary anachronisms that bump comically against the slangy *Phooey!, Phoo!, Pfui!* It is as if through language the concubine is trying to escape her fate. Her clowning is an attempt to see things clearly and to spit the old clichés out of her mouth for good. But the attempt itself undercuts her.

Mark Twain tells the story of Olivia's effort to cure him of swearing. Collecting all of the offensive words into a long catalogue, she one day spouted them back at him to show him how unpleasant they could sound coming from her. Twain listened quietly, and when she was done merely commented, "You've got the words right, but you haven't got the tune." The concubine has the words right here, but she hasn't got the tune. The three spellings of *Phooey, Phoo, Pfui* suggest that even in rejecting the artificiality of her surroundings she is trapped by a necessity to make artificially refined distinctions. Her "rebellion" thus turns into a polite, refined game. Stevens plays a stylistic joke on the reader here. The first two lines promise a conventional love lyric or romantic spring song. The slangy third line pulls the rug out from under the reader's expectations, making him take a literary pratfall. The poem is also a joke on the elegant, archaic concubine who hopes to change her life merely by changing her language. While this may be a useful first step, Stevens seems to be saying, a whole change of perspective is required as well. She has not only to change her language; she has to change her tune.

Stevens, as much as Whitman, was committed to new ways of seeing. From the elevated position of Hoon, or central man, or the singer in "Ideas of Order," he could say "Phooey" (or "Phui") to any representative of the old order, including an outmoded religion or conception of God. When Emily Dickinson satirizes her soft cherubic creatures for their inadequate religious notions she does it quietly, ironically stinging them with backhanded attacks that masquerade as compliments. Dickinson's method is that of the *eiron*, and her goal is not to reject the women's religion or their God, but to puncture their delusions about themselves. In Stevens's "A High-Toned Old Christian Woman," he satirizes in the mode of the *alazon*, adopting the role of egotist and boaster in order to shout down not only the absurd old woman but her religion, her moral laws, and her God as well. Stevens becomes the boisterous, unpleasant, obnoxious clown, taunting the old woman with his own high-toned slapstick, substituting his own Whitmanesque jovial hullabaloo for her pale, outmoded hymns.

Stevens not only exposes the old woman ("widowed," since her god is dead), but he taunts her with the very clowning and bawdiness and poetry he knows she abhors. The poem is structured as a contrast between the windy, haunted, sexless, humorless heaven of old Christians and the pagan, human, sexual, comic earth of new poets. With mock politeness, mimicking and exaggerating her own high tone, the poet opens with a boast, a heresy, and a parodic attack:

> Poetry is the supreme fiction, madame. (p. 59)

God is not the supreme being, the speaker smugly insists. God is a fiction. And God isn't even the supreme fiction—poetry is. What follows is a disquisition delivered by a pompous mock orator, full of tricks of logic calculated to insult and offend his victim. Although the woman never speaks in the poem, we can hear her sputtering throughout. Much like Margaret Dumont at the hands of Groucho Marx, she is alternately outraged, speechless, confused, and foolish in her struggle to follow the volley of mock logic and sift insult from flattery. "Take the moral law" and stuff it, we hear the clownish speaker about to say, but then he defuses objections by proceeding with what seems a logical metaphor: "and make a nave of it." Is there a knave in the nave? Before we have time to decide, the speaker races on to "build haunted heaven." The phrase sounds objectionable, but the speaker swiftly moves to "palms," a just reward for a life of "conscience." Both conscience and palms are undercut, however, by the comparison with "windy citherns hankering for hymns." "Windy" suggests empty and baseless. "Hankering" evokes the earthy as in Whitman's "hankering, gross, mystical, nude":

> We agree in principle. That's clear.

The line is a total misrepresentation. What is clear is that they don't agree in principle. The statement in no way follows logically from the preceding argument; the speaker is tricking the old woman into an agreement she would never consciously accept. But before she has time to object or even to register the contradiction, the speaker is off again proposing another metaphor, another joke on her. He directs her to "take / The opposing law" (poetry, one presumes) and make not a church of it, but a "masque," an "art," built on a "peristyle." The word of classical origins prepares the way for the *Jove*-ial hullabaloo later in the poem. This masque, this bawdiness, also converts to "palms," though they are sexual palms "squiggling like saxophones." The speaker has proposed a kind of faulty enthymeme: the moral law produces palms; poetry produces palms; therefore, poetry is the moral law. The speaker triumphantly concludes:

> And palm for palm,
> Madame, we are where we began.

Actually, we are not where "we" began at all. We are where the speaker began. Having "proved," absurdly and cockily, the opening statement, the speaker continues his mock logic:

> Allow,
> Therefore, that in the planetary scene
> Your disaffected flagellants, well-stuffed,
> Smacking their muzzy bellies in parade,
> Proud of such novelties of the sublime,
> Such tink and tank and tunk-atunk-tunk,
> May, merely may, madame, whip from themselves
> A jovial hullabaloo among the spheres.

The "disaffected flagellants" (that is, the speaker and his bawdy poet friends) have now somehow become "*Your* disaffected flagellants," implicating the woman in their activity. And these flagellants resemble not at all the traditional Christian ascetics with whom the speaker would compare them; these flagellants are comically well stuffed. The oxymoron both deflates and elevates them, as does the juxtaposition of the old romantic "sublime" with the nonsense ditty, "tink and tank and tunk-atunk-tunk." The banjos and guitars and jazz and free verse that are to come are incongruous with the sonorous organs and droning old hymns they will replace. And if the woman at the end has finally caught up to the tricks that have been played on her, if she is wincing at the parade of belly-slapping Whitmanesque backwoodsmen, why even her wincing will

turn against her, serving as inspiration and ammunition for the muzzy
poets:

> But fictive things
> Wink as they will. Wink most when widows wince.

For the speaker of the poem, the widow's world view is an example of the
mechanical encrusted on the living. His method of confronting it is to
adopt a boisterous *élan vital*, inflating himself and his own energy and
egotistically fast-talking his way beyond whatever hold high-toned old
Christianity might try to have on him.

For Stevens, as for Whitman, the old dispensations are mechanical and
inert, representing a fixity that restricts rather than renews human imagination and possibility. Dickinson and Frost question the Christian God in
hopes of finding him (or finding him out). Stevens and Whitman blow
God away in hopes of replacing him. For Stevens, "Jehovah and the great
sea-worm" have been replaced by the sensuous things of this world, "Ca-
naries in the morning, orchestras / In the afternoon, balloons at night.
That is / A difference, at least" (p. 142). All that is left of the old Christian
concept is a residue, "A vermillioned nothingness" (p. 328), or a dangerous fiction, a "Herr Gott" (p. 349). The only God that can sustain us is
a God who is as real as New Haven (p. 485) and who, though he may not
provide much conventional consolation, is an Emperor of Ice-Cream
(p. 64).

If this world is all there is, notions of heaven become targets for comedy. Heaven becomes "the blank" (p. 217), and the means of getting there
is a chariot that parodies Dickinson's fine carriage:

> Out of the tomb, we bring Badroulbadour,
> Within our bellies, we her chariot.
> Here is an eye. And here are, one by one,
> The lashes of that eye and its white lid.
> Here is the cheek on which that lid declined,
> And, finger after finger, here, the hand,
> The genius of that cheek. Here are the lips,
> The bundle of the body and the feet.
> . . . .
> Out of the tomb we bring Badroulbadour. (pp. 49–50)

The poem parodies a Dickinsonian carriage ride as well as Whitmanesque
notions of eternal recurrence. As a literalist of the imagination, Stevens
can have fun both with the romantic Christian belief in resurrection and
with the more pantheistic belief of an eternity of change in nature. Whit-

man suggests that we look for him under our bootsoles, and that is precisely where Stevens will look for Badroulbadour. The Arabian nights princess will be rewarded with eternal life as befits her station, but she will be conveyed to that life by worms, who comically speak the poem in chorus. The poem is a kind of worm work song, chanted by the worms as they go about their appointed task of carrying the princess, piece by piece, out of the tomb toward the only heaven there is. The structure of the poem itself suggests the circularity of the activity, and the ellipsis of the penultimate line reflects its insensible drudgery and blankness. At this point in the poem there is nothing else to do but repeat the chant. The Dickinsonian parody clearly deflates the Christian idea of resurrection; the Whitmanesque parody both laughs at and celebrates the idea of an eternity in nature, with a certain joyfulness in the careful dismantling of Badroulbadour. The black comedy makes the rather gruesome truth acceptable, even engaging. If Stevens sees no transcendence in the procession, he shares with Whitman a refusal to be terrified in the face of it, preferring to view it comically. Stevens didn't quite buy Whitman's version of an immortality in the eternal recurrence of things, but he liked its "classical sound" and could have fun with it. Dickinson and Frost hope to get to heaven eventually, if there is one. Whitman knows he will get to heaven because his heaven is under his bootsoles and everything eventually ends up there. Stevens knows he won't get to heaven, but that in itself is a good reason for enjoying the here and now, which includes the worms and their patient processions.

The worms carry Badroulbadour out of the tomb toward heaven's gates. What they find beyond those gates, Stevens describes in another poem, "Of Heaven Considered as a Tomb." Here, the dead are merely "the darkened ghosts of our old comedy" and Stevens asks the "interpreters" (clergymen? biblical scholars? the reader?) to mediate for them. The poem is structured as a series of questions ostensibly addressed to experts by an ignorant speaker who wants answers. Gradually, however, it becomes apparent that the questioner himself knows the answers and the experts are the ignorant ones. The questions themselves are foolish, and the fact that the experts take them seriously itself undercuts those experts. Stevens knows that the men "Who in the tomb of heaven walk by night" aren't in heaven at all; they are in the tomb. And they only "walk" because we have imagined that they do—they are the ghosts of our old comedy, our old notions of the afterlife. Do these people who don't exist except in your imagination, says Stevens, think they are "Freemen of death?" (the phrase itself is an oxymoron). Or have they finally figured out that death is an end, a nothingness?

The questions that are ostensibly addressed to the dead through their interpreters are finally addressed to the living, to the interpreters themselves, and the poem is a satire on them. "Do you still believe foolishly in an afterlife," Stevens asks us, "or have you finally faced the truth? Go ahead, ask your imaginary dead," he suggests. "See if they'll answer you." Stevens expects no answers to his questions. He merely uses them as a means of poking fun at conventional ways of thinking, while offering some sly advice to the ignorant:

> Make hue among the dark comedians,
> Halloo them in the topmost distances
> For answer from their icy Élysée. (p. 56)

Although Stevens appears to be asking innocent questions of the experts, he is really satirizing them. Heaven is a tomb, an icy élysée, and to call to the dead is foolish. Stevens's final advice to the experts thus works in two ways. He is directing the experts to act foolishly, to halloo these dead ghosts who only exist in the experts' own minds. But he is also suggesting the proper approach to death or to dead ideas. "Make hue" can mean both make noise and make color. To make noise in the silence, to make color in the dark, to make rowdy and elegant burlesque of the solemn, is to employ Stevens's and Whitman's characteristic methods of staying alive and vital. By travestying the exalted, they indulge their own exaltation.

Stevens's method in this poem is more Dickinsonian or Frostian than usual since he adopts the pose of the *eiron* to unmask the *alazons*. But his ultimate advice is Whitmanesque: Make hue. Make a jovial hullabaloo. Stevens's and Whitman's characteristic mode is to "remember the cry of the peacocks"; that is, to oppose color, strut, ego, and noise to death, blank, and loss (p. 8): "Poetry / Exceeding music must take the place / Of empty heaven" (p. 167). Finally, for Stevens, death isn't something to be teased into friendship with Emily Dickinson, or politely evaded with Robert Frost, or even blabbed and bragged away with Walt Whitman. It is instead something to be acknowledged without embroidery or transformation, to be seen steadily and clearly for the literal fact it is. There are no men walking in heaven. There is no resurrection other than that afforded by the worms. The fact need not occasion despair; it can instead intensify enjoyment of the here-and-now, engendering a deeper appreciation of the human comedy.

In summary, Stevens shares with Whitman a belief in the self, in this world, and in new ways of seeing. Like Whitman he often adopts a version of the backwoods voice of American humor. Stevens's backwoods dandy makes jovial hullabaloo in the face of high-toned conventionalism, replacing God and heaven with the supreme fiction of poetry. Like Whitman, Stevens also makes fun of himself, using comedy to qualify and undercut even his deepest beliefs. The speaker of "A High-Toned Old Christian Woman," for example, is himself rather high-toned, obnoxious, and closed-minded. His *alazon* qualities prevent complete identification with him. And the all-knowing attitude of Hoon and the questioner in "Of Heaven Considered as a Tomb" reveals an egotism that tempers the "truths" implied in the poems. Stevens thus uses his inflated persona as Whitman does in the first half of "Song of Myself," simultaneously to celebrate and to laugh at himself.

For all his strut and brag, however, Stevens ultimately remains less confident and more skeptical than does Whitman. By the end of "Song of Myself" Whitman has triumphed over conventions and created a new world with himself as center. The self-parody of the earlier sections gives way to Whitman's emergence as comic god, reborn and waiting for us to follow. Stevens never becomes God, preferring instead, like Frost and Dickinson, to preserve a comic balance of attitudes. Throughout Stevens's poetry we hear two voices playing against each other—the voice of elevation and the voice of deflation. In the early poems these two voices occasionally split into two separate characters who both affirm and reject Whitmanesque assertions:

> Chieftain Iffucan of Azcan in caftan
> Of tan with henna hackles, halt!
>
> Damned universal cock, as if the sun
> Was blackamoor to bear your blazing tail.
>
> Fat! Fat! Fat! Fat! I am the personal.
> Your world is you. I am my world.
>
> You ten-foot poet among inchlings. Fat!
> Begone! An inchling bristles in these pines,
>
> Bristles, and points their Appalachian tangs,
> And fears not portly Azcan nor his hoos. (pp. 75–76)

"Bantams in Pine-Woods," a paradigmatic Stevens poem, can be (and has been) interpreted in several contradictory ways, none of them "right," or all of them "right" if taken together. Two common misconceptions confuse interpretations of the poem: first, that the poem is an allegory in which one figure is the imagination and the other is reality; and second, that the reader is supposed to choose one over the other. The poem is structured on the conflict between the universal cock and the inchling.

Since the poem is a kind of animal fable, it is natural to look for human correspondences. But the comedy of the poem actively works against any allegorical equations, warning us not to choose one side over the other.

The usual approach to the poem is to see the universal cock as a boastful egotist and impostor, an imagination grown too large and insistent, Whitman claiming to be God. In his self-importance and egotism this cock, puffed up by his gaudy appearance, imagines that he is "the intelligence of his soil." He assumes that the world revolves around him and that the sun is but a servant to him. From his inflated perspective he thinks that he could move the sun, like Whitman or Davy Crockett, if need be. His world is he, and, behind his majestic armor of caftan and hackles, he is isolated from reality.

If the universal cock is an *alazon*, a boastful impostor, the imagination on its high horse, then the inchling is an *eiron*, a Dickinsonian self-deprecator, reality. He knows that the soil is his intelligence, and from this diminished perspective he can puncture and deflate the cock. The inchling is aware of his limitations, and that awareness is itself a strength, keeping him in touch with the world rather than isolating him from it. The language of the poem itself seems to undercut the universal cock. His name conceals a taunt, "if you can," and an expletive, "fuck!" And there is a hint of "ash can" in his place of origin. Further, there is some evidence outside the poem to support this interpretation. In "Notes Toward a Supreme Fiction" Stevens expresses his impatience with an Arabian whose "damned hoobla-hoobla-hoobla-how" reflects an effort imaginatively to distort reality. And in a note on the meaning of *hooing* in "The Man with the Blue Guitar," Stevens explains the word as a derisive portmanteau coinage of *booing* and *hooting*, suggesting that the "hoos" that follow the cock around in "Bantams in Pine-Woods" are boos and hoots.[11]

The inchling would clearly like this interpretation that makes him the comic spirit and the cock the comic butt. But can we trust the truculent, diminutive loudmouth to speak for Stevens? In some ways the inchling is as much an *alazon* as is the cock. He is no true self-deprecator and wit, but is instead an impostor, a boaster of modesty, as surely as the cock is a boaster of grandeur. He reveals an overweaning pride about his smallness and uses it to cut himself off from others as effectively as the cock is cut off. Like the speaker in Frost's "Mending Wall" he falls victim to the very attack he makes on someone else. His military bearing ("halt!") and pompous tone are comically incongruous with his avowed smallness. His smug and fatuous blathering backfires on him.

If the inchling is unreliable, his version of the cock (which is all we have in the poem) may be seriously flawed. Perhaps the universal cock is an image of Stevens, whose own portly frame recalls the cock's. Perhaps the poem is about a large-spirited poet surrounded by inchling poetasters and critics. Indeed, the cock's attitude toward experience is identical with that of Hoon in "Tea at the Palaz of Hoon," who also sees his world as an imaginative projection of himself. In that poem Stevens seems to support Hoon's quiet confidence and power. Perhaps the cock's "hoos" are followers from the palace of Hoon. I mentioned earlier that Stevens explained the word *hooing* as a combination of *booing* and *hooting*. In the same note, however, he virtually reverses that explanation by suggesting that *hooing* might instead mean "making Bing Crosby"; that is, performing in an accomplished way.[12] And in "The Man with the Blue Guitar" the slick trombones "hoo" down the false god by "making Bing Crosby" (p. 177). Perhaps the universal cock is also supposed to call up a kind of Bing Crosby calmness and capability and music.

Where does Stevens stand in all this? He could be the cock, surrounded by but well beyond the scrabbling little inchlings. Or he could be the inchling, deflating the pompous and self-aggrandizing cock. And he could be both. Stevens's hint about Bing Crosby provides an analogy that may, in part, explain his comic method in the poem. If the cock is indeed a kind of Bing Crosby figure, the mellow crooner who is master of his world and always gets the girl, the inchling could be seen as a kind of Bob Hope figure, the abused clown, aspiring and incompetent, who always loses out. Like the inchling, Hope expresses his dismay in petulance and complaint, but ultimately manages to bumble through to his own small triumph, fast-talking all the way. Crosby is mellifluous and capable but is also a bit of a cock, all too ready to sacrifice his friend for his own pleasure. Hope is foolish and inept but more human than Crosby in knowing his limits and needs. In the "Road" pictures we may be romantically drawn to Crosby and glad that he gets Dorothy Lamour in the end, but we probably see more of ourselves, our own realistic problems and ineptitudes, in Hope and are glad that he survives happily. Ultimately we do not choose one character and reject the other; both characters are necessary halves of a whole, and we watch the comedy play itself out between them.

No matter what we call them—cock and inchling, Crosby and Hope, universal and personal, imagination and reality, *alazon* and *eiron*, exaggeration and deflation—both sides in the drama are necessary, and both sides are undercut and embraced. For Stevens, the poet is both God imagining his world and inchling charting his weather and landscapes. The comic interplay between the bantams, and not the separate sides in the drama, is what most engages and fascinates Stevens. The ultimate goal is a comic balance in which neither side "wins." It is not a dialectic in which two sides argue toward some resolution; it is a comic drama in which the conflict itself militates against any simplistic, one-sided view. When the cock gets too big, the inchling pulls him down; when the inchling gets too petty, the cock brings him up. The ensuing balance is the triumph of the comic spirit, which, for all its clowning, always pulls toward moderation and harmony.

Simultaneous praise and put-down is the comic method Stevens uses in one of his most popular and Whitmanesque poems, "The Comedian as the Letter C." The poem is often seen as a kind of spiritual autobiography of the early Stevens and a farewell to the Harmonium mode of writing, since Stevens stopped publishing for ten years after writing the poem and never returned to quite the "essential gaudiness" of his early style. While the poem certainly is a spiritual autobiography, it is more than that. It is a way of looking at life and experience, and a quest for new ways of knowing and seeing. The central focus of the poem is the comic alternation of fluidity and fixity, of movement and inertia in an individual's life. Stevens explores how people's urges to pursue new ways of seeing and knowing harden or atrophy, requiring renewed pursuit. Crispin is not just a comic version of Stevens but a representative of the human comedy in general.

Crispin's goal in "The Comedian" is remarkably similar to Whitman's in "Song of Myself":

> What was the purpose of his pilgrimage,
> Whatever shape it took in Crispin's mind,
> If not, when all is said, to drive away
> The shadow of his fellows from the skies,
> And, from their stale intelligence released,
> To make a new intelligence prevail? (p. 37)

Like Whitman, Stevens sends his character on a quest for a new world in which the "essential prose" will "wear a poem's guise at last" (p. 36). Both characters are a trifle absurd in their exaggerated views of their own capabilities. But both also imagine greatly, live largely, and, after suffering a ritual death at sea (Whitman with John Paul Jones, Crispin in his Atlantic crossing), incorporate more of experience into their "rude aesthetics" than they could have at the outset of their quests. If Stevens's poem stops short of Whitman's transcendental affirmation, it nevertheless parodies that affirmation, employing a similar comic structure and method.

Like "Song of Myself," "The Comedian" is structured on a combination of two traditional comic plots, satiric exposure comedy and romance comedy. In "Song of Myself" Whitman adopts an *alazon* persona, exposing his egotism and excess by exaggerating them and submitting the character to a ritual death that leads to a rebirth. The usual fate of the *alazon* is to be expelled or converted, but Whitman swerves from the traditional pattern by turning himself into a comic god and envisioning a new world around himself. Stevens, like Whitman, adopts the persona of boastful impostor and fool. The persona is exposed in a number of ways, suffering several ritual deaths and experiencing a kind of rebirth in Carolina. But while Whitman swerves from the typical pattern at the end of "Song of Myself," allowing his character to transcend it and absurdly assert himself, Stevens follows the conventional pattern, reforming his character and integrating him into society. At the end of "The Comedian" Crispin is married, has daughters, and is firmly ensconced in domestic social life. Although Stevens's ending is more realistic, it also seems something of a comedown for the hero, leading readers to see him as a failure. In earlier comedy the reformation and integration of the aberrant character would have seemed appropriate and affirmative. In a modern context, and in contrast to Whitman's absurd triumph, such an ending may seem merely a trap, a new fixity, a rejection of all Crispin has learned.

Like "Song of Myself," however, "The Comedian" is also structured on a pattern of romance comedy. Whitman's persona is a kind of comic swain who pursues his soul and the reader, overcomes various blocks to his happiness, and finally triumphs. At the end of the poem he confidently awaits the promised union with his lover. Crispin is also a kind of comic paramour who seeks a union with poetry, the landscape, and the real. Like Whitman's persona, Crispin overcomes the blocks to his happiness and prepares to celebrate a union. But the union proves to be other than he had expected. While Whitman ends "Song of Myself" at the moment before marriage (the usual ending of a romance comedy), Stevens swerves from that expectation and takes his poem beyond the usual romance-comedy ending to its realistic outcome: domestic life and a gaggle of children.

Thus, while the two poems are structured similarly on a combination of typical comic plots, their departures from expectation establish their differing focuses. Whitman has his character transcend the ending of the usual satiric comedy and become a god, while Stevens has his character fit neatly into the usual ending and become a converted clown. Whitman allows his character the usual romance comedy ending, a promised union with his paramour, while Stevens takes his character beyond the usual ending, showing what marriage "really" means. In Stevens's parodic version of "Song of Myself," Crispin aspires greatly but suffers a comic pratfall from which he never quite recovers, remaining unable to attain any mythic heroism.

Stevens was not Whitman. Whitman, the philosophical idealist, could overturn the comic conventions and absurdly assert his own "aberrant" program. Stevens, the philosophical realist, could only affirm his character's aspirations to do that while also comically exposing his all-too-human limitations. But Crispin's "failure" in no way makes him a tragic figure. If he doesn't attain Whitman's transcendent heroism, he is a more accurate picture of "things as they are." And by parodying Whitman, Stevens not only undercuts such affirmations but uses them at the same time. A closer look at Stevens's comic method will clarify Crispin's role and Stevens's theme.

Like Whitman, Stevens casts his protagonist in the role of *alazon*—boaster, egotist, hyperbolic poet. Whitman's use of the first person narrator, however, led numerous readers to equate the persona with Whitman himself and consequently miss the comedy. Using the third person narrator in "The Comedian," Stevens avoids any confusion. As narrator he is clearly the *eiron* who exposes and deflates Crispin's *alazon*. The reader sees Whitman's persona solely through that persona's eyes, making it difficult to discriminate the serious from the comic. The reader sees Crispin not only through Crispin's eyes but also from the larger perspective of the narrator's comic vision.

As *alazon*, Crispin derives from a long line of comic figures. Stevens himself points to Crispin's lineage in "Anecdote of the Abnormal": "Crispin-valet, Crispin-saint!" (*OP*, p. 24). As valet, Crispin appeared in seventeenth- and eighteenth-century French drama. He was the tricky slave—timid, boasting, and knavish by turns—who had ambitions beyond his class but eventually ended up marrying a milkmaid or kitchen wench. The figure goes back even further to Horace, who faulted Crispinus for producing "an abundance of bad verses" and nicknamed him "the Babbler."[13] He also appears in Ben Jonson's "The Poetaster," where he is forced to vomit up such wordy gobbets as "retrograde," "reciprocall," "turgidous," and "oblatrant."[14] And a more recent version of this valet figure appears in the comic film *Monsieur Beaucaire*, in which Bob Hope plays a rather incompetent barber in the court of Louis XIV who, disguised as king and hero, resiliently comes to believe he is just what he pretends to be, only to be routed time and again. In "The Comedian" Crispin carries on the tradition of comic valet and jack-of-all-trades, assuming the roles of barber, valet, sailor, musician, botanist, philosopher, pedagogue, poet, sophomore, emigrant, colonizer, hermit, apprentice yeoman, hero, husband, and father.

The poem opens with Crispin's philosophic motto, which could be taken as a paradigm of egotism, "man is the intelligence of his soil" (p. 27). From the outset Crispin is the universal cock, a comical Hoon, a Whitmanesque egotist who believes that his intelligence is central and the world flows out from it. He is Socrates, musician, and preceptor, ruler over himself and his environment. He is the European classicist, but he also bears some resemblance to the swaggering hero of the American tall tale, who sees nothing funny about his bombastic claims. Like Whitman, he is able to propose "an aesthetic tough, diverse, untamed, / Incredible to prudes, the mint of dirt, / Green barbarism turning paradigm" (p. 31).

For all his swagger and blab and pompous posing, however, it is also clear from the outset that Crispin is the little man—the Thurber, the Woody Allen, the Chaplin, the Keaton, the Bob Hope—deluded into thinking he is something more than he is. Language itself undercuts him. Although as poet Crispin might be expected to control language, it is language that comically controls and abuses him. In much the same way that Shakespeare's valets sometimes mock their masters, undercutting their foolishness with witty metaphor, nonsense, doubling, humorous conundrums, and noise, so language in "The Comedian" mocks its supposed master, Crispin. While the narrator of the poem is not Crispin, he uses the language Crispin might have used, but uses it against him. Bergson describes the method in his essay on laughter:

> A comic theme with which we are well acquainted [is] that of the "robber robbed." You take up a metaphor, a phrase, an argument, and turn it against the man who is, or might be, its author, so that he is made to say what he did not mean to say and lets himself be caught, to some extent, in the toils of language.[15]

The description closely fits Stevens's method in the poem. Crispin is the barber barbered, the rhetorician rhetoricked. Adopting and exaggerating Crispin's own hyperbolic language, Stevens undercuts Crispin with his own words. The language in effect doubles Crispin by pretending itself to be large, with its Latinate words, its French borrowings, and its sophisticated diction. At the same time it continually bumps up against the common, the small, and the idiomatic, just as Crispin bumps up against real life. Crispin is a Socrates, all right—of snails; a musician—but of pears, not spheres; an intelligence—not of the soil, but soiled with its own delusions. One of Stevens's favorite stylistic devices for undercutting Crispin is just these oxymoronic couplings that deny themselves by asserting themselves. Crispin is thus a "marvelous sophomore," an "auditor of insects," a "nincompated pedagogue," a "lutanist of fleas," a "lexicographer of . . . greenhorns," an "imperative haw of hum." When Crispin gets too high on himself and the doubling language is too elevated and pretentious, Stevens brings it all crashing back to earth with a homely juxtaposition. In section 2 the opulence of Mayan sonneteers deflates to "A new reality in parrot-squawks" (p. 32). And in section 4 Crispin's whole aesthetic program goes out the window in a phrase: "exit lex, / Rex and principium, exit the whole / Shebang" (pp. 36–37). The homely idioms pull the rug from under Crispin's grand aspirations and send him sprawling.

Stevens himself drew attention to the comic role of the language in the poem in a way that no critic has sufficiently followed up. On three separate occasions over a span of twenty years, Stevens found it necessary to comment on the title of the poem in order to clarify one of his central intentions. In his notes to the Italian translation of his poetry by Renato Poggioli in 1954, Stevens writes:

> *It may be a little difficult to translate* The Comedian as the Letter C. *The sounds of the letter C, both hard and soft, include other letters K, X, etc. How would it be possible to translate a line like*
>   Chequering from piebald fisks unkeyed,
> *and preserve anything except the sense of the words? However, it is true that the poem has made its way without reference to the sounds of the letter C.*[16]

Years earlier, in a letter to Hi Simons, Stevens is even more specific:

> It is true that the letter C is a cypher for Crispin, but using the cypher was meant to suggest something that nobody seems to have grasped. I can state it, perhaps, by changing the title to this: THE COMEDIAN AS THE SOUNDS OF THE LETTER C . . . . Now, as Crispin moves through the poem, the sounds of the letter C accompany him . . . . You have to read the poem and hear all this whistling and mocking and stressing and, in a minor way, orchestrating, going on in the background. . . . The natural effect of the variety of the sounds of the letter C is a comic effect.[17]

And five years earlier, in a letter to Ronald Lattimore, Stevens insists:

> I ought to confess that by the letter C I meant the sound of the letter C; what was in my mind was to play on that sound throughout the poem. While the sound of that letter has more or less variety, and includes, for instance, K and S, all its shades may be said to have a comic aspect. Consequently, the letter C is a comedian . . . . Moreover, I did not mean that every time the letter C occurs in the poem it should take the stage. The reader would have to determine for himself just when that particular sound was being stressed, as, for example, in such a phrase as "piebald fiscs unkeyed," where you have the thing hissing and screeching. As a rule, people very much prefer to take the solemn views of poetry.[18]

Stevens goes on in the letter to say, as he said repeatedly throughout his life, that he had "the greatest dislike for explanations." The fact that despite his dislike he explained the importance of the sound of the letter C in the poem on three occasions over twenty years suggests its importance for him. Although Stevens specifically says that the comedian in this poem is the letter C itself, critics still continue to assume that the comedian is Crispin. Crispin is the comic hero, but, as Stevens suggests, he is not the comedian at all. The letter C is.

The letter C functions as a kind of Meredithian comic spirit, showering its silvery laughter on Crispin throughout the poem, but reserving the harshest attacks of its slapstick for those moments when Crispin is most egotistical or most deluded. Just as slang was a Shakespearean clown for Whitman, the sounds of the letter C function like a Launce or Speed for Stevens. Standing slightly off stage-center and hissing, sputtering, whistling, clucking, and chortling, they wittily undercut their master without the master being the wiser. The letter C thus resembles Enid Wellsford's classic definition of the fool:

> The Fool or Clown is the Comic Man, but he is not necessarily the hero of comedy, the central figure about whom the story is told . . . . As a dramatic character he usually stands apart from the main action of the play, having a tendency not to focus but to dissolve events, and also to act as an intermediary between the stage and the auditorium. . . . The Fool, in fact, is an amphibian, equally at home in the world of reality and the world of imagination.[19]

The sounds of the letter C are an *eiron* to Crispin's *alazon*, an inchling to his universal cock. Hissing and screeching Crispin down from his high horse, they put Crispin in his place and warn the reader not to take him too solemnly.

Reading the poem with our ears, we hear the letter C slapping at Crispin from the outset: "sovereign," "Socrates," "snails," "musician," "Principium," "sed quaeritur," "nincompated," "preceptor," "snouts," "mustachios," "inscrutable." In section 1 he is so "washed away by magnitude" (his own) that "The whole life that still remained in him / Dwindles to one sound strumming in his ear, / Ubiquitous concussion, slap and sigh" (p. 28). The one sound is the sound of the letter C, squawking at him no less than seven times in one line.

Having faced the sea in section 1, he must face the C further in section 2 when he arrives at his first destination, the Yucatan. With a force equal to that of the thunderstorm that sends the tough aesthete flying, the sounds of the letter C rain down on Crispin throughout the section, hissing and clucking their tongues at his foolishness: "Yucatan," "falcon," "toucan," "rocking," "insect," "sonneteers," "dissertation," "vicissitude," "destitution," "stupor," "cadaverous," "intrinsic," "squawks," "façade," "swallowed," "shadows," "scruples," "yuccas."

Crispin learns something from the stormy C's, and in sections 3 and 4 as he approaches Carolina and his new aesthetic, the sounds subside, replaced by long vowels and a more sonorous lyricism that reflects his movement toward a truer vision. In section 5, as the new aesthetic itself begins to harden into convention and Crispin settles into a nice shady home, the sounds of C return to taunt him: "Discontent," "prickling," "confect," "chits," "infected," "confined," "confused," "calamitous," "obliquities." The meaning of the C words here, as well as their sounds, establishes the mood. And section 6 begins with a veritable concatenation of sound as Stevens invokes the C ironically to bell Crispin's last deduction:

> Portentous enunciation, syllable
> To blessed syllable affined, and sound
> Bubbling felicity in cantilene,
> Prolific and tormenting tenderness
> Of music, as it comes to unison,
> Forgather and bell boldly Crispin's last
> Deduction. Thrum with a proud douceur
> His grand pronunciamento and devise. (p. 43)

Fully half the words in the passage contain the sounds of the letter C, warning us to keep our distance from this well-meaning but clumsy would-be poet and friend of the earth. The C functions something like John Berryman's interlocutor in the *Dream Songs*, as a comic spirit that punctures the protagonist's ignorance but remains a friend as well, keeping him sane by accompanying him on his journey.

Exposed by the language itself and by the discrepancy between his words and his actions, Crispin, like Whitman's persona in "Song of Myself," suffers several ritual deaths that lead to renewed vision. Having held an inflated old-world view of the self, Crispin ventures out on the elemental sea and finds that the charms that gained control over gelatins and jupes don't work in a larger context. The old mythologies vanish with an insubstantial triton, and Crispin is purged of imaginative embroideries to "some starker, barer self / In a starker, barer world" (p. 29). Freed from old ways of seeing, "the last distortion of romance / Forsook the insatiable egotist" (p. 30). Facing the "veritable ding an sich" (p. 29) is the first step toward a new, more vital imagination.

If the world without imagination is stark, inhuman, alien, and deadening, the world with too much imagination is a fantasy land of Maya sonneteers. The "green barbarism" of Crispin's new aesthetic proves to be so many parrot squawks, and he undergoes another ritual death in the storm that is "more terrible / Than the revenge of music on bassoons" (p. 32). The line smacks of nonsense, suggesting a storm that isn't very terrible at all. It is, however, terrible indeed. The revenge of music on a part of itself would be like the revenge of poetry on a poet, or of life on a living being. The revenge of the whole on one of its component parts would be terrible because it would risk damaging not only the part but the whole as well. Crispin has been so obsessed with his own importance that he can't see his place in the whole orchestra. He has been playing his bassoon in an effort to drown out the world around him. The music of poetry thus takes its revenge on him, attacking him with C's and showing him that rather than trying to play the music of the spheres, he should place himself within the sphere of music. The storm in Yucatan teaches him "something harsher than he learned" at sea, that he must be a part of the universal harmony, not its lone soloist.

Errant bassoonist, Crispin leaves the opulent south behind and journeys north to what he hopes will be a polar region. While it is not, and while he finds instead a spring "abhorrent to the nihilist" (p. 35), the "burly smells" and "arrant stinks" dissipate his moonlight fictions and help him to "round his rude aesthetic out" (p. 36) with the "essential prose." Reformed by ridicule in the manner of the traditional *alazon*, Crispin arrives at a more modest conclusion: "Nota: his soil is man's intelligence. / That's better. That's worth crossing seas to find" (p. 36). As an "aspiring clown" Crispin will participate in landscape and weather. Instead of being a dictator to snails, pears, and fleas, he will be a valet to the world. He will find no ideas but in things. According to Crispin's new program everyone will sing his own soil: the man in Georgia will be pine spokesman; the natives of the rain will be rainy men. Reformed, his egotism purged from him, Crispin hopes to build a colony around himself informed by his new vision of himself and the world.

What he achieves, however, is not a Whitmanesque vision of a new world, but rather the conventional end of an exposure comedy—integration in a preexistent society. Married and content, Crispin decides that plums will outlast their poems, and he opts for daughters over visionary experiences. In conventional comedy the return to social nature is a cause for celebration. The aberrant character realizes the error of his ways and reenters the society of the beginning of the play, refreshed and renewed. In Crispin's case the "happy" ending is less unambiguously happy, his chits chiding him with their own cacophonous music. But despite Crispin's "failure" to be Whitman, despite Crispin's acceptance of a "diminished" domestic life, Stevens will not abandon him to tragedy. He *has* aspired, he *has* come to appreciate his own human limitations, and he *has* worked out a suitable arrangement with reality.

If Whitman is more ecstatically attractive in his triumphant exuberance, Crispin is more realistically recognizable. It is not Whitman's ecstatic vision that informs contemporary life and poetry, but Stevens's domestic comedy. The characteristic voice of many young American poets today is not that of the Whitmanesque kosmos, but that of the little man, the aspiring clown, the Chaplin, the Keaton, the Crispin, making do as best he can in the difficult world around him. Our poets aren't out in the weather with Whitman, but inside with Crispin writing poems about plums. If Crispin "stops in the dooryard of his own capacious bloom" (Whitman's words mocking him), he has had his journey, he has had his vision, and he has seen things as they are.

It is thus important to remember, as many readers do not, that the end of the poem is finally no more a "failure" for Crispin than it is a "success." Stevens manages to balance notions of success and failure so carefully that no choice can finally be made between them. "Jovial Crispin" refuses to wear "calamitous crepe"; he refuses to "bray," or "blubber," or "scrawl a tragedian's testament," or participate in a "dirge." If he hasn't built "loquacious columns," he *has* built a cabin, and "In the presto of the morning" he is "still curious" (p. 42). He may be "sapped by the quotidian," but he nevertheless pours the "quotidian sap" into a wife who produces chits. Crispin is the victim of an exposure comedy, but he is also the hero of a romance comedy, overcoming the blocks to his happiness and achieving a fertile union. Indeed, although he seems to have stopped writing at the end, he has done what Whitman only promised to do: "Singing the song of procreation, / Singing the need of superb children."

In "I Sing the Body Electric" Whitman romanticizes the kind of scene in which Crispin finds himself in the end: "I have perceiv'd that to be with those I like is enough, / To stop in company with the rest at evening is enough, / To be surrounded by beautiful, curious, breathing, laughing flesh is enough."[20] Stevens both laughs at and affirms Crispin's domestic life. In the lines he cited to demonstrate his use of the sounds of the letter C, lines he worried would not translate into Italian (and are difficult enough to translate into English), Stevens summarizes the quotidian:

> For all it takes it gives a humped return
> Exchequering from piebald fiscs unkeyed. (p. 43)

Domestic life pays back as well as takes in. The state treasury is unlocked by inserting and withdrawing the sexual key from its vault. "Humping" produces a return. If Crispin isn't rewarded with divine progeny, he is rewarded with human progeny. His daughters make their own music like "four blithe instruments." With their "differing struts" they make the dark "hilarious" by their "spread chromatics." The daughters are "chits" (sprouts or shoots, or vouchers for debts incurred). They are "sounds of music coming to accord / Upon his lap" (p. 45). If they are also "gew-gaws" of "din and gobble," tink tank a-tunk and rou cou cou, bassoons and tambourines and a clatter of the idiomatic and the elevated, so is the essential gaudiness of poetry. Crispin may be bald at the end, but his daughters have musical curls. Crispin's own "green brag" continues in these "green crammers of the green fruits of the world, / Bidders and biders for its ecstasies." And the "green world" is the traditional destiny of the romance hero.

Finally, Crispin's cabin even takes on a religious aura. It is a "phylactery" and a "halidom" (p. 43), reminding us that Crispin is not merely valet but saint, the patron saint of shoemakers, an appropriate occupation for a traveler and a father. Although the ending goes beyond the point of the usual romance comedy, exposing also the reality of the symbolic marriage, it is nevertheless a "happy" ending. Crispin may not have transcended the human comedy; indeed, he has ended as one of us, huddled "with us all in an ignoble assimilation"—yet perhaps not so ignoble. In "The Noble Rider and the Sound of Words" Stevens laments:

> There is no element more conspicuously absent from contemporary poetry than nobility. There is no element that poets have sought after, more curiously and more piously, certain of its obscure existence. . . . For the sensitive poet, conscious of negations, nothing is more difficult than the affirmations of nobility.[21]

One way of affirming nobility still possible for a modern writer, Stevens discovered, was by parodying it. Crispin's aspirations to abandon the stale or irrelevant European traditions and instead to face twentieth-century America with its own stalenesses and irrelevancies may be clownish, but it is not ignoble. By parodying Whitman's epic affirmations, Stevens is able to affirm them. Parodying nobility, he can affirm nobility.

To preserve the balance of elevation and deflation, Stevens provides two endings for the poem, endings which reflect the two comic plots that combine to structure Crispin's adventure. Stevens's refusal to choose one ending over the other, to decide whether the point of the poem is "anabasis or slump, ascent or chute," is a final joke on the reader's expectations of unambiguous closure. The first ending resembles that typical of romance comedy. The sounds of music come to accord on Crispin's lap in "Seraphic proclamations of the pure" (p. 45). The "strident" anecdote grows "muted, mused." The ending thus resembles Shakespeare's *Two Gentlemen of Verona*, in which Proteus loves Julia but journeys to another country where he falls in love with Sylvia, is pursued by Julia, and finally is forced to drop his romantic imaginings and capitulate to reason as Julia comes to accord upon his lap. Similarly, Crispin loves the old ways of seeing but journeys to another country where he becomes enamored of new ways of seeing, is pursued by reality, and eventually settles into the same salad beds from which he began. Crispin's activity in the poem may, like Proteus's, have seemed "strident," but despite his failings he attains a kind of "music" in the end.

Stevens's second possible ending more closely resembles that of satiric exposure comedy.

> If the music sticks, if the anecdote
> Is false, if Crispin is a profitless
> Philosopher, beginning with green brag,
> Concluding fadedly . . .
> And so distorting, proving what he proves
> Is nothing, what can all this matter since
> The relation comes, benignly, to its end? (p. 46)

In this ending Crispin seems more like Meredith's Sir Willoughby Patterne in *The Egoist*, who also "concludes fadedly," reformed through ridicule into humbling himself before Laetitia Dale.

Stevens doesn't choose one ending over the other. He prefers to keep the two plots intertwined and his protagonist ambiguously both success and failure. The last line is rife with possibilities:

> So may the relation of each man be clipped. (p. 46)

Its four C sounds laughing at our desire for answers, the line can be read in a number of ways. It could be purely descriptive: Stevens's narrative of Crispin's story, with its two endings, could reflect anyone's life. It could be more fatalistic: all people die and their stories end, so what does it matter anyway? It could be an observation on aesthetics: the relationship of poet to reader can be one of severance or connection; it can be clipped off or clipped on. It could be a kind of prayer: may each person's story end so benignly. There are other possibilities. In any case, the final line incorporates contradictory possibilities, as does the whole poem. Walter Kerr notes, "Comedy is not a form that reaches conclusions. It is a form that is interrupted."[22]

Stevens refuses to choose between the two endings; he also refuses to choose between Crispin's two stated aesthetic programs. Most critics assume that the second *nota* is good and the first is bad, that it is preferable for the soil to be man's intelligence than for man to be the intelligence of the soil. But the whole poem is finally not so much a progress as a cycle, not so much a choice between opposites as a balance of opposites. If the first *nota* seems egotistical and overweening, just as did the universal cock in "Bantams in Pine-Woods," it also recalls the Whitman of "Song of Myself," and Hoon, and the woman in "The Idea of Order at Key West." For all the fun Stevens has with it, that same first *nota* is what encourages Crispin to venture forth in pursuit of a colony in the first place. In "The Noble Rider and the Sound of Words" Stevens defines the poet's role in terms that directly parallel the first *nota*: "What makes the poet the potent figure that he is, or was, or ought to be, is that he creates the world to which we turn incessantly and without knowing it and that he gives to life the supreme fictions without which we are unable to conceive of it."[23] The soil is not an intelligence capable of such poetry.

The problem with the first *nota* is not so much its perspective as its fixity. The idea has atrophied, hardened into a convention that proves distorting and enervating. In that the second *nota* represents a change, it is better, since change and motion in Stevens's poetry are concomitant with vitality. "There must be no cessation / Of motion . . . / And, most, of the motion of thought / And its restless iteration" (p. 60). But the second *nota*, too, can harden or atrophy, becoming merely a new fixity. Thus Stevens pokes fun at it as well, turning Crispin into a comical "clerk of experience" (p. 39). The first *nota* causes Crispin to swell with extravagance; the second *nota* causes him to flatten to simplemindedness. Both impose a rigidity on man and place, and a switch from one to the other won't change man's essential nature. A florist asking aid of cabbages seems every bit as comic and self-delusive as a Socrates giving aid to snails. Stevens won't be "the lunatic of one idea / In a world of ideas" (p. 325).

In "Notes Toward a Supreme Fiction," Stevens reflects:

> He had to choose. But it was not a choice
> Between excluding things. It was not a choice
>
> Between, but of. He chose to include the things
> That in each other are included, the whole,
> The complicate, the amassing harmony. (p. 403)

Comically, the one *nota* is included in the other, and the movement in the poem from one to the other is merely part of a recurrent cycle that structures Stevens's poetry and his view of experience. The real hero of the poem is finally not Crispin but the narrator, who can see beyond the simple oppositions to the harmonious whole. Stevens explains in a letter to Hi Simons:

> I suppose that the way of all mind is from romanticism to realism, to fatalism and then to indifferentism, unless the cycle re-commences and the thing goes from indifferentism back to romanticism all over again. No doubt one could demonstrate that the history of the thing is the history of a cycle. At the moment, the world in general is passing from the fatalism stage to an indifferent stage: a stage in which the primary sense is a sense of helplessness. But, as the world is a good deal more vigorous than most of the individuals in it, what the world looks forward to is a new romanticism, a new belief.[24]

If "The Comedian as the Letter C" recounts the revenge of music on bassoons, the bassoons may rise up again and shout down the music or lead it in a new direction. And "Crispin-valet, Crispin-saint," exhausted realist that he may be, may behold "His tattered manikin arise, / Tuck in the straw, / And stalk the skies" (*OP*, p. 24).

The role of romanticism in the continuing drama of reality and imagination was a problem that was to engage Stevens all his life. As with most things, his attitude was contradictory, implying a choice, not *between*, but *of*, sides. In the essay "Imagination as Value" he insists: "We must somehow cleanse the imagination of the romantic. . . . The imagination is one of the great human powers. The romantic belittles it. The imagination is the liberty of the mind. The romantic is a failure to make use of that liberty."[25] But in an essay on Marianne Moore he qualifies. The "romantic in its other sense, meaning always the living and at the same time the imaginative, the youthful, the delicate and a variety of things which it is not necessary to try to particularize at the moment, constitutes the vital element in poetry. . . . It means, now-a-days, an uncommon intelligence" (*OP*, p. 252). Comedy enables Stevens to embrace such contradictory ideas simultaneously.

Finally, it is important to remember that Stevens is not a philosopher, he is a poet, more interested in the *texture* of words and sounds and ideas than in any consistent program of thought. Stevens's comedy can take the form of humor, achieving a Whitmanesque celebration of the self as in "Tea at the Palaz of Hoon" and "The Idea of Order at Key West"; it can adopt satire or irony, attacking old ideas and beliefs as in "A High-Toned Old Christian Woman" or "Of Heaven Considered as a Tomb"; it can employ parody as a means of ridiculing and reusing outmoded styles and concepts, seeing truth in all its contradictoriness, as in "The Comedian as the Letter C," "Sailing after Lunch," and "Bantams in Pine-Woods." But finally it is the sheer play of language, which suffuses the poems from early to late, that distinguishes Stevens's originality.

When Robert Frost complained that Stevens wrote about "bric-a-brac" and Stevens countered that Frost wrote about "subjects," both poets were doing more than merely trading insults.[26] They were defining their own comic aesthetics. Frost adopted the persona of the plain Yankee farmer, Stevens that of the oxymoronic backwoods dandy. Frost wanted to re-affirm the old values and ways of seeing; Stevens wanted to reject them and find new ways. Frost practiced quiet evasion, the humorous offstage whisper; Stevens preferred loud confrontation, the farcical onstage slap-stick. The opposing comic stances are ultimately directed toward the same end—balancing opposites, fighting on both sides at once. But Frost and Stevens differ most obviously in their attitude toward language. Frost's plain style, which refuses to draw attention to itself so much of the time, directs the reader to subjects—characters, narratives, landscapes. Stevens's gaudy style, his parody of the baroque, draws attention to itself and away from subjects. Stevens's commitment to contradictory attitudes, his effort to balance imagination and reality, is not just the subject of his poems; it is deeply embedded in the bric-a-brac of the language itself.

By having language disguise itself as a living comedian with outrageous costumes, props, and antics, Stevens gives our imagined constructs their own life and shape, their own reality. By itself becoming a living thing, language counters its own properties of abstraction, artifice, and inertia, drawing attention to its fiction and making us believe in it at the same time. By making language move and change and fluctuate and confuse, Stevens is closer to a reality that moves and changes and fluctuates and confuses. Whether we end with a parrot squawk, a pht, and a phooey, or a hey-di-ho, a hoo, and a rou-cou-cou, hilarity clips high seriousness, and, balanced on its wordy nose, the world keeps moving.

VI

John Berryman
Me, Wag

T. S. Eliot remarks in "Tradition and the Individual Talent," "Some one said: 'The dead writers are remote from us because we *know* so much more than they did.' Precisely, and they are that which we know."[1] Berryman knew well the dead (or dying) writers discussed thus far in this study, both rejecting them and incorporating them into his own work. He reserved places in his *Dream Songs* for Dickinson, Frost, Stevens, and Whitman, among others, a fact that would indicate to Harold Bloom a certain amount of anxiety. Although Berryman's (and most poets') anxieties usually involve matters more threatening than influences, Berryman's combination of the voices and techniques of earlier poets helps to define his own uniqueness. Although he is clearly ambivalent about most of his poetic forebears, he imagines "Miss Dickinson—fancy in Amherst bedding hér" (#187), and he devotes a trilogy of songs to Robert Frost, evincing a grudging respect for him: "His malice was a pimple down his good / big face . . . / he couldn't hear or see well"; but "Quickly, off stage with all but kindness, now," he was "an unusual man" (#37). Dickinson's and Frost's underlying tragic sense and their ambivalent attitudes toward the self, God, and religion appealed to Berryman and inform his own comic method.

Wallace Stevens and Walt Whitman have even more interest for Berryman. Stevens prods him into a rowdy quibble: "He lifted up, among the actuaries, / a grandee crow. Ah ha & he crowed good. / That funny money-man." Berryman clearly appreciates Stevens's comic method. Adopting Stevens's oxymoronic humor ("grandee crow," "He mutter spiffy"), Berryman sees Stevens as both a funny money-man and a funny-money man, suggesting that while his poems are comic, they may also be counterfeit. What is missing for Berryman in Stevens, what is "not there in his flourishing art," is a capacity to "wound": "It is our kind / to wound, as well as utter / a fact of happy world." Berryman's ambivalence is clear in his final assessment of Stevens, who is "brilliant . . . / better than us; less wide" (#219). The comment suggests that Stevens is both less wide (has less breadth and range) than Berryman and less wide of the mark. Stevens's gaudy language and his method of exaggeration and deflation appealed to Berryman. Although he criticizes Stevens for a lack of heart, he couldn't dismiss him. The question mark in the title of Dream Song #219, "So Long? Stevens" (one of the few titles in *The Dream Songs*), suggests his ambivalence.

Berryman drew on Dickinson, Frost, and Stevens, but he felt the closest affinity with Walt Whitman. In his sensitive essay on "Song of Myself" in *The Freedom of the Poet*, Berryman confesses, "I like or love Whitman unreservedly." Berryman loved "Song of Myself" for its sense of "Welcome, self-wrestling, inquiry, and wonder . . . (not exulting as over an accomplished victory, but gradually revealing, puzzling, discovering)."[2] The description is a good one of *The Dream Songs* as well; Berryman's own long poem is consciously modeled on Whitman's: "I think the model in *The Dream Songs* was the other greatest American poem—I am very ambitious—'Song of Myself.'"[3] But if Berryman admired Whitman's poem unreservedly, he was not prepared to duplicate it. Like Stevens, he lacked Whitman's transcendental faith; like Dickinson and Frost, he had a sense of potential tragedy and loss that qualified Whitman's exaggerated optimism.

Thus *The Dream Songs* becomes a kind of parody of "Song of Myself," embuing Whitman's barbaric yawp with more sadness, doubt, worry, and fear than Whitman would have acknowledged. Whitman begins his poem in health and optimism: "I, now thirty-seven years old in perfect health begin, / Hoping to cease not till death" (sec. 1, p. 29). Berryman ends his poem in ill health and ambiguity: "I, Henry Pussy-cat, being in ill-health / & 900 years old, begin & cease, / to doubt" (#365). Likewise, while Whitman can boldly insist that the persona of "Song of Myself" is himself, Berryman must distance his persona by insisting that it is an imaginary character, not himself. Berryman quotes Whitman's statement in his essay on "Song of Myself"—"to put *a Person*, a human being (myself, in the latter half of the Nineteenth Century, in America) freely, fully and truly on record"—and then parodies that statement in a note on his own *Dream Songs*, which are "essentially about an imaginary character (not the poet, not me) named Henry, a white American in early middle age" (p. vi). Whitman claims to be writing about himself while clearly writing about a symbolic figure; Berryman, like Dickinson, claims to be writing about a fictional character while clearly writing about himself.[4]

Thus Berryman's characteristic comic voice and method reflect a combination of the backwoods and Yankee strains of American humor we have seen so far. For Whitman, comedy is a mode of celebration, a means of absurdly affirming a transcendent faith in the self. For Dickinson and Frost, comedy is more often an evasive tactic, a way of seeing truth aslant. For Stevens, comedy is a means of achieving a balance, of keeping things and ideas moving, vital, and alive. For Berryman, comedy is a combination of these things, incorporating celebration and sadness, self-aggrandizement and self-deprecation, attack and evasion, into an essentially confessional mode. Berryman adds to the inherited voices a more personal note, a new self-consciousness about his own capabilities and inadequacies. For Berryman, comedy is a means of confession and a tactic for facing fear and dread without seeming lugubrious or self-pitying. Death is omnipresent; God is a bad joke; life is boring or painful; people's capacities fall woefully below their aspirations. By exaggerating his suffering comically, Berryman is able both to express it and to rebuke it.

Constance Rourke prophesied the coming of Berryman in her 1931 study of American humor when she described the "minstrel voice." According to Rourke, the two major strains of American humor, the Yankee and the backwoods voice, were merging into a third strain, best evidenced in the Negro minstrel show. Combining the Yankee's characteristic pose of ignorance and witty self-deprecation with the Kentuckian's characteristic pose of omnipotence and boastful self-aggrandizement, the minstrel voice added its own distinct note of melancholy. "Triumph was in his humor," suggests Rourke, "but not triumph over circumstances. Rather this was an unreasonable headlong triumph launching into the realm of the preposterous."[5] Combining the language, banter, dance, ego, and flamboyance of Whitman and Stevens with the sadness, doubt, uncertainty, private pain, and humiliation of Dickinson and Frost, Berryman adopted the mode of the Negro minstrel show as a paradigm for his own life.

In general, the critics quickly perceived the spirit of The Dream Songs. Robert Lowell, in a review of the first 77 Dream Songs, notes, "This great Pierrot's universe . . . is more tearful and funny than we can easily bear."[6] William J. Martz concurs that Berryman "is preeminently a poet of suffering and laughter."[7] Berryman himself knew the effect the songs would have on an audience. He warned a Harvard audience in 1966, "Prepare to weep, ladies and gentlemen. Saul Bellow and I almost kill ourselves laughing about The Dream Songs and various chapters in his novels, but other people feel bad. Are you all ready to feel bad?"[8]

Although readers immediately responded to the minstrel combination of sadness and laughter in The Dream Songs, they didn't as immediately understand Berryman's actual use of minstrel show characters and devices in his long poem. Indeed, despite all of Berryman's efforts to explain his method, readers continue to confuse the various minstrel characters in the songs. As recently as 1979 two poet-critics, Diane Ackerman and Donald Davie, independently and erroneously distinguished Henry and Mr. Bones as separate characters, failing to see that they are merely two

names for the same character.[9] Earlier, William J. Martz made a similar
error, concluding that Dream Song #76 is flawed by inconsistencies of
voice. The "inconsistencies," however, disappear when the relationship
between minstrel characters is properly understood.[10]

In an important *Harvard Advocate* interview in 1967, Berryman carefully clarifies his method. Asked why Henry is called Mr. Bones, Berryman replies, "There's a minstrel show thing of Mr. Bones and the interlocutor. . . . I wanted someone for Henry to talk to, so I took up another
minstrel, the interlocutor, and made him a friend of my friend, Henry."[11]
Since some critics apparently didn't read the *Harvard Advocate* interview, Berryman added an explanatory note to the complete collection of
The Dream Songs in 1969:

> It is idle to reply to critics, but some of the people who addressed them-
> selves to the *77 Dream Songs* went so desperately astray . . . that I permit
> myself one word. The poem then, whatever its wide cast of characters, is
> essentially about an imaginary character (not the poet, not me) named
> Henry, a white American in early middle age sometimes in blackface, who
> has suffered an irreversible loss and talks about himself sometimes in the
> first person, sometimes in the third, sometimes even in the second; he has a
> friend, never named, who addresses him as Mr Bones and variants thereof.
> (p. vi)

With all this help, it seems curious that critics continue to go astray. It is
useful, therefore, to examine more closely the minstrel show background
of *The Dream Songs*, observing how Berryman adapted the characters,
devices, and structure of the minstrel show to his own purposes.

In his otherwise excellent study of the epic poem in America, James E.
Miller implies that we do not know the source of one of Berryman's epi-
graphs for *The Dream Songs*, "Go in brack man, de day's yo' own." We
do know that source, and reference to the book from which Berryman got
his information on minstrel shows is instructive. Berryman's epigraph is
taken from Carl Wittke's history of the American minstrel show, *Tambo
and Bones*, a book that helps clarify both character and structure in *The
Dream Songs*.[12]

Wittke traces the origins of the American minstrel show to Daddy "Jim
Crow" Rice, who in 1828 corked his face black and imitated the comical
strut of an old black cripple on stage in Louisville. Rice's mimicry was an
immediate hit and became known as "jumping Jim Crow." Although it
may be difficult to understand how such a seemingly unfunny performance would have become so popular, one has only to consider the comical treatment of hunchbacks on the late-night television show "Fridays,"
or Dan Aykroyd's comical version of a midget Toulouse-Lautrec on "Sat-

urday Night Live," to remember that physical deformity has been a significant focus of comedy from Plautus to the present. Indeed, Rice's performance was so well received both in this country and abroad that it
eventually developed into the loosely structured but elaborate minstrel
shows of the 1830s and 1840s. Berryman pays tribute to Daddy Rice in
his Dream Song #2, referring to Rice's "Big buttons" (gold coins, an extravagance that eventually led to his downfall) and to the "cornets" that
were used in the advance parade announcing the show. It is appropriate
that Berryman begins his own minstrelsy with Rice, the father of minstrelsy, and with the cornets of the advance parade. As Wittke notes,
Rice's performance hovered somewhere "between tragedy and farce" and
the audience "cried and laughed" as he jumped Jim Crow. Berryman expects the same response from his audience as he jumps and sings his
Dream Songs.

From Rice's act, the minstrel show developed into a loosely structured
variety show, combining humor, song and dance, and theatrical performance. As it came to be standardized by such troupes as the Christy Minstrels, the show divided into two parts, the first part consisting of humorous repartee between the black-faced white "end men" in a semicircle and
the white "interlocutor" in the center. The end men, called Mr. Bones and
Mr. Tambo after the instruments they played, were ignorant darky clowns
who suffered greatly but were eternally resilient. They put on airs, made
humorous mistakes, got comeuppances, and remained blissfully unaware
of their own foolishness. Like Berryman's Mr. Bones, the minstrel end
men drank too much, loved not wisely but too well, and had periodic literary aspirations and delusions of adequacy. According to Wittke, the end
men were supposed to cultivate an eccentric vocabulary complete with
faulty pronunciation, bad grammar, and bombastic ignorance, answering
the interlocutor's serious questions with puns, spoonerisms, willful misunderstandings, and conundrums. When not talking, the end men's job
was to keep the audience laughing by grimacing while the balladists performed, or by performing their own comic songs and grotesque dances in
parody of the serious entertainers.

The interlocutor, responsible for running the show, was a humorless
straight man who served as a foil to the end men, exposing both their
foolishness and his own and sometimes being unwittingly undercut by
their antics. The end men were humorous in their ignorance and ineptness and willfulness. The interlocutor was humorous in his pompousness
and humorlessness and authority. But the interlocutor's main function
was not self-exposure, as one can easily perceive in the recently reprinted
Minstrel Gags and End Men's Hand-Book.[13] His main function was to

serve as a friend, confidant, and critic of Bones and Tambo. He kept the
end men talking or shut them up when it was time for a ballad. He deflated their foolishness when they put on airs, and he cheered them up
when they fell into humorous excesses of despair.

The relationship between end men and interlocutor was adapted by
subsequent comic duos like Abbott and Costello, Martin and Lewis,
Burns and Allen, and Crosby and Hope. Abbott, Martin, Burns, and
Crosby played the role of interlocutor to Costello, Lewis, Allen, and
Hope, who played the role of end man or clown. John Berryman also
adapted the traditional conflict for his own purposes in *The Dream
Songs*. Berryman is not writing a minstrel show, and his characters don't
always correspond to the traditional roles (Berryman's Mr. Bones never,
for example, undercuts the interlocutor, and Berryman's interlocutor occasionally puts on blackface himself, something the traditional figure
never did). But the parallels are instructive, clarifying the conflicting
voices in the poem and reflecting the poem's tone and spirit. Generally,
there are three voices in *The Dream Songs*: Henry, who is variously the
feisty but lovable Henry Pussycat, the solid Henry House, the pompous
Dr. Bones, and the lugubrious Mr. Bones; an unnamed voice who is variously the interlocutor, Tambo, critic, confidant, and friend; and the poet
himself. The three voices are all elements of a single individual struggling
to be whole and keep his balance.

Thus, when Henry/Mr. Bones puts on airs and gets too high on himself,
the unnamed voice assumes the role of Mr. Interlocutor, soberly bringing
Henry down. In Dream Song #25, for example, when Henry's literary
pretensions get out of hand (a favorite pretension of the minstrel Mr.
Bones as well, who is always writing his own biography or aspiring to be
a great author), the interlocutor steps in to calm him: "Euphoria, / Mr
Bones, euphoria." In Dream Song #69 when Henry lusts after the body of
Miss Boogry (Berryman must have chuckled at the dirty joke implicit in
the number), the interlocutor similarly steadies him: "Mr Bones, *please*."
Conversely, when Henry/Mr. Bones gets too low, benumbed by fear and
dread (another favorite topic of the traditional minstrel repartee), the interlocutor himself puts on blackface and tries to pull Henry up: "you is
bad powers," he mocks in Dream Song #50. And in Dream Song #76:
"You is from hunger, Mr Bones." Often, the interlocutor is merely moder-
ator and straight man, as in Dream Song #26: "What happen then, Mr
Bones?" he repeats in each stanza to keep Henry talking.

As Berryman clearly knew, the comic conflict that structures his *Dream
Songs* extends further back in the comic tradition than the American minstrel stage. Berryman's characters, and their minstrel predecessors as well,

are merely modern versions of the two archetypal comic characters we have seen before in Whitman, Dickinson, Stevens, and Frost—the *eiron* and the *alazon*. In his quirky study of Stephen Crane, Berryman himself defines these archetypes in a way that seems more applicable to his own work than to Crane's:

> Specifically, early Greek comedy presented a contest between the *Alazon* (Impostor) and the *Eiron* or Ironical Man: after vauntings and pretensions, the *Alazon* is routed by the man who affects to be a fool. The Impostor pretends to be more than he is, the Ironist pretends to be less. Now in most of the criticism of Stephen Crane that displays any sensitivity, whether outraged or not, one nearly makes out a nervous understanding that this author is simultaneously *at war with* the people he creates and *on their side*— and displays each of these attitudes so forcibly that the reader feels he is himself being made a fool of. . . . Who are the creations Crane is most at war with? His complex ones, his "heroes"? Or his simplest ones, his babies, horses, dogs, and brooks. With the first class his art is a Greek comedy, a contest with the impostor. . . . So far as his creations of the first class are striving to become members of the second class, they become candidates for pathos or tragedy; so far as they fail, they remain figures of (this deadly-in-earnest) comedy. Crane never rests. He is always fighting the thing out with himself, for he contains both *Alazon* and *Eiron*; and so, of course, does the reader; and only dull readers escape. As comedy, his work is a continual examination of pretension—an attempt to cast overboard, as it were, impediments to our salvation. . . .
> There is regularly an element of pathos, therefore, in his ironic (oppositional) inspection, and an element of irony regularly in his pathos. A Crane creation, or character, normally is *pretentious* and *scared*—the human condition; fitted by the second for pathos, by the first for irony.[14]

If one were simply to substitute Berryman's name for Crane's here, one would have an accurate description of Berryman's technique in *The Dream Songs*. Henry/Mr. Bones is the pretentious but scared *alazon* who, in his baby talk and babbling, seems to strive to become baby or brook. The unnamed voice or interlocutor is the *eiron*, or ironical man, who continually jostles Henry into remaining comic and human. Berryman, containing both *eiron* and *alazon*, is both at war with Henry and on his side, balancing his pathos and irony with minstrel humor. The result is Berryman's "deadly-in-earnest" comedy. When Berryman, referring to Crane, says, "We have met Henry Fleming and Henry Johnson, and we shall meet a Henry stranger still, later on," we must wonder whether he isn't prophesying his own future persona.

In only a fraction of the poems in *The Dream Songs* are the minstrel antagonists actually on stage together, but their presence permeates the whole. Embedded in tone, voice, and the language itself, the *eiron-alazon* debate is at the heart of Berryman's comedy.

The characters in *The Dream Songs* are drawn from the archetypal characters of the minstrel stage; the structure of the poem as a whole also reflects the influence of minstrelsy. Critics have had little success describing the structure of *The Dream Songs*, concluding, probably correctly, that the poem is a rather loosely organized series of events in Henry's life characterized by risings and fallings and by certain thematic clusters. Berryman himself dismissed any efforts to ascertain some secret structural principle in *The Dream Songs*. In the *Harvard Advocate* interview he insists that the poem has no "ulterior structure": "*Il n'y en a pas!* . . . mostly, they just belong to areas of hope and fear that Henry is going through at a given time."[15] In the later *Paris Review* interview he expands on his earlier comments, suggesting a more conscious concern for structure:

> The narrative such as it is developed as I went along, partly out of my
> gropings into and around Henry and his environment and associates,
> partly out of my readings in theology . . . and third, out of certain partly
> preconceived and partly developing as I went along, sometimes rigid and
> sometimes plastic, structural notions.[16]

While I wouldn't want to argue for any rigorous structural principles, Berryman's "partly preconceived and partly developing as I went along, sometimes rigid and sometimes plastic structural notions" may well reflect the minstrel model in particular and comic plot patterns in general.

According to Wittke, the minstrel show came to be divided into two parts—the "first part" and the "olio." The first part featured colorful costumes and gaudy sets. It focused on the comic repartee between end men and interlocutor and interspersed grotesque jokes with lovely lyrical ballads. The second part, or olio, often began with a parodic stump speech or sermon and then featured solo performances of dances and songs and parodies of well-known people and poets.

Although the parallels are not exact, *The Dream Songs* do seem to reflect the general structure of the minstrel show. Like the minstrel show, Berryman's poem is divided into two parts. The first part features repartee between Henry/Mr. Bones and an unnamed interlocutor, juxtaposing ribaldry and lyricism. In Dream Song #26, for example, Berryman says of Henry, "his loins were & were the scene of stupendous achievement," the kind of boastful claim Mr. Bones characteristically made of himself. And in Dream Song #27 the focus shifts abruptly to a lovely lyric of the sort that punctuated minstrel repartee:

I'll die;
live you, in the most wild, kindly, green
partly forgiving wood,
sort of forever and all those human sings
close not your better ears to, while good Spring
returns with a dance and a sigh.

The second part of *The Dream Songs,* like the second part of the minstrel show, focuses a variety of individual performances, with references to well-known political figures as well as poets like Frost and Stevens. Indeed, Berryman may have gotten the idea for the opening of his second part from Wittke's reference to a typical mock sermon delivered by Dan Emmet at the beginning of the olio:

Suppose, frinstance, dat yoa eat yoa full ob possam fat an' hominy; yoa go to bed, an' in de mornin' yoa wake up an' find youseff dead! Whar yoa speck yoa gwine to? Yoa keep gwine down, down, down, till de bottam falls out![17]

Perhaps it shouldn't have been so surprising when Berryman began the second part of his *Dream Songs* with Henry's death and resurrection. He had a clear precedent in the minstrel show.

The structure of *The Dream Songs* thus loosely resembles that of the minstrel show. It also reflects the typical comic structure we saw in "Song of Myself" and "The Comedian as the Letter C." All three poems begin with a version of the poet's self—an aspiring clown-poet, a boaster and egotist—who, after a series of misadventures with the self and others and his own art, suffers a ritual death (Whitman in Texas and with John Paul Jones, Crispin at sea and in the Yucatan, Henry in the underworld) and recovers to new life. Whitman is reborn as a kind of comic God; Crispin and Henry settle for a comfortable, shady home with daughters. As do Whitman and Stevens, Berryman draws on both Meredithian exposure comedy and Shakespearean romance comedy for his plot, first exposing Henry through his own excesses and finally integrating him into domestic life. Although Berryman said that he modeled his poem on Whitman's, his method is really closer to Stevens's. Unable to share Whitman's transcendental convictions, Berryman and Stevens affirm his exuberance through parody.

The patterns of traditional comedy thus inform the structure of *The Dream Songs.* And the patter of the American minstrel stage gives Berryman's comedy its unique resonance. Negro minstrelsy appealed to Berryman for several reasons. By putting on blackface Berryman could identify with the Negro as outsider, as member of a long-suffering and abused race. He could tap into that long history of grief and sorrow which characterized the Negro experience in America, using it as a metaphor for his own sense of personal pain and frustration and powerlessness. More importantly, the blackface role enabled him to make fun of himself and of the very excesses of sorrow and fear that he wanted to express. As Imamu Baraka points out, originally "the cake-walk," a popular dance in the minstrel show, was a "Negro parody of white high manners in the manor house." Baraka muses, "I find the idea of white minstrels in black-face satirizing a dance satirizing themselves a remarkable kind of irony."[18] The white minstrels were unaware that in satirizing the blacks they were really satirizing themselves. Berryman is clearly aware of it and thus becomes both victim and victimizer. Henry/Mr. Bones, on the other hand, remains ignorant. Berryman notes in an interview with Richard Kostelanetz, "Now Henry is a man with, God knows, many faults, but among them is not self-understanding."[19] Berryman himself does have the fault of self-understanding, seeing that "we were all end men, end men and interlocutors." And he uses those characters as metaphors for the human predicament in a world that seems at best arbitrary and at worst consciously hostile to our needs and aspirations. Berryman's minstrelsy becomes a means of gaining perspective and distance on himself, a means of "rebuking fear," excess, and foolishness, while at the same time expressing them.

With the minstrel background clearly in mind, we can look more closely at Henry, Berryman's end man and everyman. Like his minstrel ancestors, Berryman's Mr. Bones exaggerates his terror, ineptitude, and mistreatment; he boasts about his sexual and literary endeavors; and he is capable of insult and attack while undercutting himself or being undercut by his friend and antagonist, the interlocutor.

Carl Wittke notes that fear and suffering were important topics for comic treatment in the minstrel show, and Berryman indicates that they are his major themes as well. In his *Paris Review* interview Berryman told Peter Stitt, "I do strongly feel that among the greatest pieces of luck for high achievement is ordeal. . . . My idea is this: the artist is extremely lucky who is presented with the worst possible ordeal which will not actually kill him. At that point, he's in business. . . . I hope to be nearly crucified."[20]

The ordeal in Berryman's life that he felt was tantamount to a crucifixion was the death of his father. In 1926, when Berryman was eleven, his father shot himself through the left chest. Although there is some uncertainty about Berryman's immediate reaction to the death, throughout his life he believed that his father's suicide had shattered his own equilibrium.

Alternating between compassion and loathing for the man, he returned again and again to the suicide in his Dream Songs, making it the focus of his wretchedness.[21]

Whitman exaggerates his joy and happiness and health; Berryman exaggerates his fear and sadness and wretchedness, reflecting Walter Kerr's speculation about the future of comedy: "What if despair is the new heroic posture, the new pretense to greatness? What if there is, after all, an aspiration open to ridicule: contemporary man's aspiration to be known as the most wretched of all beings?"[22] Thus Henry is Berryman's heroic posture. Boaster of loss and braggart of deficiency, Henry aspires to be the most wretched of all beings. "Come & diminish me," he pleads in Dream Song #13, "& map my way." In exaggerating his griefs comically, Berryman makes Henry into both noble hero and egotistical fool.

Dream Song #29 is one of the bleakest of the sequence, describing Henry's existential angst in terms so painful that the small residue of humor almost gets lost completely:

> There sat down, once, a thing on Henry's heart
> só heavy, if he had a hundred years
> & more, & weeping, sleepless, in all them time
> Henry could not make good.
> Starts again always in Henry's ears
> the little cough somewhere, an odour, a chime.

The depression (caused, one suspects, by his father's suicide) is a kind of monstrous entity that sits parasitically on Henry's heart, keeping him eternally down. The final stanza extends the notion of a suffering caused by objectless existential guilt, while adding a thin note of humor that makes the pain bearable:

> But never did Henry, as he thought he did,
> end anyone and hacks her body up
> and hide the pieces, where they may be found.
> He knows: he went over everyone, & nobody's missing.
> Often he reckons, in the dawn, them up.
> Nobody is ever missing.

The motiveless guilt is so hard to bear that Henry longs for a reason to feel guilty. Humorously, it would be better if he had killed someone (his father, perhaps, whom he does disinter and hack up later in Dream Song #384), so that he would at least know why he felt so bad. Unfortunately, nobody is ever missing. The reversal has just enough comic edge both to intensify the horror Henry feels and to keep it just short of a crucifixion.

Berryman himself said of the poem, "Whether the diction of that is consistent with blackface talk, heel-spinning puns, coarse jokes, whether the end of it is funny or frightening, or both, I put up to the listener."[23]

Berryman treats the same theme—a longing for something bad to happen in order to justify feelings of fear and guilt—in Dream Song #76, a poem that is more consistent with blackface talk but is as ambiguously funny and frightening as Dream Song #29:

> Nothin very bad happen to me lately.
> How you explain that?—I explain that, Mr Bones,
> terms o' your bafflin odd sobriety.
> Sober as man can get, no girls, no telephones,
> what could happen bad to Mr Bones?
> —*If* life is a handkerchief sandwich,
>
> in a modesty of death I join my father
> who dared so long agone leave me.
> A bullet on a concrete stoop
> close by a smothering southern sea
> spreadeagled on an island, by my knee.
> —You is from hunger, Mr Bones,
>
> I offers you this handkerchief, now set
> your left foot by my right foot,
> shoulder to shoulder, all that jazz,
> arm in arm, by the beautiful sea,
> hum a little, Mr Bones.
> —I saw nobody coming, so I went instead.

This is the poem that William Martz misinterprets because of a misidentification of the speaking characters. Assuming that Henry and Mr. Bones are separate characters, Martz concludes that the poem is flawed. Martz erroneously describes the poem as beginning with a dialogue between Henry and Mr. Bones, then abandoning the minstrel setting to allow Berryman to speak directly in stanza two, and then returning to the minstrel stage at the end of stanza two and in stanza three. Martz is right to see that the comedy of the poem springs from Henry's premise that he normally expects something very bad to happen to him every day. Indeed, Henry's tone is not merely surprise that nothing bad has happened lately, but actual consternation, suggesting that he only feels good when he feels bad, that things are only right when they are wrong. But Martz's misidentification of characters persuades him that the poem breaks apart in the middle and suffers from a lack of unity. When one correctly identifies the characters, however, the poem falls neatly in place, evidencing great unity.

The poem is a dialogue not between Henry *and* Mr. Bones, with interpolations by the poet, but between Henry *as* Mr. Bones and the interlocutor, who temporarily assumes the role of Tambo to cheer Henry/Mr. Bones up.

Henry speaks the first line and a half, setting up the comic premise—Henry's expectation of daily anguish. The interlocutor/Tambo answers in the next three-and-a-half lines, in words calculated to distract Henry from his morbidity, calling Henry "Mr. Bones" as one might call someone Mr. Despair to jar him out of self-pity. Henry remains oblivious and continues through stanza two to try to see himself as the wretchedest of all men. For Henry, life is thus a handkerchief sandwich, an unnourishing veil of tears. If life is so bad, perhaps he should commit suicide and join his dead father. The interlocutor/Tambo breaks in mockingly at the end of stanza two, and then offers Henry a real handkerchief with which to dry his tears. Finally, he suggests that they go offstage together arm in arm, inviting Henry to accept friendship, song, and dance. Thus the two characters balance each other here. Henry/Mr. Bones is the morose *alazon*, wretched because nothing very bad has happened to him lately. The interlocutor/Tambo is the witty *eiron*, gently undercutting Henry's pretentious grief and offering to merge with him offstage as a healthy individual. The last line, spoken by Henry, remains ambiguous. In the rhythm of "Swing low, sweet chariot," the line could represent Henry's recovery of balance, his making music of his sorrows. Or it could be read more negatively as Henry's continued obliviousness to his *eiron* half and his determination to join his father (which is what he does in the "Opus posthumous" poems almost immediately following).

The tone of melancholia prevails in poems like Dream Songs #29 and #76, but Berryman often goes to rowdier lengths to expose Henry's pretensions to wretchedness. Dream Song #50 is a good example:

> In a motion of night they massed nearer my post.
> I hummed a short blues. When the stars went out
> I studied my weapons system.
> Grenades, the portable rack, the yellow spout
> of the anthrax-ray: in order. Yes, and most
> of my pencils were sharp.
>
> This edge of the galaxy has often seen
> a defence so stiff, but it could only go
> one way.
> —Mr Bones, your troubles give me vertigo,
> & backache. Somehow, when I make your scene,
> I cave to feel as if

de roses of dawns & pearls of dusks, made up
by some ol' writer-man, got right forgot
& the greennesses of ours.
Springwater grow so thick it gonna clot
and the pleasing ladies cease. I figure, yup,
you is bad powers.

The poem begins with Henry exaggerating his fearful and dangerous
position in melodramatic terms that immediately establish the comic context. He is now the victim of intergalactic forces. The stars go out in a
comic apocalypse, and Henry studies his weapons system—an incongruous catalogue if ever there was one: grenades, for modern infantry com-
bat; the portable rack, a medieval torture, its portability humorously
modern; the anthrax ray, a futuristic science-fiction device; and his sharpened pencils. The catalogue is comic in its juxtaposition of modern, ancient, and futuristic weapons, preparing Henry for all kinds of foes. The
addendum of pencils, with the detail about their being sharpened, may
elevate the power of the pencil, but it also deflates the catalogue of
weapons.

Despite his elaborate preparations, Henry knows that the battle can go
only one way: he must die. At this midpoint in the poem the interlocutor
enters to deflate Henry's pretensions, serving as *eiron* to Henry's *alazon*:
"Mr Bones, your troubles give me vertigo, / & backache." In stanza three
the interlocutor switches to blackface in an effort to jolt Henry out of his
fatalistic fantasies. The interlocutor/Tambo wants to remind Henry of the
joys and beauties of life: "roses," "dawn," "green," "spring," "maidens."
But the images are clichés and can't be asserted with any power or meaning. The only way to assert such traditional affirmations is to do it comically. "Yup," he mocks, "you is such bad powers that you've banished the
roses and dawns and pearls and greennesses and springwater and ladies."
By mocking Henry, the interlocutor is able to assert the old values in the
face of Henry's paranoia. The last line, "you is bad powers," is both satiric and literal. "You sure are a tough guy and we're all scared of you,"
the interlocutor mocks. But at the same time he means it; Henry *is* powerful enough to destroy himself (and consequently his world). The interlocutor may also be reminding Henry (in the sense that *bad* means *good*
in black dialect) that Henry has the potential to be a power for good, if
only he will forgo his morbidities.

In Dream Songs #50 and #76, the *eiron-alazon* conflict is embodied in
separate voices that make up a single character. In Dream Song #14 the
single voice of Henry embodies the conflicting poles:

Life, friends, is boring. We must not say so.
After all, the sky flashes, the great sea yearns,
we ourselves flash and yearn,
and moreover my mother told me as a boy
(repeatedly) "Ever to confess you're bored
means you have no

Inner Resources." I conclude now I have no
inner resources, because I am heavy bored.
Peoples bore me,
literature bores me, especially great literature,
Henry bores me, with his plights & gripes
as bad as achilles,

who loves people and valiant art, which bores me.
And the tranquil hills, & gin, look like a drag
and somehow a dog
has taken itself & its tail considerably away
into mountains or sea or sky, leaving
behind: me, wag.

The poem is paradigmatic of Berryman's comic spirit. Once again the speaker (not exactly Henry, not exactly the interlocutor or Tambo, not exactly Berryman, and a kind of combination of all three) is depressed with his life. At the end he feels that life, God, reality, and nature have somehow gone away, leaving him as just the tail end. He is helpless; the world "wags" and controls him at its whim. And yet he is also the "wag," the comedian who can see humor in his situation. Despite his bitterness he is able to chuckle throughout the poem, putting his boredom in perspective. The joke of the mother's archetypal response to a child who has nothing to do sets the comic tone; the repetition of "boring" itself becomes comic; and the contrast of Henry with Achilles humorously deflates and elevates Henry. If Henry is "as bad as achilles," the opposite may be true as well: perhaps he is as good as Achilles. Berryman, wagged by the world, is also the wag of the world, able to characterize his suffering as "General Fatigue," "Captain Fatigue," "pale Corporal Fatigue" (#93), able to continue humorously despite his ennui and melancholia since he has "a living to fail" (#67).

Comedy is thus a means for Berryman to confess his inadequacies and fears and humiliations without being enmired in self-pity. When Henry gets too low, comedy pulls him up. Conversely, when Henry gets too high on himself, comedy pulls him down to size. Two areas in which Henry and his traditional minstrel counterpart boast superiority but perpetually

get their comic comeuppances are love and fame, or more characteristically for Henry, lust and ambition.

   If Henry/Mr. Bones is the world's greatest sufferer, he is also the world's
greatest sexual athlete. "His loins were & were the scene of stupendous
achievement" (#26). He exercises by climbing "trees, / & other people's
wives" (#350). He is perpetually interested in women's "tops & bottoms /
& even in their middles" (#350) and is prepared to exploit them for both
his physical and literary satisfaction: "He published his girl's bottom in
staid pages / of an old weekly" (#122). For Whitman, sex is evidence of
cosmic continuity. For Henry it is more often an arena of conquest and
personal triumph. His lust for Miss Boogry in Dream Song #69, for example, "would launch a national product / complete with TV spots &
skywriting / outlets in Bonn & Tokyo / I mean it."

   Throughout *The Dream Songs* Henry's lust, like his suffering, ultimately renders him grotesquely comic. The appellation *Mr. Bones* may
itself be a dirty joke. And for all his aspirations to sexual godhood and
dionysiac frenzy, Henry remains rather pussycatish and harmless, lusting
from afar:

> Filling her compact & delicious body
> with chicken páprika, she glanced at me
> twice.
> Fainting with interest, I hungered back
> and only the fact of her husband & four other people
> kept me from springing on her
>
> or falling at her little feet and crying
> "You are the hottest one for years of night
> Henry's dazed eyes
> have enjoyed, Brilliance." I advanced upon
> (despairing) my spumoni.—Sir Bones: is stuffed,
> de world, wif feeding girls.
>
> —Black hair, complexion Latin, jewelled eyes
> downcast . . . The slob beside her feasts . . . What wonders is
> she sitting on, over there?
> The restaurant buzzes. She might as well be on Mars.
> Where did it all go wrong? There ought to be a law against Henry.
> —Mr. Bones: there is. (#4)

The juxtaposition of sex and food, romantic ecstasy and chicken, worship
and animality, is comic. The only "advances" Henry is able to make are
on his spumoni. And the interlocutor's appellation, "Sir Bones," caps off

the incongruity between Henry's inflated lust and his pretensions to courtly love. Late in *The Dream Songs* Henry is further reduced to envisioning not woman as food, but food as woman: "Melons, they say, though, / are best—I don't know if that's correct— / as well as infertile, it's said" (#222).

Without the comic perspective, Henry's lust would be merely outrageous or offensive, alienating the reader. Treated comically, the lust participates in a more affirmative comic tradition as well. Traditional comedy is rooted in sexual urges and energies, sometimes civilized into respectable images of marriage, spring, and festivity as in Shakespearean comedy, and sometimes allowed to take a more Dionysian form as in Aristophanic comedy. Contemporary comedy more often strips the social forms away to deal with the basic urges themselves. The Henry of *The Tropic of Cancer* and *The Tropic of Capricorn*, for example, comically rejects sexual taboos, satirizing a repressed society and affirming joy and life. Although Berryman's Henry isn't so affirmative an example of sexual energy, his lusts are both farcical and transcendent, undercutting him while elevating him as well. Laughing at the way sexual urges and energies control him, Berryman is able to assert their importance.

Similarly, Berryman is able to assert his ambitions, his "spellbinding powers," by exaggerating and undercutting them:

> Spellbound held subtle Henry all his four
> hearers in the racket of the market
> with ancient signs, infamous characters,
> new rhythms. On the steps he was beloved,
> hours a day, by all his four, or more,
> depending. (#71)

Henry boasts his transcendent powers as poet to hold spellbound "by the heart & brains & tail, because / of their love for it" exactly four followers. The small number of followers, juxtaposed with the almost religious faith in himself and his powers, is a comic, but nevertheless serious, affirmation of his art. A few Songs later (#75), Henry stops preaching on the steps of the market and puts "forth a book." "No harm resulted from this," jokes Berryman with a deadpan face, though not all the critics were respectful:

> Bare dogs drew closer for a second look
>
> and performed their friendly operations there.
> Refreshed, the bark rejoiced.

Even if the critics pissed on the book, Berryman will see their "opera-
tions" as "friendly." At least it makes the book and the critics feel better,
"refreshed." Eventually, "surviving Henry" gets the last laugh as his book

> began to strike the passers from despair
> so that sore on their shoulders old men hoisted
> six-foot sons and polished women called
> small girls to dream awhile toward the flashing & bursting tree! (#75)

If Henry has been crucified, he will rise again.

Berryman satirizes himself, using exaggeration and deflation to ridicule
and assert his claims of being the wretchedest of all men and the greatest
of poets and sexual athletes. He also uses satire as a mode of attack,
ridiculing attitudes or people he finds wanting. "I ask for a decree / doom-
ing my bitter enemies to laughter advanced against them" (#132). He satirizes other poets both by name and more generally: "Yvette's ankles /
are slim as the thought of various poets I could mention" (#289). And since
Coleridge, Rilke, and Poe have died, "Toddlers are taking over. O / ver!"
(#12). He satirizes political figures, as in the punningly titled "The Lay
of Ike":

> This is the lay of Ike.
> Here's to the glory of the Great White—awk—
> who has been running—er—er—things in recent—ech—(#23)

He dismisses Iowa as a place so low that people "get the 'bends'" coming
from there (#189). But Berryman's most consistent satire is reserved for
the literary profession, the critics and scholars who will eventually determine the worth of his work. It is the critics, "the Professional-Friends-of-
Robert-Frost" who turn literature "abrupt" into "an industry" (#38).
Berryman has "a sing to shay" about the Modern Language Association,
the phrase suggesting both his drunken rowdiness in the solemn surroundings and the appropriate vehicle (a shay) for conveying so flimsy an
organization (#35). *The Dream Songs* contain numerous warnings to the
MLA members who might address themselves to his work: "These Songs
are not meant to be understood, you understand" (#366). And again:

> —I can't read any more of this Rich Critical Prose,
> he growled, broke wind, and scratched himself & left
> that fragrant area.
> When the mind dies it exudes rich critical prose,
> especially about Henry, particularly in Spanish, and sends it to him
> from Madrid, London, New York.

Now back on down, boys; don't express yourself. (#170)

And yet, even here, Berryman implicates himself in the satire. He is, after all, himself a critic and professor of literature ("my o'ertaxed brain . . . even keeps an office hour"), and although he ridicules the annotators of his work, he covets them as well (#274). In Dream Song #373 he asks, "Will assistant professors become associates / by working on his works?" The question laughs at the whole institutionalization of the critical enterprise, but at the same time expresses the hope that readers will become *his* associates by reading him. Comedy enables Berryman to be arrogant and humble at the same time, both attacking his enemies and exposing himself.

The dramatic play between end man and interlocutor, between *alazon* and *eiron*, that prevents *The Dream Songs* from degenerating into self-pity or self-aggrandizement is evident (as it was in Whitman and Stevens also) in the language itself. As we have seen, Berryman wanted to express his sense of personal suffering, disintegration, and pain without self-pity or mawkishness or cliché. By comically exaggerating his difficulties, Berryman renders Henry's pretensions to wretchedness both ridiculous and heroic. Treating the clichés of alienation, despair, and angst comically, he is able to use and renew them. Berryman's language itself reflects a similar strategy. Just as Henry claims to be the most wretched of men, so the language itself seems crippled, struggling helplessly and heroically along on its rubbery legs, confined in its arbitrary three-stanza form, the form in which, according to Howard Nemerov, most jokes are cast. Language, for Berryman, doesn't merely *report* a self, it *is* a self. Quirky, funny, sad, it breaks prescribed codes of behavior, offends good sense, and continually asks for sympathy. Just as Henry exposes his inadequacies, language exposes *its* inadequacies, tripping over itself, evading understanding, confusing pronouns, reversing word order, making grammatical mistakes, and dissipating into baby talk and nonsense.

Like Henry, Berryman's language is crippled and wretched. Like Henry, it is also comic, its juxtapositions of high and low style and its surprising incongruities keeping its pretensions in check. When Berryman's language gets too lugubrious, it picks itself up much the way the interlocutor picks up Henry, with a put-down or a sudden shift of pace and tone. In Dream Song #175 when Henry, that "merry old soul," concludes that neither his pipe nor his bowl nor his fiddlers three will ever heed his call, the scene is set for despair. But true to the nursery rhyme opening, the language intrudes to make a joke that rights things:

> This world is a solemn place with room for tennis.

The juxtaposition of "solemn place" and "tennis" and the subsequent slant rhyme of "tennis" and "anus" prevents the potential solemnity from taking over. Similarly, when Henry fractures his arm, "no joke to Henry," the language refuses any sympathy, making a joke instead. Berryman explains that the arm is "fractured in the humerus," the pun defying Henry's pain (#165). The world that boasts "the ultimate gloire" is often caught in its "underwear" (#123).

Just as language itself comically deflates Henry's claims to wretchedness, it can also elevate Henry's celebration. As we have seen, Berryman wanted to affirm romantic love and bardic power, two old notions that neither he nor his contemporary readers could take quite seriously any longer. By viewing Henry's parallel aspirations comically, exaggerating love into lust and bardic power into bathetic pretension, Berryman could celebrate what would otherwise have been sentimental, egotistical, or clichéd. Berryman's language, too, reveals a desire to celebrate the romance of its own power while exposing its limits and inadequacies simultaneously. Like Stevens, Berryman laughs at the clichéd language in order to use it. To say that humor is "fatal to bardic pretension" as Berryman does in "Images of Elspeth"[24] is only half the story. By parodying its romantic tendencies, language is able to use those tendencies. Parodying bardic pretension is a way of being bardic.

Dream Song #171 provides a good example:

> Go, ill-sped book, and whisper to her or
> storm out the message for her only ear
> that she is beautiful.
> Mention sunsets, be not silent of her eyes
> and mouth and other prospects, praise her size,
> say her figure is full.
>
> Say her small figure is heavenly & full,
> so as stunned Henry yatters like a fool
> & maketh little sense.
> Say she is soft in speech, stately in walking,
> modest at gatherings, and in every thing
> declares her excellence.
>
> Forget not, when the rest is wholly done
> and all her splendours opened one by one
> to add that she likes Henry,
> for reasons unknown, and fate has bound them fast

> one to another in linkages that last
> and that are fair to see.

The poem is a parody of Waller's "Go Lovely Rose" (or perhaps a parody of Pound's parody of that poem), using the language and assumptions of the traditional love song by parodying them. The juxtapositions of the formal and idiomatic, the intrusion of the unromantic into a romantic context, and the humorous elaborations of the theme all add to the comedy. The courtly love elevation of woman as goddess (she is "beautiful," "heavenly," "modest," "excellent," and "fair") is undercut by the poet's evident carnality (he is drawn to her "mouth and other prospects," "and all her splendours opened one by one"). The archaic, even biblical language ("maketh," "forget not," "be not silent," "bound them fast / one to another") collapses under the deflating juxtaposition of the colloquial ("storm out," "yatter," "mention sunsets"). The syntax, the gags, the colloquialisms, and the tag phrases, here and elsewhere in *The Dream Songs*, enable Berryman to use language that would otherwise seem too sentimental, abstract, romantic, and conventional.

Finally, the playful language, in its vitality, nonsense, and buffoonery, strives against the power of despair and nightmare that permeates the whole of *The Dream Songs*. The comedy of the language may not neutralize the horror, but it qualifies and distances it. The clowning play of language, like the clowning drama between Berryman's minstrel characters, is Berryman's way of dealing with his most threatening antagonist—death. *The Dream Songs* are pervaded by death. Henry is smitten with the deaths of friends and colleagues and obsessed by intimations of his own impending death. If the name *Mr. Bones* refers to a minstrel character and to a sexual obsession, it is also a kind of *memento mori*, an image of death which the interlocutor constantly places before Henry. By calling Henry *Mr. Bones*, the interlocutor takes on another identity, one about which Berryman left some rather cryptic clues.

Most critics have accepted Berryman's explanation in the *Harvard Advocate* interview of the origins of Henry's name. Berryman explains, "One time my second wife and I were walking down an avenue in Minneapolis and we decided on the worst names that you could think of for men and women. We decided on Mabel for women, and Henry for men. So from then on, in the most cozy and adorable way, she was Mabel and I was Henry; and that's how Henry came into being." True or not, the explanation has drawn attention away from Berryman's challenge to readers to discover the name of the unnamed interlocutor. Later in the same interview Berryman refers to Henry's "friend": "He is never named; I know

his name, but the critics haven't caught on yet. Sooner or later some assistant professor will become an associate professor by learning the name
of Henry's friend." [25] In his book on Stephen Crane, Berryman notes,
"The names authors give their characters seldom receive sufficient attention unless the significance of a name is immediately striking." [26] And in
an interview in *Shenandoah* Berryman reveals, "One has secrets, like any
craftsman, and I figure that anyone who deserves to know them deserves
to find them out for himself." [27] Berryman's three comments seem to fit
together as a kind of challenge to the reader. He says that he has secrets a
worthy reader will discover; names are more important than most critics
think; the interlocutor's name is one of Berryman's secrets, the discovery
of which will effect the promotion of some assistant professor to the rank
of associate.

Although I am already a full professor, and therefore perhaps not qualified to guess the friend's name, I would like to suggest a possibility. Henry
and Mr. Bones are variant names for a single character in *The Dream
Songs*, a character who, despite Berryman's protestations, quite closely
resembles Berryman. In fact, *Henry Mr. Bones* is almost an anagram for
John Berryman. If one sets *Henry Mr. Bones* and *John Berryman* side by
side and deletes all of the letters they have in common, three letters remain: *JAS. J. A. S.* are the initials of Berryman's father, John Allyn Smith
(Berryman adopted his stepfather's surname), whose suicide when Berryman was eleven informs the tone and themes of *The Dream Songs*. Although this may be purely coincidence, it may also provide a clue to the
identity of the unnamed "friend."

If Henry's friend is his dead father, then Berryman is participating in an
old comic tradition. Aristophanes, for example, has Dionysus bring his
poetic "father," Aeschylus, back from the dead in "The Frogs"; Dante re-
lies on Virgil to guide him through hell in his *Divine Comedy*; and most
recently, James Merrill calls on his poetic father, Auden, to help him in his
own *Divine Comedies*. Further, I have suggested that the relationship between Henry/Mr. Bones and the interlocutor/Tambo resembles the relationship between the members of the comic film teams like Martin and
Lewis, Abbott and Costello, and Burns and Allen. These teams are also
based on father-child relationships, with Martin, Abbott, and Burns serving as father figures to Lewis, Costello, and Allen, who are clearly childlike.

In any case, Henry's friend in *The Dream Songs* does seem to function
much like a father figure for Henry. Throughout *The Dream Songs* the
friend intrudes to remind Henry that he is mortal, human, and comic,
three important things (signified by the name Mr. Bones) that Henry is

constantly in danger of forgetting. In poems like Dream Song #25, #36, and #256, for example, the interlocutor reminds Henry that he will die, something a dead father does by example: "Fate clobber all," he intimates in Dream Song #25; "Sah. We hafta *die*. / That is our 'pointed task," he insists in Dream Song #36; "Mr Bones, the Lord will bring us to a nation / where everybody only rest," he explains in Dream Song #256. And the friend appears in four of the "Opus posthumous" poems that begin the second part of *The Dream Songs*. What better friend could Henry talk with in the grave than a dead father?

The interlocutor reminds Henry (as a dead man would) that he will die. He also comforts Henry as a father would. In Dream Song #76, for example, the interlocutor offers his arm to Henry: "Now set / your left foot by my right foot, / shoulder to shoulder, all that jazz, / arm in arm, by the beautiful sea." The "smothering southern sea," we recall, is where Berryman's father took his own life. And in Dream Song #143, the interlocutor sings a song of Henry's feelings about his father's suicide, feelings only Henry, and perhaps his father, would know:

> —That's enough of that, Mr Bones. *Some* lady you make.
> Honour the burnt cork, be a vaudeville man,
> I'll sing you now a song
> the like of which may bring your heart to break:
> he's gone! and we don't know where. When he began
> taking the pistol out & along,
>
> you was just a little; but gross fears
> accompanied us along the beaches, pal.
> My mother was scared almost to death.
> He was going to swim out, with me, forevers,
> and a swimmer strong he was in the phosphorescent Gulf,
> but he decided on lead.
>
> That mad drive wiped out my childhood. I put him down
> while all the same on forty years I love him
> stashed in Oklahoma
> besides his brother Will. Bite the nerve of the town
> for anyone so desperate. I repeat: I love him
> until *I* fall into coma.

The poem begins in the middle of the minstrel show, with Mr. Interlocutor characteristically interrupting Mr. Bones's female impersonation, a popular comic bit on the minstrel stage. The interlocutor ribs Henry, and then introduces a song sung by himself, "which may bring your heart to break." The song he sings is Henry's song, the song Henry would sing if he could, the song J. A. S. might want his son to sing about him. The pronoun shift from third to first person blurs the distinction between Henry and the singer, bringing them together in a memory of the formative incident.

Whether we assume that the friend is Henry's father or not, it is clear that he focuses the central theme of *The Dream Songs* and of much of the comic poetry discussed in this book—death. Death for Whitman was an illusion or a blowhard; for Dickinson it was a terrible numbness, a trivial fly, or a kindly suitor; for Frost it was a seductive force, best avoided; for Stevens, it was an end of motion and change. Death for Berryman is a fascinating horror. In his *Harvard Advocate* interview he defines his attitude: "There's a wonderful remark, which I meant to use as an epigraph, but I never got around to it. 'We were all end-men.' . . . Isn't that adorable?"[28] For Berryman, Henry and all of us are "end" men, comic and condemned to death. Rather than evade the fact with Frost, who sneaks out the back window while death knocks on the lockless door, Berryman "called for a locksmith, to burst the topic open" (#335).

Berryman's "complex investigations of death" discover extremes. Sometimes, as for Whitman, death is for Berryman "lucky," a "happy ending" (#288). In Dream Song #26, for example, death provides Henry with an escape from discontent: "I had a most marvelous piece of luck. I died." And in Dream Song #86 it frees him from guilt, as the mock lawyer of this Opus posthumorous poem argues at the final judgment that Henry cannot be held guilty for any crimes committed after he died. Henry is "Not Guilty by reason of death." In Dream Song #319 the amputation of a leg provides the same comic protection from guilt and pain that the amputation of a self does: "*there* was one leg no more could happen to— / I thrust a knife into it, it doesn't hurt." Death is merely the "top job" to be "undertaken" (#46).

Death as the happy escape from suffering is counterbalanced by death as the ultimate horror. Berryman can rage at the death he sees around him, feeling his own utter helplessness to stop it: "The high ones die, die. They die" (#36). As it is for Sylvia Plath, death is for Berryman "a German expert" (#41). Henry's grief and outrage over his father's death lead him, as they led Plath before him, to a ritual revenge. In Dream Song #384, laughing and raging like a madman, Henry visits his father's grave. "O ho alas alas" he raves:

> I'd like to scrabble till I got right down
> away down under the grass

and ax the casket open ha to see
just how he's taking it, which he sought so hard
we'll tear apart
the mouldering grave clothes ha & then Henry
will heft the ax once more, his final card,
and fell it on the start.

Succumbing to despair over his father's suicide, Henry wants to murder the man who started Henry's own painful life and thereby condemned him to death.

If Berryman thus ranges to extremes in his attitudes toward death, both welcoming it as lucky and attacking it as a horror, he more characteristically combines the extremes, making death a character in the grand minstrel show. Death is a kind of straight man or interlocutor, a humorless reminder of mortality. Berryman, as end man, will keep death off balance with one-liners, comic reversals, and distracting antics while looking it straight in the face: "He stared at Ruin. Ruin stared straight back" (#45). As in a silent film comedy, Berryman's language and characters move quirkily, in fast action. They continually get knocked down and rumpled and continually bounce back up brushing themselves off, adjusting their bowlers, and fiddling with their neckties, their attitude one of surprise, consternation, and comically outraged dignity. When "he went to pieces. / The pieces sat up & wrote" (#311).

The "Opus posthumous" poems (Dream Songs #78–#91) provide a good example of Berryman's method. These fourteen poems read something like a minstrel end-man monologue, with appropriate interpolations by Mr. Interlocutor, Mr. Bones's friend and nemesis. The whole sequence is centered on Henry's outrageous claim, the kind of absurd claim that characterized the humor of his minstrel predecessor—he is dead. In the first of the series, Dream Song #78, Berryman recounts how Henry "sheared / off" down to his minimal self, a residue of Whitman's "orbic flex," Crane's "pain," and Henry's "powerful memory." With his "parts . . . fleeing" (the comic terminology undercutting any solemnity here), Henry knows that "His soul is a sight" (#80), and he broods on what is to come:

the knowledge that they will take off your hands,
both hands; as well as your both feet, & likewise
both eyes,
might be discouraging to a bloody hero. (#81).

It might be, but isn't finally for Henry. In Dream Song #81 he reasons that the body "wasn't so much after all to lose, was, Boyd?" but is reminded by Mr. Interlocutor that "Mr Bones, you needed that." In Dream Song #82 Henry discovers that God isn't around, the "great Uh" (#80) is a fiction left back above ground, and "we was had" (#82). But from the "cozy grave" he will "rainbow . . . scornful laughings" (#82). Although he does regret the lack of typewriters in the grave with which to sing his new knowledge, he is glad to be rid of deadlines that have become "ancient nonsense— / no typewriters—ha! ha!—no typewriters— / alas!" (#83). The indecorous "plop" of the earth falling on his coffin makes him feel like a lobster in a pot, as the enormity of his situation begins to trouble him. But he describes the lobster so well that Mr. Interlocutor intrudes, willfully misunderstanding Mr. Bones as is the traditional interlocutor's wont: "Sound good, Mr Bones. I wish I had me some" (#84). In Dream Song #85 Henry poses Dickinson's punning question "How will the matter end?" and engages in her kind of speculations: "Who's king these nights?" Nevertheless, he keeps a Stevensesque perspective on his plight. Like Badroulbadour he knows the "Worms are at hand" and jokes "I daresay I'm collapsing. . . . I am breaking up." In this poem, the midpoint of the sequence, although he vaguely recalls the minstrel summons ("Go in Brack man de day's yo own"), he reaches bottom, coming to a "full stop" where even language is a closed system: "The cold is cold" (#85). By Dream Song #86, however, he has been judged "Not Guilty by reason of death," and it is rumored that he will, like Christ and Whitman and Crispin before him, do what Frost only threatened to do—return from the dead "in triumph, keeping up our hopes" (#87). But he puts his remaining time in the underworld to good use, visiting the dead and picking their brains, even having a bevy of female companions, his coffin "like Grand Central to the brim / filled up" (#89). "The Marriage of the Dead" represents for him but "a new routine," reminding us that this is just a stage show after all, with its own lovely visions: "O she must startle like a fallen gown" (#89). Before making his comeback he envisions an afterlife where "In the chambers of the end we'll meet again" (#90). The poems that follow his resurrection day show Henry recovering from illness, then drinking, breeding, and celebrating himself once again.

The "Opus posthumous" sequence, revelling in one-liners, puns, and self-deprecating and self-aggrandizing jokes, thus resembles the minstrel stage, and death itself becomes a kind of minstrel figure. Late in *The Dream Songs*, in #373, Berryman summarizes the sequence in a single poem:

> My eyes with which I see so easily
> will become closed. My friendly heart will stop.
> I won't sit up.

Nose me, soon you won't like it—ee—
worse than a pesthouse; and my thought all gone
& the vanish of the sun.

The vanish of the moon, which Henry loved
on charming nights when Henry young was moved
by delicate ladies
with ripped-off panties, mouths open to kiss.
They say the coffin closes without a sound
& is lowered underground!

So now his thought's gone, buried his body dead,
what now about the adorable *Little* Twiss
& his fair lady,
will they set up a tumult in his praise
will assistant professors become associates
by working on his works?

Once again Henry imagines his own death—the rot and decay, the vision of women, the reaction of his wife, and the possibility of a kind of immortality, all choreographed in a comic minstrel dance. Replete with incongruous lines and images, with solipsism and redundancy, the poem informs us that when Henry is dead he "won't sit up" and will start to smell bad. The juxtaposition of "delicate ladies" and "ripped-off panties" further sets the incongruous tone, and the exclamation mark at the end of stanza two underlines the mock-innocence of the speaker—as if it is real news to him and to us that coffins are lowered underground. The third stanza, with its references to his wife and daughter, recalls Dream Song #345, in which Berryman notes that "relevant experts / say the wounds to the survivors is / the worst of the Act." But the speaker in Dream Song #373 ridicules the whole notion by speculating on the "tumult" they might "set up . . . in his praise," like some monument or foundation. The whole proceeding is trivialized by the familiar reference to assistant professors struggling to become associates by working on his work. The poem, a perfect example of Berryman's technique in dealing with death, comically exposes anyone who would elevate death or ignore the plain facts of stink and inaction. It also comically chastizes those who would use or abuse the speaker after his death with grief or praise. He was, after all, no saint; he was capable of ripping ladies' panties off for his pleasure. But there is a certain sadness here, too, a longing for precisely what the speaker satirically rejects. He would like the romanticism, the moon and the lovely ladies, the wife's tumult, and the critical recognition. The only way to have those things, or to express those things, is through comedy.

Berryman's ambivalence about death is paralleled by his ambivalence about God and religion. On the one hand, Henry rejects God as his "enemy" (#13). He is "cross with God who has wrecked this generation" (#153). God is a "slob" who should be "curbed" (#238). God is full of morbid surprises "like / when the man you fear most in the world marries your mother" (#168). Like Whitman and Stevens, Berryman would prefer to dismiss this Dr. God, this "great Uh," the "high chief," "that abnormally scrubbed and powerful one" from the whole picture, and to substitute something else. But like Dickinson and Frost, Berryman is not so sure of himself and his own power. Henry and his world are just too flimsy to go it on their own, and Henry continues to ponder religion's place in the scheme of things: "Hankered he less for youth than for more time / to adjust the conflicting evidence, the 'I'm— / immortal-&-not' routine" (#347).

In *The Freedom of the Poet*, Berryman characterizes *Don Quixote* as a work of fervent though disenchanted piety. The description fits Berryman's work as well. Periodically in *The Dream Songs* Henry reveals his longing to love God and to believe that eternity is more than a "sort of forever" (#27), but there is a communications problem:

> He yelled at me in Greek,
> my God!—It's not his language
> and I'm no good at—his is Aramaic,
> was—I am a monoglot of English
> (American version) and, say pieces from
> a baker's dozen others. (#48)

The picture of Christ yelling at Berryman in a language he can't understand and the subsequent disquisition on the linguistic confusion render the colloquy somewhat ludicrous. The linguistic comedy further leads to some theological comedy, as Henry connects the symbolic resurrection with seeds and with bread falling and rising. The idea of resurrection is "troublesome to imaginary Jews, / like bitter Henry," and especially troublesome for a man who so values suffering. For a Christian, the idea is the opposite of "troublesome." It assures, in fact, the end of earthly trouble and the beginning of eternal life in heaven. But for Henry, the death of "the death of love" would be terrible because it would undercut all of his heroic pain. The next Song, #49, extends the theme as Henry "*wants* to have eaten" (the communion from the preceding poem, perhaps), but instead drinks his wine in his favorite bar and falls asleep.

If Henry can't accept God's grace, perhaps he can court his wrath. Living in a state of "chortle sin" (#57) Henry implores God:

If all must hurt at once, let yet more hurt now,
so I'll be ready, Dr. God. Push on me,
Give it to Henry harder. (#194)

The invocation recalls Berryman's comment in the *Paris Review* interview that he would like to be nearly crucified, since that would help his writing.

Berryman's fervent but disenchanted piety is evident throughout *The Dream Songs*, but his most impressive religious poetry appears in his next book, *Love and Fame*, a book that provides an interesting contrast to *The Dream Songs*. Indeed, the failure of the first sections of *Love and Fame* helps to clarify the success of the final section and provides an instructive contrast by which to measure Berryman's comic method in general. Like *The Dream Songs*, *Love and Fame* is a kind of spiritual autobiography of the poet. But while the comic strategy of *The Dream Songs* is continually to qualify and undercut Henry's excesses of lust and ambition, *Love and Fame* allows the excesses to go unchecked. Lacking the minstrel voice of *The Dream Songs*, *Love and Fame* becomes a noisy self-indulgence, glorifying the young Berryman's monstrous ego. Berryman's annoyed insistence that the ironical religious prayers in the final section of the book are meant to serve the *eiron* function by putting the protagonist's boasting and posturing in a comic context, and his reference to ironies in the first parts of the book, are intriguing but ultimately unpersuasive. The ironies he claims for the first sections simply are not there, and the prayers at the end are too far removed from the narrative to undercut it successfully. Trying to pull off Whitman's technical coup (investing his *alazon* hero with such confidence, energy, and exuberance that he overcomes all conventional responses and triumphs over society's and the reader's restrictions and hesitations), Berryman fails, and we are left with a protagonist who seems merely sophomoric and boorish, a protagonist who watches Marx Brothers and Chaplin films but learns nothing from them.

The concluding eleven prayers are another matter entirely. In his "Eleven Addresses to the Lord," although they are certainly more muted and quiet, Berryman returns to the comic strategy of *The Dream Songs*, using parody to enable him to say what he could not say otherwise. Berryman remarks, "You know, the country is full of atheists, and they are really going to find themselves threatened by those poems."[29] If not threatened, the modern reader might at least be bored or put off by straight conventional prayer as he is bored and put off by the straight boasting in sections 1–3 of *Love and Fame*. By parodying the language and sentiment of the prayer, Berryman is able convincingly to pray. The first poem in the sequence is a good example of the religious longing that had been evident as an undercurrent in the wilder and more painful *Dream Songs*:

Master of beauty, craftsman of the snowflake,
inimitable contriver,
endower of Earth so gorgeous & different from the boring Moon,
thank you for such as it is my gift.

I have made up a morning prayer to you
containing with precision everything that most matters.
"According to Thy will" the thing begins.
It took me off & on two days. It does not aim at eloquence.

You have come to my rescue again & again
in my impassable, sometimes despairing years.
You have allowed my brilliant friends to destroy themselves
and I am still here, severely damaged, but functioning.

Unknowable, as I am unknown to my guinea pigs:
how can I "love" you?
I only as far as gratitude & awe
confidently & absolutely go.[30]

The juxtaposition of levels of diction sets up the linguistic comedy. Colloquial phrases like "different from the boring Moon" and "It took me off
& on two days" undercut the more elevated conventional religious diction, enabling Berryman to use it. The tone is loving but also wry, as Berryman manages to inject some of his doubts about God's goodness into
the ostensibly humble invocation. As in *The Dream Songs*, but without
their accusing tone, Berryman notes that God has allowed Berryman's
brilliant friends to destroy themselves and has used Berryman (and all
people) as guinea pigs. Thus Berryman still can't "love" God or truly
know him, and he remains somewhat dissatisfied with God's inscrutable
program. But he accepts God now and is able to express awe and gratitude. All eleven of the poems are similarly lyrical and comical. They are
some of the most persuasive modern prayers we have, incorporating faith,
doubt, humility, and ego into a parody of the conventional form.

   The prayers, and Berryman's last two books in general, have not met
with the kind of critical acclaim afforded *The Dream Songs*, which will
continue to be regarded as Berryman's comic masterpiece. Full of profound truths and divine aberrations, eloquent insights and absurd obses-
sions, lyrical high-mindedness and nonsensical hanky-panky, and mawk-
ish self-aggrandizement and witty self-deprecation, *The Dream Songs*
succeed in offending, disarming, shocking, seducing, cajoling, wheedling,
tickling, charming, slapping, joking, jostling, and caressing the reader
into acceptance. Combining the flamboyant language and banter and
dance of Whitman and Stevens with the sadness and doubt and pain of

Dickinson and Frost, Berryman uses his comedy as a means of facing fear, dread, and anguish without seeming lugubrious or self-pitying, a means of facing ruin and going to pieces while affirming the self and its absurd aspirations:

> Why then did he make, at such cost, *crazy* sounds?
> to waken ancient longings, to remind (of childness),
> to make laugh, and to hurt,
> is and was all he ever intended. (#271)

VII

Envoi
Dance with Dread and Tweedle

In the fairy tale "The Flying Trunk," a merchant's son who has been mistaken for a god by the king's daughter because of his magnificent magical trunk is invited to appear before the royal family:

> "Will you tell us a story?" asked the Queen, "one that has
> deep meaning and is instructive?"
> "But a story I can laugh at," added the King.
> So the merchant's son told a story—one that was both
> instructive and funny, which was not easy to do.[1]

As I have suggested in this study, American poets have characteristically assumed the role of the merchant's son, sometimes masquerading as a god, telling stories that are both instructive and funny in order to avoid the king's wrath or win the king's daughter—which is not easy to do. Walt Whitman, adopting the backwoods voice of American humor to elevate himself (and his reader) to the role of comic God, and Wallace Stevens, assuming the guise of a backwoods dandy to pursue Supreme Fictions, used rhapsodic language to fly in the face of convention. Emily Dickinson and Robert Frost, preferring the quieter Yankee voice of American humor, adopted the roles of innocent child or New England farmer, using self-deprecation and understatement to fly aslant of danger and despair. John Berryman, combining rhapsody and understatement, used the magic trunk of minstrelsy to keep himself moving and alive in a world that seemed bent on his destruction. Whether adopting the tactics of the ring-tailed roarer, the Yankee peddler, the minstrel, or some combination of the three, our poets have used irony, satire, parody, and farce, but above all humor, to attack atrophied ideas and beliefs, defend against destructive impulses from within and without, and celebrate language and life by embracing absurdities and humiliations as well as joys and triumphs.

The tradition of American humor as defined by Whitman, Dickinson, Frost, Stevens, and Berryman continues in contemporary American poetry, with our more recent poets adopting their predecessors' rhapsodic, Yankee, and minstrel voices to their own purposes. The rhapsodic backwoods voice of Whitman, for example, is carried on most audibly by the

Beat poets (Ginsberg, Corso, Ferlinghetti) and the New York school (O'Hara, Koch, Ashbery) of the fifties and sixties. And "carried on" is an apt description of their antics and nonsense, their vision of poetry and language as play. Reacting against the cool irony and detachment of "academic" verse, these postwar poets reject the well-wrought lyrical urn in favor of outrageous posturing, sudden bizarre juxtapositions, the free play of language over craftsmanship and form.

Of the Beats, Ginsberg is probably most often paired with Whitman. Ginsberg's "Howl," despite its clearly more bitter and frenzied tone, has obvious roots in Whitman's "barbaric yawp." A darker version of "Song of Myself," "Howl" once again lifts the poet's boastful self to center stage where it can rage and take pratfalls. Similarly, "America" approaches Whitman's buoyant innocence and sweep as Ginsberg laughs at his country and himself:

> America this is quite serious.
> America this is the impression I get from looking in the television set.
> America is this correct?
> I'd better get right down to the job.
> It's true I don't want to join the Army or turn lathes in precision parts
>   factories, I'm nearsighted and psychopathic anyway
> America I'm putting my queer shoulder to the wheel.[2]

Or in "Sunflower Sutra" Ginsberg comically lectures a sunflower on its identity, clowning in a manner that recalls Lawrence's criticism of Whitman:

> You were never no locomotive, Sunflower, you were a sunflower!
> And you Locomotive, you are a locomotive, forget me not![3]

If the sunflower needs no reminder of what it is, perhaps we, with our penchant to mechanize the universe, do. And if the locomotive is no sunflower, perhaps it can be transformed into a forget-me-not. Ginsberg's humor, like Whitman's, is that of the boaster or ring-tailed roarer who laughs us back to our humanity.

Similarly, Gregory Corso combines a Stevensesque nonsense with a Whitmanesque boast and blab in his own songs of the open road. In his "Poets Hitchhiking on the Highway" he and his companion engage in a kind of verbal joust or backwoods tournament in which each tries to unseat the other as master wordsmith and purveyor of nonsense:

> So we fought:
> He said: "The apple-cart like a
>   broomstick-angel

> snaps & splinters
> > old dutch shoes."
> I said: "Lightning will strike the old oak
> > and free the fumes!"
> He said: "Mad street with no name."
> I said: "Bald killer! Bald killer! Bald killer!"
> He said, getting real mad,
> > "Firestoves! Gas! Couch!"
> I said, only smiling,
> > "I know God would turn back his head
> > if I sat quietly and thought."
> We ended by melting away,
> > hating the air!⁴

The mock-heroic conflict celebrates the sheer pleasure of words and companionship and imagination.

The rhapsodic tradition is also evident in the zany antics of the New York school, with its epistemological skepticism, its references to pop culture, and its deliberate clichés, archaisms, surrealism, and nonsense. Frank O'Hara, often considered the father of this school, recalls Whitman in his democratizing impulse, his celebratory lists, his praise of the ordinary, and his effort to get the urban trivia of life into the poem, practices that naturally result in comic juxtapositions and surprising inclusions:

> The white chocolate jar full of petals
> swills odds and ends around in a dizzying eye
> of four o'clocks now and to come. The tiger,
> marvelously striped and irritable, leaps
> on the table and without disturbing a hair
> of the flowers' breathless attention, pisses
> into the pot, right down its delicate spout.
> A whisper of steam goes up from that porcelain
> urethra. "Saint-Saens!"⁵

Kenneth Koch, like O'Hara, acknowledges his affinities with Whitman. Indeed, in his hilarious "A Poem of the Forty-eight States" he boasts to be nothing less than Whitman reincarnated. The poem begins with Whitman ecstatically touring the country once more before dying. Although in section 4 he speculates "I reckon I am about as big and dead as a whale!," he doesn't actually "die" until section 6:

> O Charleston! why do you always put me in the mood for kidding?
> I am not dead yet, why do you make me say I am?

. . . .
O Charleston, why do you always do this . . . Gasp! Goodbye!

But you can't keep a good gray poet down for long, and in section 8 Whitman celebrates his "rebirth in the poems of Kenneth Koch" and ends by promising the reader, "I like Pennsylvania too, we could have a lot of fun there, / You and I will go there when Kenneth is dead." [6] Partly humorous self-aggrandizement on Koch's part, partly celebration of Whitman's immortality, the poem transports Whitman's characteristic humor of excess and hyperbole into the present.

John Ashbery adapts this same tall-tale tradition to his own purposes in a poem like "Farm Implements and Rutabagas in a Landscape." In this mysterious sestina, the world is strangely alien, full of unexpected occurrences and unexplained juxtapositions. Evil, in the form of the sea hag, threatens to take over Popeye's house, but Popeye, like his backwoods forebears, boasts great powers. His thunder can wreak havoc from a great distance, enabling him to "chuckle" and "scratch his balls," concluding "it sure was pleasant to spend a day in the country." [7] Ashbery explains that he turned to the sestina as a means of "getting into remoter areas of consciousness. The really bizarre requirements of a sestina I use as a probing tool. . . . I once told somebody that writing a sestina was rather like riding downhill on a bicycle and having the pedals push your feet. I wanted my feet to be pushed into places they wouldn't normally have taken." [8] In "Farm Implements" the *reader* is riding downhill on the sestina, its pedals pushing him so unexpectedly that logical connections continually fail, making the ride both pleasantly surprising and frustrating. The poem, like many of Ashbery's, is in some ways a joke on the reader, giving him discontinuity, illogic, and simultaneity when he expects (and wants) continuity, logic, and sequence. Reflecting both "the illusion of life and the distinct impression of a mechanical arrangement" by which Bergson defined the comic, Ashbery's Popeye provides a contemporary version of the all-powerful, mythic backwoodsman whose physical strength can triumph over any foe. If the figure has degenerated into a cartoon, it is nevertheless imbued with the saving residue of our comic romance.

While poets of the Beat movement and the New York school in the 1950s and 1960s were celebrating themselves through outrageous antics, bluff poses, surprising language, and humorous hyperbole and excess, other poets (whose voice is more characteristic of the 1970s and 1980s) were exploring the quieter Yankee mode of self-deprecation, preferring the wry smile and the low profile to the guffaw and the spotlight. Forgoing the verbal pyrotechnics and flamboyance of Whitman and Stevens, poets like Maxine Kumin, Ted Kooser, Richard Hugo, David Wagoner, William Dickey, and James Wright, among others, have moved to the more understated Frostian voice—strongly imagistic, often narrative, quiet, restrained, lyrical.

Thus, Maxine Kumin has written a series of wry poems about a New England Yankee neighbor, Henry Manley, flavoring the portraits with a gentle, loving humor:

> My neighbor in the country, Henry Manley,
> with a washpot warming on his woodstove,
> with a heifer and two goats and yearly chickens,
> has outlasted Stalin, Roosevelt and Churchill
> but something's stirring in him in his dotage.

The "but" supplies the humorous twist here as Kumin goes on to describe Henry's (for him) peculiar behavior:

> Last fall he dug a hole and moved his privy
> and a year ago in April reamed his well out.
> When the county sent a truck and poles and cable,
> *his* Daddy ran the linemen off with birdshot
> and swore he'd die by oil lamp, and did.

Kumin weaves a note of minstrel sadness into the humor of her portrait. Henry's cantankerous refusal to give in to "progress" and his tenacity of spirit have represented for Kumin a valuable way of life that is disappearing. Henry's "changes" threaten Kumin with the loss of an America she holds dear. The poem ends when Henry, who has

> walked up two miles, shy as a girl, comes calling
> to tell me he has a phone now, 264, ring two.
> It rang one time last week—wrong number.
> He'd be pleased if one day I would think to call him.
>
> Hello, hello Henry? Is that you?[9]

Kumin's call in the last line is a gesture of friendship, an acknowledgment of a new link of communication between them, and a concerned question about Henry's new self.

Kumin's playful portrait draws on Frost's plain style and wry bemusement. Ted Kooser, another offspring of Frost, combines some of Emily Dickinson's impulses to light verse and witty linguistic juxtaposition in his portrait of a midwestern small businessman in "At the Bait Stand":

> Part barn, part boxcar, part of a chicken shed,
> part leaking water, something partly dead,

> part pop machine, part gas pump, part a chair
> leaned back against the wall, and sleeping there,
> part-owner Herman Runner, mostly fat,
> hip-waders, undershirt, tattoos and hat.[10]

The opening description of the bait stand is partly a description of its part owner, whose last name humorously contradicts his essential character. Like Kumin's portrait of Henry Manley, Kooser's portrait reflects an America that seems increasingly archaic, usurped by telephone lines and commercial worm farms, but an America we would nevertheless like to preserve and affirm. Humor keeps the portrait from being unduly romantic or sappily nostalgic.

Whereas language for the Beats and the New York poets functioned something like that of Groucho Marx, drawing attention to itself, collapsing logic and meaning under the sheer weight of its own nonsense, language for Kumin and Kooser is more often a means of creating "real" characters and evoking humorous circumstances with a straight face. Often, the speaker of such poems assumes the role of a Woody Allen, a Chaplin, or a Keaton, a Thurberesque "little man" who, while exposing his innumerable faults and failings, nevertheless continues to bounce back up every time he is knocked down, proving the resilience of his weakness. Thus Richard Hugo, whose poetry is often characterized by a stoic sense of loss and pain reflected in blighted landscapes, broken towns, and bad weathers, keeps his balance with a sense of humor. In his last, and best, book, *The Right Madness on Skye*, Hugo insists on "keeping / tears in check by thinking bad jokes."[11] Hugo's one-liners spice the book, as the following brief catalogue demonstrates:

> You might note on my stone in small letters:
> Here lies one who believed all others his betters.
>
> If you hear anything bad about me, believe it.
>
> When you're a skeleton, it's hard to find a lover.
>
> I have a theory. It's not good but hear me.[12]

Hugo's humorous exposure of his own inadequacies is a way of keeping off tears. David Wagoner's similar exposure is more often a way of celebrating himself. Like Frost's and Dickinson's, Wagoner's self-deprecation is often a means of self-elevation. His humorous confessions are affirmations. If Wagoner is the "bad fisherman" whose "haywire backswing" catches only branches overhead,[13] the cornet player who sits in the "seventh chair / Out of seven" with his "embouchure / A glorified Bronx cheer,"[14] and the reluctant actor of the role of boy Jesus in a pageant, he nevertheless always ends up with our identification, sympathy, and support. His strategy is clear in "Boy Jesus":

> When they made me the boy Jesus
> In the Sunday school Christmas pageant, oh Jesus,
> I would have given almost anything
> To be anybody else in the world but a made-up Jesus.
>
> But suddenly it was too late to say anything
> Polite against it or do anything
> Desperate in my knee-length toga, while my squirming friends
> Snickered in the pews, or even *feel* anything.

At this point in the poem the reader is both victim and victimizer, recalling similar moments in his own life when he snickered or was snickered at. Wagoner continues, denouncing his qualifications for the part:

> Why had they picked on me? Jesus and I
> Gave each other a pain: I couldn't stump preachers, could I?
> No dove had come flapping down when I was baptized, I was no boy
> Genius, and we were Laurel and Hardy carpenters, my father and I.

Having comically exposed his humiliation, Wagoner concludes the poem with an affirmation:

> From that day on, I put my fidgity faith in my own words
> And later in love—in ugly, profane, beautiful words,
> Instead of going hook, line, and sinker for Jesus—
> No Gospels for the Fishers of Men, but love in other words.[15]

The comedy here is that of the victim, the little man and bumbler, the weakling and loser, who nevertheless carries on and eventually triumphs by moving beyond the manipulation of others to an affirmation of himself and his own words. The verse form of the poem itself reflects the comic theme as the poet manages to sing within the formal chains imposed upon him by the mechanically repeating end words. What begins as a confession of embarrassment, failure, and inadequacy turns into an affirmation of purpose, success, and mastery.

William Dickey uses a similar strategy in his wonderful "The Food of Love," with humor deflating and elevating him simultaneously:

> I could never sing. In the grade-school operetta
> I sat dark offstage and clattered coconut shells.
> I was the cavalry coming, unmusical, lonely.

For five years I played the piano and metronome.
I read Deerslayer in small print while I waited for my lesson,
and threw up after the recital at the Leopold Hotel.

I went to a liberal college, but I never learned
how to sit on the floor or help the sweet folk song forward.
My partridge had lice, and its pear-tree had cut-worm blight.

Yet this song is for you. In your childhood a clear falsetto,
now you sing along in the bars, naming old songs for me.
Even drunk, you chirrup; birds branch in your every voice.

It's for you, what I never sing. So I hope if ever
you reach, in the night, for a music that is not there
because you need food, or philosophy, or bail,

you'll remember to hear the noise that a man might make
if he were an amateur, clattering coconut shells,
if he were the cavalry, tone-deaf but on its way.[16]

The confession of failure at the beginning comes full circle by the end. What seemed to be ineptitude is transformed into a wonderful aptitude.

This version of the Yankee voice—the persona of the Thurberesque "little man," the impotent bumbler, the inadequate failure, the clown who establishes his superiority by claiming his inferiority—is a favorite with our younger contemporary poets. Stephen Dunn's difficulties with garage mechanics, Greg Kuzma's with insurance men, and Larry Levis's with the poem itself come immediately to mind. By presenting supposedly unsympathetic qualities sympathetically, by affirming indecisiveness, insecurity, and impotence over the opposite qualities that the culture requires, the poets both undercut that culture and elevate their persona in all his absurdity and limitation. For all his difficulties and failures, he is clearly preferable to the society that impinges upon him.

Robert Benchley, a master of this kind of humor, has said that the world can be divided into two kinds of people, those who divide the world into two kinds of people and those who don't. Having just divided contemporary poets into two voices—the backwoods and the Yankee— and being of two minds about it, I should like to insist that the categories aren't at all rigid. Such categorizing is of course artificial and potentially distortive, especially in the case of contemporary poets who, as Constance Rourke predicted they would, have tended to merge the voices of American humor into "a single generic figure."[17] Indeed, Gregory Corso, whom I've put in the backwoods tradition, rather uncooperatively claims allegiance to Frost. In *Long Live Man* he responds to Frost's recently published *In the Clearing* by addressing the author: "You undoubtedly think unwell of us / But we are your natural children."[18] Similarly, Ashbery's recent work has moved away from the swaggering unmeaning of the New York school toward a quieter, more accessible voice in which (as Ashbery himself puts it) "meaningfulness" manages to keep "up to the pace of randomness."[19] In his "Self-Portrait in a Convex Mirror" Ashbery's deadpan comic vision enables him to play around Parmigianino's and his own art, affirming both without resorting to illogic or obscurity.

As Corso and Ashbery incorporate Yankee understatement into their often rhapsodic voice, Wagoner, Kumin, and Hugo incorporate backwoods rhapsody into their often understated voice. One of Wagoner's favorite stylistic devices is the humorous Whitmanesque catalogue. When a panhandler says "God bless you," Wagoner rails:

> God bless *me*? *Me* be one for the cloud-capped, holy-
> For-showbiz, smug, sharkskinny, hog-certain, flowery Chosen
> Harping for glory? Thumbs-upping glissandos on pure-gold G-strings?
> I couldn't stagger, let alone clodhop, to such music.[20]

Later in the poem Wagoner gives the panhandler another quarter, "to hope I'll be worth a damn." Kumin is similarly rhapsodic in her praise of Whitmanesque subjects, celebrating *shit* in an affirmation of cosmic continuity.[21] And Hugo can wax rhapsodic over his sorrow and endurance, exposing his own incongruous silliness. In "Maratea Porto: The Dear Postmistress There," for example, Hugo equates the suffering and stoicism of surviving ten days with no mail to the heroism of Odysseus, Genghis Khan, and Michelangelo.[22]

The most typical fusion of the Yankee and backwoods voice in contemporary American poetry involves the combination of the Yankee plain style of Frost and the tall-tale exaggeration of Whitman. The incongruity of style and content augments the humor. Nancy Willard, for example, in the lovely title poem of her *Carpenter of the Sun*, uses the simplest lyrical language to tell a tall tale about her son and the sun:

> My child goes forth to fix the sun,
> a hammer in his hand and a pocketful of nails.
> Nobody else has noticed the crack.
>
> Twilight breaks on the kitchen floor.
> His hands clip and hammer the air.
> He pulls something out,
>
> something small, like a bad tooth,
> and he puts something back,
> and the kitchen is full of peace.

All this is done very quietly,
without payment or promises.[23]

Without their rhapsodic swagger, Willard tells as tall a tale as Davy Crock-ett's about freeing the sun and "introducin' people to the fresh daylight with a piece of sunrise in my pocket" or Walt Whitman's about himself replacing the sun ("Flaunt of the sunshine I need not your bask—lie over! / You light surfaces only. I force surfaces and depths also" [sec. 40, p. 73]).

The tall tale is taken to further and more surreal extremes by other con-temporaries. Russell Edson, for example, rejecting "little constipated lines that are afraid to be anything but correct, without an ounce of humor, / that gaiety that death teaches!," adapts Frost's plain style to the prose poem. Drawing on not "the banal, high-schoolish snickering that one sees so often in so-called prose poems, but the humor of the deep, uncomfor-table metaphor,"[24] Edson describes men so fat that their own bodies de-vour them and sheep so small that they fit into a test tube like a "sub-stitute for rice, a sort of wooly rice" (a reversal of Benjamin Franklin's tall tale of sheep whose tails are so heavy that they must be trailed in little carts behind them).[25]

What Edson does on a small scale, James Merrill does on a large scale, using humor to enable him to articulate cosmic truths. Merrill's penchant for combining backwoods and Yankee humor is most evident in his recent *Divine Comedies*, in which elegant language and a parlor-game fascina-tion with the ouija board invoke a visionary myth involving such tall-tale touches as talking atoms and ghost counselors. Merrill's elegant measures may seem less like the yawp and blab of a Whitman than like the spiffy mutterings of a Stevens, but like both of them he has imagined grandly, writing comic dramas of the self and society. Combining backwoods boasting with Yankee self-deprecation, Merrill is able to make claims he could not otherwise make.

The fusion of voices from traditional American humor can produce sat-ire. Robert Bly, for example, fiercely satirizes the perpetrators of the Viet-nam war, who worked to shrink human beings to the size of statistics ("If we could only make the bodies smaller, / Maybe we could get / A whole year's kill in front of us on a desk!").[26] David Wagoner similarly attacks the Weyerhauser Company for the "selective logging" practices that deci-mate forests.[27] Sharon Olds exposes the Republicans' insensitivity to all but the wealthy.[28] And Marge Piercy scorns male chauvinism in a poem like "A work of artifice."[29] But satire has not been a central mode for con-temporary poets, whose comedy usually tends more to humor.

Often a contemporary poem that exhibits satiric tendencies moves to-ward humor in the end. James Wright's prose poem "The Wheeling Gospel Tabernacle" is a good example. The subject matter—a pair of revival-ist preachers whose own belief is shallow or nonexistent—could lend itself to the kind of satire that Emily Dickinson directed against her "soft cherubic creatures" or that E. E. Cummings directed against his "cam-bridge ladies." However, Wright finally not only exposes the con men for what they are, but also personally identifies with their methods and thus implicates himself in the laughter at the same time. In the poem, Homer Rhodeheaver, evangelist Billy Sunday's psalmodist and shill at the offer-tory, escapes the Pittsburgh cops who are after him on a paternity suit. How did he escape?

> Some thought that Dr. Sunday ascended. I lean toward the
> opinion that the two laborers in the vineyards of the Lord
> skinned the populace of Benwood down the river the next day,
> and that possibly Homer had time between hymns to make some
> lonely widow happy.

Wright sees the two preachers as lovable rapscallions, somewhat like the King and the Duke in Twain's *Huckleberry Finn*, and jauntily gives them the benefit of the doubt. Although Rhodeheaver was a ladies' man, maybe he was the Lord's man as well:

> For all I know, Homer Rhodeheaver really was a glorious
> singer of the great hymns down home. For all I know,
> he carried a better tune than he knew. Women heard him
> in Pittsburgh. Maybe women heard him in the Wheeling Gospel
> Tabernacle. Maybe Jehovah was drowsing, and Eros heard the
> prayer and figured that love after all was love, no matter
> what language a man sang it in, so what the hell.
>   Little I know. I can pitch a pretty fair tune myself, for
> all I know.[30]

The poem ends with typical Yankee self-deprecation: "for all I know." Wright claims ignorance while backhandedly aligning himself with the Yankee con artist and pitchman. Wright's own "fair tune" is pitched to celebrate the humorous anecdote, an anecdote that enabled Wright's par-ents one chance "to laugh like hell for the sheer joy of laughter before the Great Depression began." When asked in an interview, "What value do you place on humor in poetry?," Wright replied, "I could not do without it."[31]

Wright has no desire to reform Rhodeheaver through ridicule, for that would cancel the opportunity to laugh like hell for the sheer joy of laugh-ter before the great depression begins, an attitude that defines the mode of the humorist. How dull a world it would be, the humorist seems to say, if folly were reformed. Thus most of our contemporary poets, like Wright, reflect Morton Gurewitch's recent definition of humor. For Gurewitch, humor "either copes with disaster or thrives on whimsy and joy," seeking "not to expunge folly, but to condone and even to bless it, for humor views folly as endearing, humanizing, indispensable."[32]

Contemporary comic poetry incorporates not only the voices of traditional American humor, but also the characteristic themes as well. As it was for Whitman, Dickinson, Frost, Stevens, and Berryman, death is a central and continuing concern. Like Whitman, who used humor to transcend or dismiss death, Emily Dickinson, who used it to befriend him or trick him into powerlessness, Frost, who used it to elude him or evade him, and Stevens and Berryman, who used it to clown around him or meditate on him, our contemporary poets have used humor to deflate, decoy, or deliberate death. Ihab Hassan explains that comedy, "broadly conceived, may be understood as *a way of making life possible in this world, despite evil or death.*"[33]

Thus Richard Hugo combines Whitman's rhapsodic voice with a portion of Yankee pretense to become larger than death in the title poem of his last collection, *The Right Madness on Skye*. Posing as a dead "dumb" crofter, Hugo delivers instructions for his own funeral, insisting that only "feigned tears" and "plastic" flowers be allowed in the procession. Hugo claims that he is dead throughout the poem as he describes the slow movement of the horse-drawn hearse bearing his body. But he wryly tips off the reader, "it's fun to be dead with one eye open." The poem ends with Hugo's boast, "I was holding my breath all the time. Didn't I fool you?" Hugo will finally have nothing of Harry of Nothingham (the absentee landlord driver), preferring to dance with the oxen: "Take my word. It's been fun."[34]

In "The Right Madness on Skye" Hugo comically elevates himself above death. In "The Minneapolis Poem" James Wright jokes his way around it. Like Dickinson and Frost before him, Wright playfully puts death (and Minneapolis) down:

> But I could not bear
> To allow my poor brother my body to die
> In Minneapolis.
> The old man Walt Whitman our countryman
> Is now in America our country
> Dead.
> But he was not buried in Minneapolis
> At least.[35]

Dying may be bad, suggests Wright, but it is not half so bad as being buried in Minneapolis. This Dickinsonian or Frostian playfulness in the face of death often acquires a rougher edge in contemporary poetry, incorporating a harsher or more ominous tone. X. J. Kennedy, for example, parodies Dickinson's cordial relations with death in his "In a Prominent Bar in Secaucus One Day":

> "For when time takes you out for a spin in his car
> You'll be hard-pressed to stop him from going too far
> And be left by the roadside, for all your good deeds,
> Two toadstools for tits and a face full of weeds." [36]

The sexual elements of Dickinson's outing with her gentleman caller are here made painfully and comically explicit.

More often, the sense of helplessness occasioned by death forces our poets into defensive postures. Adopting the role of the "little man" beset by forces too large for him, Greg Kuzma casts death in the shape of two insurance men come to sell him a bill of goods he cannot refuse:

> One's sober as death.
> He looks modeled out of clay or wax.
> His smile seems broken through hard rock
> to reach his face.
> The effect is painful,
> what they want.
>
> The other, fat, gesticulates,
> although he doesn't have the facts
> (the other holds the book like a name book—
> the cover is black)
> he argues for commitment.
> He says, "Suppose an early death"
> and tries to lead me
> while I live to see you Barb
> and Jackie eating grass
> or bleared by shame,
> the Mustang getting towed away
> to please a creditor.
>
> "Suppose a death at fifty-five
> when the policy's matured."
> (I see it in my top drawer
> swollen like a leech
> or spilling dimes into the corners.) [37]

Laughing at the inability to cope with the fact of death is actually one way of coping with it. Michael Van Walleghan, incorporating some poignant minstrel sadness into his self-portrait of the little man, confesses:

> But then I seem to have always had trouble with the obvious.
> Once, when a friend died, and after my parents had told me he
> had died, I came around the next morning anyway to call him
> out for school. His mother came to the door weeping and told
> me Orville couldn't go to school that day.[38]

The poem combines laughter and sadness in a way that is reminiscent of Berryman's quieter poems and characteristic of the recent poetry of many of our younger poets. Michael Heffernan provides a vivid example of this mode in a poem from his sonnet sequence, "The Crazyman's Revival."

> When it got specially bad he began to think
> He thought about the sick dog by the road
> he found one time and put a bullet in its head
> He thought about the spot that bullet made
> on the dog's brow, wonderfully round and pink
> He thought about the things he knew for sure
> how men were lonely and lived lonely lives
> how even the sun was lonely and on fire
> He thought about the cry of Oliver Hardy
> how he would dance with dread and tweedle his derby
> and send his clear soprano up from all his tonnage
> whenever the deadly husband with the knives
> the murderous sailor or their own relentless wives
> were about to do him and his pal some permanent damage.[39]

The helplessness, the existential sense of people's puniness in a vast indifferent cosmos, the inexplicableness of death, all contract to the cry of Oliver Hardy. But to see our terrors treated as farce is to take the first step toward controlling them. While in no way rejecting the real strain and threat aroused by the poem, the reference to film comedy puts them in perspective. The "damage" done to Laurel and Hardy is never "permanent," and if we tweedle our derbies nervously, we can nevertheless take dread as our partner and dance. Sylvia Plath, whose own sense of humor is too often underplayed, summarizes the power of laughter in her recently published "Perseus: The Triumph of Wit Over Suffering." For Plath, Perseus's method of overcoming "not a basilisk-blink, nor a double whammy, / But all the accumulated last grunts, groans, / Cries and heroic couplets," all human suffering collapsed into the gorgon's grimace, is to be "Armed with feathers to tickle as well as fly" until "the cosmic / Laugh

does away with the unstitching, plaguey wounds / Of an eternal sufferer"
and establishes "the celestial balance / Which weighs our madness with
our sanity."[40]

Death remains a persistently troublesome force for our contemporary
comic poets. Religion, however, has diminished to a merely minor annoy-
ance. For Whitman, God was a power to be reckoned with. In order to
set himself up as a god, Whitman first had manfully to reject God or ab-
sorb God into himself. Indeed, Whitman's comic replacement of God
with himself at the end of "Song of Myself" was outrageous and persuasive precisely because it was such an unexpected and humorous action.
Dickinson's banter with God also served very serious and essential purposes. Humor allowed Dickinson to express her skepticism while embracing God as a central and crucial necessity. Even Frost's and Berryman's
attacks on God often seem calculated more to make him show his face
than to dismiss him. For all of these poets, religion figures importantly as
a force to question or reject or embrace, a real force that cannot be
ignored.

The difference between the modern and contemporary poets in their
attitude toward religion rests partially in their initial assumptions. Many
modern poets grew up with traditional beliefs and proceeded to lose,
question, or reaffirm them. Most younger contemporary poets grow up
with the death of God and the loss of religion not as painful conflicts to
face but as givens, facts of life, something one is born with. Thus for
Gregory Corso heaven is "syrupy . . . oppressively sweet" and God is a
"gigantic fly paper."[41] And for Maxine Kumin it is no consolation when
Billy Graham announces that angels are God's secret agents, watching
over us:

> It's no consolation, angels,
> knowing you're around
> helplessly observing like
> some sacred CIA.[42]

The diminishment of God and religion has in some ways resulted in a
diminishment of theme. Religious doubt and questioning and celebration
have been central inspirations for great poetry. When a contemporary
poet turns to God, there is apt to be less urgency about it. Peter Meinke's
sonnet "The Poet, Trying to Surprise God" is a case in point. For Meinke,
God is a kind of prop, a straight man, an impotent comic foil who
provides light comic relief while allowing the poet to elevate himself.
Whereas the conflict between poet and God in earlier comic poetry was

often a real and uncertain one, in this whimsical contemporary version,
God doesn't have a chance:

> The poet, trying to surprise his God
> composed new forms from secret harmonies,
> tore from his fiery vision galaxies
> of unrelated shapes, both even & odd.
> But God just smiled, and gave His know-all nod
> saying, "There's no surprising One who sees
> the acorn, root, and branch of centuries;
> I swallow all things up, like Aaron's rod.
>
> So hold this thought beneath your poet-bonnet:
> no matter how free-seeming flows your sample
> God is by definition the Unsurprised."
> "Then I'll return," the poet sighed, "to sonnets
> of which this is a rather pale example."
>
> "Is that right?" said God. "I hadn't realized. . . ."[43]

The poem isn't really a poem about belief or religion; it is a poem about
the poet's cleverness. God here is an *idea* of omnipotence, a deflated idea,
perhaps more a metaphor for a smug reviewer, a literary critic, or a pretentious reader. In the course of the poem, God claims that he can't be
surprised, and then he is surprised that the poem is a sonnet. God is
merely the fool, the fop, the *alazon* who pretends to be more than he is,
while being undercut by the *eiron* poet who tricks him by playing dumb. I
do not mean to denigrate the poem, which is charming, witty, and surprising, a technical achievement that is both adept and memorable. But the
mere presence of God in a poem can no longer add a spiritual dimension
of power as it could in the past. Indeed, Meinke has no intention of doing
that—he knows how he and his audience regard the deity.

And yet, there remains on the part of our poets the desire to keep the
possibilities of religion open. Thus Richard Hugo claims, "If I can't enter
the church, at least / I can go on peeking" and insists "Just because / I've
no religion don't say heaven can't welcome me back / under the new ma-
jority quota now in effect."[44] Similarly, Howard Nemerov humorously affirms the need for religious celebration:

> When I report at the funerals of friends,
> Which happens nowadays oftener than it did,
> I am astonished each time over again
> At the fucking obsequiousness addressed to God:

O Thou, &c. He's killed this one already,
And is going to do the rest of us
In His own good time, then what in the world
Or out of it's abjection going to get
For either the dead or their smalltime survivors?
Who go to church at ordinary times
To pray to God, who does not go to church.

As for those masses and motets, no matter:
He happens to be tone deaf (or is it stone deaf?
My hearing's not so good either). But once in a way
The music takes me, if it doesn't Him,
The way Bach does the Et In Terra Pax,
Or Mozart does the Tuba Mirum, where
We doomed and damned go on beseeching anyhow.
Does He, when He hears that heavenly stuff, believe?
And at the Lacrimosa does He weep for us?
No end, my friends, to our inventiveness:
God doesn't matter. Adoration does.[45]

In the first stanza Nemerov registers his exasperation with people who
lavish adoration on a God who is, after all, a murderer and who doesn't
attend church. As in the Meinke poem, God is for Nemerov a foil, a joke,
a phantom, an invention, whose real purpose in the poem is to point up
something else. In Meinke's poem, God is there to point up the poet's superiority. In Nemerov's poem, God is there to point up people's need to
invent, create, praise, and adore. Nemerov would probably agree with
Galway Kinnell's assessment of his own belief:

I say "God"; I believe,
rather, in a music of grace
that we hear, sometimes, playing to us
from the other side of happiness.[46]

Thus when our religious poems do succeed, they are often couched as
humorous praise of *this* world as the only possible paradise. Kinnell, for
example, embodies his religious praise in the figure of a huge sow and her
suckling piglets, and Maxine Kumin achieves a sacramental level in "The
Excrement Poem" "as God disposes" from "the least cast of worm to
what must have been / in the case of the brontosaur, say, spoor / of consid-
erable heft, something awesome." Kumin concludes her Whitmanesque
celebration of cosmic cycle with the punning affirmation, "We go on."[47]

God as an abstract concept retained power for Whitman, Dickinson,
Frost, Stevens, and Berryman, whether they chose to reject him or accept

him. God appears in contemporary poetry more often as the comic foil of the Meinke sonnet or the glorious sow or awesome spoor of Kumin and Kinnell. The fact that God is no longer a troublesome concept is itself troublesome to some of our best poets. In order to invoke him at all, they often invoke him comically.

The fairy tale "The Magic Trunk," with which I began this chapter, has a rather sobering ending. The merchant's son, enthralled with the powers of the trunk, decides to play his godlike role to the hilt. Carrying fireworks with him, he flies across the sky in a blaze of splendor, filling the king and queen and townspeople with awe. Unfortunately, the trunk itself catches fire and burns to ashes. His deception exposed, the poor youth is forced to flee without honor, hope, or the king's daughter.

As if in an effort to avoid the fate of the merchant's son, our recent poets have eschewed the flamboyant, boastful backwoods voice of American humor and the breathless antics of the minstrel for the self-deprecation of the Yankee or some combination of the three voices. Poetry itself, which was looked on as a kind of substitute for religion by some modernist poets, has lost much of the prestige and aura that once surrounded it. Although there are probably more poems being written today than ever before, there are probably also fewer people reading them. Pogo's joke about the bear who wrote prolifically but could not read has proved prophetic. Faced with a culture that seems at best hostile and at worst indifferent to their efforts, our poets have turned to comedy as a restorative, not merely of outdated romantic notions, but of poetry itself. Avoiding the fireworks of a Stevens, a Whitman, or a Berryman, adopting the wry smile of a Dickinson or Frost, retaining a comic perspective on themselves and their art, our poets have been able to celebrate themselves and the potentially magical healing power of poetry. Paul Zimmer, one of our best serious comic poets, puts it well in a poem that is both instructive and funny:

> When asked, I used to say,
> "I want to be a doctor."
> Which is the same thing
> As a child saying,
> "I want to be a priest,"
> Or
> "I want to be a magician,"
> Which is the laying on
> Of hands, the vibrations,
> The rabbit in the hat,
> Or the body in the cup,

The curing of the sick
And the raising of the dead.

"Fix and fix, you're all better,"
I would say
To the neighborhood wounded
As we fought the world war
Through the vacant lots of Ohio.
"Fix and fix, you're all better,"
And they would rise
To fight again.
                    But then
I saw my aunt die slowly of cancer
And a man struck down by a car.
All along I had really
Wanted to be a poet,
Which is, you see, almost
The same thing as saying,
"I want to be a doctor,"
"I want to be a priest,"
Or
"I want to be a magician."
All along, without realizing it,
I had wanted to be a poet.

Fix and fix, you're all better.[48]

Notes

Chapter I:
Introduction

1. Randall Jarrell, "Some Lines from Whitman," in *Critics on Whitman*, ed. Richard Rupp (Coral Gables, Fla.: University of Miami Press, 1972), p. 52.

2. Walter Blair and Hamlin Hill, *America's Humor* (New York: Oxford University Press, 1978).

3. Louis D. Rubin, *The Comic Imagination in American Literature* (New Brunswick, N.J.: Rutgers University Press, 1973), p. xi.

4. Daniel Fuchs, *The Comic Spirit of Wallace Stevens* (Durham, N.C.: Duke University Press, 1963); Richard Chase, *Walt Whitman Reconsidered* (New York: William Sloane Associates, 1955); Constance Rourke, *American Humor* (New York: Harcourt, Brace, 1931). Some of the best work on humor in poetry can be found in the few essays on the subject: R. W. B. Lewis, "The Aspiring Clown," in *Learners and Discerners*, ed. Robert Scholes (Charlottesville: University Press of Virginia, 1964), pp. 61–108; John Vernon, "Fresh Air: Humor in Contemporary Poetry," in *Comic Relief*, ed. Sarah Blacher Cohen (Urbana: University of Illinois Press, 1978), pp. 304–23; Fred Miller Robinson, "Wallace Stevens: The Poet as Comedian," in *The Comedy of Language* (Amherst: University of Massachusetts Press, 1980), pp. 89–125; and M. L. Rosenthal, "Volatile Matter: Humor in Our Poetry," *Massachusetts Review* 22, no. 4 (Winter 1981), pp. 807–17.

5. Ogden Nash, *Verses from 1929 On* (Boston: Little, Brown and Co., 1959), p. 455.

6. *The Complete Poems of Emily Dickinson*, ed. Thomas H. Johnson (Boston: Little, Brown and Co., 1960), p. 474; subsequent references, identified by Johnson's numbers, are in the text.

7. Robert Frost, *In the Clearing* (New York: Holt, Rinehart and Winston, 1963), p. 39; subsequent references to this volume are endnoted. References to all other Frost poems are from *Complete Poems of Robert Frost* (New York: Holt, Rinehart and Winston, 1964) and are in the text.

8. Reed Whittemore, "The Two Rooms: Humor in Modern American Verse," *Wisconsin Studies in Contemporary Literature* 5, no. 3 (Autumn 1964), pp. 185–86.

9. W. H. Auden, "Notes on the Comic," in *The Dyer's Hand* (New York: Random House, 1962), p. 366.

10. Edward Field, Introduction to *A Geography of Poets* (New York: Bantam Books, 1979), p. xlii.

11. Michael Wigglesworth, *The Day of Doom*, ed. Kenneth B. Murdock (New York: The Spiral Press, 1929), p. 3; reprint of the 1662 edition.

12. Ibid., p. 54.

13. *The Complete Works of Lewis Carroll* (New York: Random House, n.d.), pp. 187–88.

14. *The Poems of H. C. Bunner* (New York: Charles Scribner's Sons, 1899), pp. 36–37.

15. T. S. Eliot, *Collected Poems* (New York: Harcourt, Brace & World, 1963), p. 85.

16. William Michael Rossetti, ed., *Humorous Poems* (New York: AMS Press, 1970), p. 471; reprint of 1879 London edition.

17. Jesse Bier, *The Rise and Fall of American Humor* (New York: Holt, Rinehart and Winston, 1968), p. 385.

18. Chase, *Walt Whitman Reconsidered.* Willard Thorp's review is in *Eight American Authors: A Review of Research and Criticism*, ed. Floyd Stovall (New York: Modern Language Association, 1956), p. 301.

19. Walt Whitman, *Leaves of Grass*, ed. Harold Blodgett and Sculley Bradley (New York: W. W. Norton and Co., 1965), sec. 24, p. 54; sec. 20, p. 47; subsequent references are in the text. "Song of Myself" is cited by section and page number.

20. George Meredith, "An Essay on Comedy," in *Comedy*, ed. Wylie Sypher (Garden City, N.Y.: Doubleday & Co., 1956), p. 4.

21. William Bysshe Stein, "Emily Dickinson's Parodic Masks," *The University Review* 36, no. 1 (Autumn 1969), pp. 54–55.

22. Dorothy Parker, Introduction to *The Fireside Book of Humorous Poetry* (New York: Simon and Schuster, 1959), p. xiii.

23. Quoted in Roger Asselineau, "Walt Whitman's Humor," *American Transcendental Quarterly* 22 (1974): 87.

24. Robert Frost, "Introduction to *King Jasper*," in *Robert Frost on Writing*, ed.

Elaine Barry (New Brunswick, N.J.: Rutgers University Press, 1973), p. 123.

25. Quoted in Chase, *Walt Whitman Reconsidered*, p. 72.

26. Quoted in Cohen, *Comic Relief*, p. 220.

27. Dave Smith, "An Interview with James Wright: The Pure Clear Word," *American Poetry Review* 9, no. 3 (May/June 1970), p. 27.

28. Howard Nemerov, *Reflexions on Poetry and Poetics* (New Brunswick, N.J.: Rutgers University Press, 1972), p. 4.

29. Ibid., p. 13.

30. Henri Bergson's "Laughter" is conveniently reprinted in Sypher, *Comedy*, as is Meredith's "An Essay upon Comedy." For Frye and Freud on comedy, see Northrop Frye, *Anatomy of Criticism* (Princeton, N.J.: Princeton University Press, 1971), and Sigmund Freud, *Jokes and Their Relation to the Unconscious*, trans. James Strachey (New York: W. W. Norton & Co., 1963).

31. Rourke, *American Humor*, p. 233.

32. Blair and Hill, *America's Humor*, pp. 258–60.

33. Rourke, *American Humor*, p. 142.

34. Ibid., p. 56.

35. *The Collected Poems of Wallace Stevens* (New York: Alfred A. Knopf, 1967), p. 65; subsequent references are in the text. Citations from *Opus Posthumous*, ed. Samuel French Morse (New York: Alfred A. Knopf, 1957), are designated by the abbreviation *OP*.

36. Blair and Hill, *America's Humor*, p. 258.

37. William Harmon, ed., *Oxford Book of American Light Verse* (New York: Oxford University Press, 1979), pp. 20–24.

38. Ibid., pp. 24–25.

39. John Berryman, *The Dream Songs* (New York: Farrar, Straus and Giroux, 1969), p. 28; subsequent references, identified by Berryman's numbers, are in the text.

40. Harmon, *Oxford Book of American Light Verse*, pp. 74–75.

41. Rourke, *American Humor*, pp. 209–10.

42. Ibid., p. 88.

43. John Hall Wheelock, *What Is Poetry?* (New York: Charles Scribner's Sons, 1963), p. 20.

44. Quoted in *The Presence of Walt Whitman*, ed. R. W. B. Lewis (New York: Columbia University Press, 1962), pp. 142–43.

45. *Letters of Wallace Stevens*, selected and edited by Holly Stevens (New York: Alfred A. Knopf, 1966), p. 294.

46. Larry Levis, "The Poem You Asked For," in *Wrecking Crew* (Pittsburgh: University of Pittsburgh Press, 1972), p. 3.

47. Auden, *The Dyer's Hand*, p. 380.

48. Frost, *In the Clearing*, p. 82.

49. E. E. Cummings, *Complete Poems* (New York: Harcourt, Brace, Jovanovich, 1972), p. 508.

50. Quoted in Bier, *Rise and Fall*, p. 18.

51. B. H. Fussell, "A Pratfall Can Be a Beautiful Thing," in *Comedy: New Perspectives*, ed. Maurice Charney (New York: New York Literary Forum, 1978), pp. 248–50.

52. Quoted in John Clendenning, "Cummings, Comedy, and Criticism," *Colorado Quarterly* 12, no. 1 (Summer 1963), p. 46.

53. Robinson, *The Comedy of Language*, p. 8.

54. Quoted in Larry Wilde, *The Great Comedians Talk About Comedy* (New York: The Citadel Press, 1968), p. 28.

55. Ibid., p. 24.

56. Ibid., p. 31.

57. Bergson, "Laughter," p. 87; italics mine.

58. Rubin, *The Comic Imagination*, p. 386.

59. Cummings, *Complete Poems*, p. 70.

60. Quoted in Walter Kerr, *Tragedy and Comedy* (New York: Simon and Schuster, 1967), p. 16.

61. Bergson, "Laughter," p. 187.

62. Quoted in Wilde, *The Great Comedians*, p. 16.

63. Meredith, "An Essay on Comedy," p. 42.

64. Hart Crane, "Chaplinesque," in *The Norton Anthology of Modern Poetry*, ed. Richard Ellmann (New York: W. W. Norton & Co., 1973), pp. 382–83.

65. Quoted in Max Eastman, *Enjoyment of Laughter* (New York: Simon and Schuster, 1936), p. 342.

66. Quoted in Hamlin Hill, "Black Humor: Its Cause and Cure," *Colorado Quarterly* 17, no. 1 (Summer 1968), p. 57.

67. Stephen Dunn, "At Every Gas Station There Are Mechanics," in *Looking for Holes in the Ceiling* (Amherst: University of Massachusetts Press, 1974), p. 14.

68. Dorothy Van Ghent, *The English Novel: Form and Function* (New York: Harper and Row, 1953), pp. 23–24.

69. Quoted in L. S. Dembo and Cyrena S. Pondram, eds., *The Contemporary Writer: Interviews with Sixteen Novelists and Poets*

(Madison: University of Wisconsin Press, 1972), p. 21.

70. M. L. Rosenthal, ed., *The William Carlos Williams Reader* (New York: New Directions, 1966), p. 24.

71. David Wagoner, "An Interview with David Wagoner," *Crazy Horse*, no. 12 (Autumn 1972), pp. 40–41.

72. John Berryman, *Love and Fame* (New York: Farrar, Straus and Giroux, 1970), pp. 85–86.

73. Harmon, *Oxford Book of American Light Verse*, p. xv.

74. Bergson, "Laughter," p. 187.

75. Meredith, "An Essay on Comedy," p. 42.

76. Ibid.

**Chapter II:
Walt Whitman**

1. Quoted in Van Wyck Brooks, *The Flowering of New England* (E. P. Dutton & Co., 1936), p. 520.

2. John Burroughs, *Walt Whitman: A Study in Rewritings* (Boston: Houghton Mifflin Co., 1904), 10:169.

3. William Michael Rossetti, ed., *Humorous Poems*, p. 471.

4. Jesse Bier, *The Rise and Fall of American Humor*, pp. 385, 387.

5. D. H. Lawrence, *Studies in Classic American Literature* (New York: Viking, 1966), pp. 164–65.

6. Quoted in Richard Rupp, ed., *Critics on Whitman*, p. 14.

7. Randall Jarrell, "Some Lines from Whitman," p. 48.

8. Constance Rourke, *American Humor*, p. 142.

9. Richard Chase, *Walt Whitman Reconsidered*, p. 58.

10. Quoted in Horace Traubel, *With Walt Whitman in Camden* (Carbondale, Ill.: Southern Illinois University Press, 1964), 5:456.

11. Walt Whitman, *An 1855–56 Notebook Toward the 2nd Edition of "Leaves of Grass,"* ed. Harold W. Blodgett (Carbondale, Ill.: Southern Illinois University Press, 1959), p. 8.

12. Walt Whitman, *The Gathering of Forces*, ed. Cleveland Rogers and John Black (New York: G. P. Putnam's Sons, 1920), 2:55–56.

13. Ibid., p. 231.

14. George Meredith, "An Essay on Comedy," p. 34.

15. Quoted in Harold Jaffe, "Bucke's Walt Whitman: A Collaboration," *Walt Whitman Review* 15, no. 3 (September 1969), p. 192.

16. Meredith, "An Essay on Comedy," pp. 51, 14.

17. Ibid., p. 36.

18. Ibid., p. 14.

19. Ibid., p. 52.

20. Ibid., p. 7.

21. Ibid., p. 48.

22. Quoted in Milton Hindus, ed., *Walt Whitman: The Critical Heritage* (London: Routledge & Kegan Paul, 1971), p. 33.

23. Quoted in Rupp, *Critics on Whitman*, p. 15.

24. Rossetti, *Humorous Poems*, p. 471.

25. Walt Whitman, *The Uncollected Poetry and Prose*, ed. Emory Holloway (New York: Doubleday & Co., 1921), 1:206.

26. Quoted in Hindus, *Walt Whitman: The Critical Heritage*, p. 34.

27. James Thurber, *Fables for Our Time* (Garden City, N.Y.: Blue Ribbon Books, 1943), p. 10.

28. Jorge Luis Borges, Foreword to *Homage to Walt Whitman*, ed. Didier Tisdel Jaén (University, Ala.: University of Alabama Press, 1969), pp. xiv–xv.

29. Walt Whitman, *Leaves of Grass and Selected Prose* (New York: Holt, Rinehart and Winston, 1967), pp. 483–84.

30. Edwin Haviland Miller, ed., *Walt Whitman: "The Correspondence II"* (New York: New York University Press, 1961), p. 305.

31. Quoted in Walter Blair and Hamlin Hill, *America's Humor*, p. 259.

32. Ralph Waldo Emerson, "The Comic," in *The Portable Emerson*, ed. Mark Van Doren (New York: Viking, 1946), p. 205.

33. Henri Bergson, "Laughter," p. 93.

34. Quoted in R. W. B. Lewis, ed., *The Presence of Walt Whitman*, pp. 142–43.

35. Henri Bergson, "Laughter," p. 71.

36. Quoted in Rourke, *American Humor*, p. 168.

37. D. H. Lawrence, *Studies in Classic American Literature*, p. 166.

38. Dale Underwood, *Etherege and the Seventeenth Century Comedy of Manners* (New Haven: Yale University Press, 1957), pp. 107–8.

39. James E. Miller, *A Critical Guide to "Leaves of Grass"* (Chicago: University of Chicago Press, 1957), pp. 6–35.

40. James E. Miller, *The American Quest for a Supreme Fiction* (Chicago: University of Chicago Press, 1979), pp. 30–49.

41. John M. Nagle, "Towards a Theory of Structure in Song of Myself," in Rupp, *Critics on Whitman*, pp. 30–49.

42. John Berryman, *The Freedom of the Poet* (New York: Farrar, Straus and Giroux, 1976), p. 285.

43. Northrop Frye, *Anatomy of Criticism*, p. 179.

44. Berryman, *The Freedom of the Poet*, p. 240.

45. J. Albert Robbins, "America and the Poet: Whitman, Hart Crane, and Frost," in *The Merrill Studies in "Leaves of Grass,"* ed. Gay Wilson Allen, p. 39.

46. Charles Alexander, *The Problem of Humor in Walt Whitman*, Ph.D. diss., University of Massachusetts, 1972, p. 221.

47. Wylie Sypher, "The Meanings of Comedy," in his *Comedy*, p. 231.

48. Whitman, *Leaves of Grass and Selected Prose*, p. 485.

49. Frye, *Anatomy of Criticism*, p. 43.

Chapter III:
Emily Dickinson

1. Constance Rourke, *American Humor*, pp. 209–10.

2. Ibid., p. 212.

3. Richard Chase, *Emily Dickinson* (New York: William Sloane Assoc., 1951), pp. 134, 228.

4. Charles R. Anderson, *Emily Dickinson's Poetry: Stairway of Surprise* (New York: Holt, Rinehart and Winston, 1960), pp. 21, 5.

5. Yvor Winters, "Emily Dickinson and the Limits of Judgment," in *The Recognition of Emily Dickinson*, ed. Caesar Blake (Ann Arbor: University of Michigan Press, 1964), p. 190.

6. Inder Nath Kher, *The Landscape of Absence: Emily Dickinson's Poetry* (New Haven: Yale University Press, 1974), pp. 14, 35.

7. Archibald MacLeish, "The Private World," in Blake, *The Recognition of Emily Dickinson*, p. 310.

8. Karl Keller, *The Only Kangaroo Among the Beauty: Emily Dickinson and America* (Baltimore: John Hopkins University Press, 1979), p. 326.

9. Quoted in Paul W. Anderson, "The Metaphysical Mirth of Emily Dickinson," *Georgia Review* 20, no. 1 (Spring 1966), p. 72.

10. Theodore LeSieg (Theodor Geisel),

Would You Rather Be a Bullfrog? (New York: Random House, 1975), pp. 3–5.

11. Quoted in Keller, *The Only Kangaroo Among the Beauty*, p. 314.

12. Thomas H. Johnson, ed., *The Letters of Emily Dickinson* (Cambridge: Harvard University Press, 1958), 3:703.

13. Ralph Waldo Emerson, "The Comic," p. 209.

14. Anderson, *Emily Dickinson's Poetry*, p. 29.

15. Mark Twain, *The Adventures of Huckleberry Finn* (New York: New American Library, 1959), p. 20.

16. Anderson, *Emily Dickinson's Poetry*, p. 115.

17. Henri Bergson, "Laughter," p. 140.

18. Keller, *The Only Kangaroo Among the Beauty*, pp. 131–35.

Chapter IV:
Robert Frost

1. Lawrance Thompson, ed., *Selected Letters of Robert Frost* (New York: Holt, Rinehart and Winston, 1964), pp. 299–300.

2. Louis Untermeyer, ed., *The Letters of Robert Frost to Louis Untermeyer* (New York: Holt, Rinehart and Winston, 1963), p. 47.

3. Robert Frost, "Education by Poetry," in *Robert Frost: Poetry and Prose*, ed. Edward Connery Lathem (New York: Holt, Rinehart and Winston, 1972), p. 334.

4. Quoted in Edward Connery Lathem, ed., *Interviews with Robert Frost* (New York: Holt, Rinehart and Winston, 1966), p. 112.

5. Dr. Seuss (Theodor Geisel), *The Lorax* (New York: Random House, 1971), p. 35.

6. Karl Keller, *The Only Kangaroo Among the Beauty*, p. 314.

7. Robert Frost, *In the Clearing*, p. 70.

8. Robert Frost, "The Constant Symbol," in *Robert Frost on Writing*, ed. Elaine Barry, p. 123.

9. Robert Frost, "Introduction to *King Jasper*," in Barry, *Robert Frost on Writing*, p. 123.

10. Radcliffe Squires, *The Major Themes of Robert Frost* (Ann Arbor: University of Michigan Press, 1963), p. 7.

11. Quoted in Donald J. Greiner, "The Use of Irony in Robert Frost," *South Atlantic Bulletin* 38, no. 2 (May 1973), p. 57.

12. Squires, *The Major Themes*, p. 55.

13. Lionel Trilling, "A Speech on Robert Frost: A Cultural Episode," *Partisan Review* 26, no. 3 (Summer 1959), p. 451.

14. Frost, *In the Clearing*, p. 15.

Chapter V:
Wallace Stevens

1. Holly Stevens, ed., *Letters of Wallace Stevens* (New York: Alfred A. Knopf, 1966), p. 294.

2. Harriet Monroe, *Poets and Their Art* (New York: Macmillan, 1926), p. 42.

3. Daniel Fuchs, *The Comic Spirit of Wallace Stevens*; Robert Pack, *Wallace Stevens* (New Brunswick: Rutgers University Press, 1958); Samuel French Morse, *Wallace Stevens: Poetry as Life* (New York: Pegasus, 1970); Fred Miller Robinson, *The Comedy of Language*.

4. Abbie F. Willard, *Wallace Stevens: The Poet and His Critics* (Chicago: American Library Association, 1978), p. 218. Willard attacks both Robert Pack and Daniel Fuchs. While her criticism of Pack is reasonable, her dismissal of Fuchs is extreme.

5. Theodore Roethke, *The Collected Poems of Theodore Roethke* (Garden City, N.Y.: Doubleday & Co., 1975), p. 258.

6. R. W. B. Lewis, "The Aspiring Clown," p. 94.

7. Morse, *Wallace Stevens: Poetry as Life*, p. 128.

8. Ibid., p. 125.

9. Wallace Stevens, *Mattino Domenicale ed altre poesie*, edited and translated by Renato Poggioli (Turino: Giulio Einaude, 1953), p. 179.

10. See p. 21 for the complete quotation and citation.

11. Stevens, *Mattino Domenicale ed altre poesie*, p. 177.

12. Ibid.

13. Edward S. LeComte, *A Milton Dictionary* (New York: Philosophical Library, 1961), pp. 79–80.

14. Ben Jonson, *Poetaster*, ed. Herbert F. Mallory (New York: Henry Holt and Co., 1905), pp. 122–23.

15. Bergson, "Laughter," p. 130.

16. Stevens, *Mattino Domenicale ed altre poesie*, p. 16.

17. *Letters of Wallace Stevens*, pp. 351–52.

18. Ibid., p. 294.

19. Enid Wellsford, *The Fool* (London: Faber and Faber, 1935), p. xii.

20. Whitman, *Leaves of Grass*, pp. 91, 96.

21. Wallace Stevens, *The Necessary Angel* (New York: Alfred A. Knopf, 1951), p. 35.

22. Walter Kerr, *Tragedy and Comedy*, p. 73.

23. Stevens, *The Necessary Angel*, p. 31.

24. *Letters of Wallace Stevens*, p. 350.

25. Stevens, *The Necessary Angel*, p. 138.

26. Quoted in Frank Lentriccia, *Robert Frost: Modern Poetics and the Landscape of Self* (Durham: Duke University Press, 1975), p. 153.

Chapter VI:
John Berryman

1. T. S. Eliot, "Tradition and the Individual Talent," in his *The Sacred Wood* (London: Methuen & Co., 1920), p. 52.

2. John Berryman, *The Freedom of the Poet*, p. 233.

3. Peter Stitt, "The Art of Poetry XVI," *Paris Review* 14, no. 53 (Winter 1972), p. 190.

4. Berryman, *The Freedom of the Poet*, p. 230. See also Thomas H. Johnson, ed., *The Letters of Emily Dickinson*, p. 412.

5. Constance Rourke, *American Humor*, p. 83.

6. Robert Lowell, review of *77 Dream Songs*, *New York Times Book Review*, 28 May 1964, p. 3.

7. William J. Martz, "John Berryman," in Denis Donoghue, ed., *Seven American Poets* (Minneapolis: University of Minnesota Press, 1975), p. 171.

8. Quoted in John Haffenden, Introduction to *Henry's Fate* by John Berryman (New York: Farrar, Straus and Giroux, 1977), p. xviii.

9. Diane Ackerman, "Near the Top a Bad Turn Dared," *Parnassus* 7, no. 2 (Spring–Summer 1979), pp. 141–50; Donald Davie, *Trying to Explain* (Ann Arbor: University of Michigan Press, 1979), p. 72.

10. Martz, "John Berryman," p. 171.

11. "An Interview with John Berryman," *Harvard Advocate* 103, no. 1 (Spring 1969), p. 6.

12. Carl Wittke, *Tambo and Bones* (Durham: Duke University Press, 1930). Miller, *American Quest*, p. 248.

13. *Minstrel Gags and End Men's Handbook* (Upper Saddle River, N.J.: Literature House, 1969; reprint of the 1875 edition published by Dick & Fitzgerald).

14. John Berryman, *Stephen Crane* (New York: William Sloane Assoc., 1950), pp. 278–80.

15. "An Interview with John Berryman," p. 5.

16. Stitt, "The Art of Poetry XVI," p. 191.

17. Wittke, *Tambo and Bones*, p. 169.

18. Quoted in William Wasserstrom, "Cagey John: Berryman as Medicine Man," *Centenary Review* 12, no. 3 (Summer 1968), p. 341.

19. Richard Kostelanetz, "Conversation with John Berryman," *Massachusetts Review* 11, no. 2 (Spring 1970), p. 346.

20. Stitt, "The Art of Poetry XVI," p. 207.

21. John Haffenden, *The Life of John Berryman* (Boston & London: Routledge & Kegan Paul, 1982), pp. 26–29.

22. Walter Kerr, *Tragedy and Comedy*, p. 328.

23. John Berryman, "One Answer to a Question," *Shenandoah* 17, no. 1 (Autumn 1965), p. 76.

24. John Berryman, *Love and Fame* (New York: Farrar, Straus and Giroux, 1970), p. 10.

25. "An Interview with John Berryman," p. 6.

26. Quoted in Wasserstrom, "Cagey John," p. 346.

27. Berryman, "One Answer to a Question," p. 17.

28. "An Interview with John Berryman," p. 6.

29. Stitt, "The Art of Poetry XVI," p. 201.

30. Berryman, *Love and Fame*, p. 85.

Chapter VII:
Envoi

1. Tasha Tudor, *The Tasha Tudor Book of Fairy Tales* (New York: Platt & Munk, 1969), p. 50.

2. Allen Ginsberg, *Howl* (San Francisco: City Lights Books, 1956), p. 34.

3. Ibid., p. 30.

4. Gregory Corso, *The Happy Birthday of Death* (New York: New Directions, 1960), p. 28.

5. Frank O'Hara, "Chez Jane," in *The Collected Poems of Frank O'Hara*, ed. Donald Allen (New York: Alfred A. Knopf, 1971), p. 102.

6. Kenneth Koch, *The Pleasures of Peace* (New York: Grove Press, 1969), pp. 39–41.

7. John Ashbery, *The Double Dream of Spring* (New York: E. P. Dutton & Co., 1970), pp. 47–48.

8. William Packard, ed., *The Craft of Poetry* (New York: Doubleday & Co., 1974), p. 124.

9. Maxine Kumin, "Hello, Hello Henry," in *The Retrieval System* (New York: Harper & Row, 1978), p. 9.

10. Ted Kooser, *Sure Signs* (Pittsburgh: University of Pittsburgh Press, 1980), p. 71.

11. Richard Hugo, "Letter to Garber from Skye," in *The Right Madness on Skye* (New York: W. W. Norton & Co., 1980), p. 58.

12. Ibid., "The Right Madness on Skye," p. 61; "Duntulm Castle," p. 31; "Kilmuir Cemetery: Stone with Two Skulls and No Name," p. 30; "Graves in Uig," p. 17.

13. David Wagoner, "The Bad Fisherman," in *Sleeping in the Woods* (Bloomington: Indiana University Press, 1974), p. 9.

14. David Wagoner, "The Junior High-school Band Concert," in *In Broken Country* (Boston: Little, Brown, 1979), p. 9.

15. Ibid., "Boy Jesus," pp. 5–6.

16. William Dickey, *The Rainbow Grocery* (Amherst: University of Massachusetts Press, 1978), p. 30.

17. Constance Rourke, *American Humor*, p. 88.

18. Gregory Corso, "After Reading 'In the Clearing,'" in *Long Live Man* (New York: New Directions, 1962), p. 89.

19. Packard, *The Craft of Poetry*, p. 121.

20. David Wagoner, "To a Panhandler Who, for a Quarter, Said 'God Bless You,'" in *In Broken Country*, p. 53.

21. Maxine Kumin, "The Excrement Poem," in *The Retrieval System*, p. 50.

22. Richard Hugo, *Selected Poems* (New York: W. W. Norton & Co., 1979), pp. 71–72.

23. Nancy Willard, *Carpenter of the Sun* (New York: Liveright, 1974), p. 19.

24. Russell Edson, "Portrait of the Writer as a Fat Man: Some Subjective Ideas on the Care and Feeding of Prose Poems," in *A Field Guide to Contemporary Poetry and Poetics*, ed. Stuart Friebert and David Young (New York: Longman, 1980), pp. 297, 301.

25. Russell Edson, "The Feet of the Fat Man" and "Counting Sheep," in *The Intuitive Journey and Other Works* (New York: Harper & Row, 1976), pp. 18, 12.

26. Robert Bly, "Counting Small-Boned Bodies," in *The Light Around the Body* (New York: Harper & Row, 1967), p. 32.

27. David Wagoner, "Report from a Forest Logged by the Weyerhaeuser Company," in *Sleeping in the Woods*, pp. 56–57.

28. Sharon Olds, "Republican Living Rooms," in *Satan Says* (Pittsburgh: University of Pittsburgh Press, 1980), p. 16.

29. Marge Piercy, *To Be of Use* (New York: Doubleday & Co., 1973), p. 3.

30. James Wright, *To a Blossoming Pear Tree* (New York: Farrar, Straus and Giroux, 1977), pp. 9–10.

31. Dave Smith, "An Interview with James Wright: The Pure Clear Word," p. 27.

32. Morton Gurewitch, *Comedy: The Irrational Vision* (Ithaca, N.Y.: Cornell University Press, 1975), p. 9.

33. Ihab Hassan, "Laughter in the Dark," *American Scholar* 33 (Autumn 1964): 636.

34. Richard Hugo, *The Right Madness on Skye*, p. 63.

35. James Wright, *Collected Poems* (Middletown, Conn.: Wesleyan University Press, 1971), p. 141.

36. X. J. Kennedy, *Nude Descending a Staircase* (Garden City, N.Y.: Doubleday & Co., 1961), p. 34.

37. Greg Kuzma, "The Insurance Men," in *Good News* (New York: Viking, 1973), p. 16.

38. Michael Van Walleghan, "More Trouble with the Obvious," in *More Trouble with the Obvious* (Urbana: University of Illinois Press, 1981), p. 37.

39. Michael Heffernan, *The Cry of Oliver Hardy* (Athens: University of Georgia Press, 1979), p. 28.

40. Sylvia Plath, "Perseus: The Triumph of Wit Over Suffering," in *The Collected Poems* (New York: Harper & Row, 1981), pp. 82–84.

41. Gregory Corso, "Transformation and Escape," in *The Happy Birthday of Death*, p. 19.

42. Maxine Kumin, "Address to the Angels," in *The Retrieval System*, p. 9.

43. Peter Meinke, *Trying to Surprise God* (Pittsburgh: University of Pittsburgh Press, 1981), p. 51.

44. Richard Hugo, "St. Clement's: Harris" and "The Right Madness on Skye," in *The Right Madness on Skye*, pp. 56, 62.

45. Howard Nemerov, "Adoration," in *Sentences* (Chicago: University of Chicago Press, 1980), p. 8.

46. Galway Kinnell, "There Are Things I Tell to No One," in *Mortal Acts, Mortal Words* (Boston: Houghton Mifflin Co., 1980), p. 59.

47. Maxine Kumin, "The Excrement Poem," in *The Retrieval System*, p. 50.

48. Paul Zimmer, "What Zimmer Would Be," in *The Zimmer Poems* (Washington, D.C. & San Francisco: Dryad Press, 1976), p. 14.

Index

Credits

233

Koch, reprinted by permission of Grove Press, Inc., and Kenneth Koch.

Lines from "At the Bait Stand" from *Sure Signs: New and Selected Poems* by Ted Kooser, ©1980 by Ted Kooser, reprinted by permission of the University of Pittsburgh Press.

Lines from "Hello, Hello Henry" and "Address to the Angels" from *Our Ground Time Here Will Be Brief* by Maxine Kumin, copyright ©1969, 1978 by Maxine Kumin, reprinted by permission of Viking Penguin Inc.

Lines from "The Insurance Men" from *Good News* by Greg Kuzma, copyright ©1973 by Greg Kuzma, reprinted by permission of Viking Press.

Lines from *Would You Rather Be a Bullfrog?* by Theodore LeSieg, copyright ©1975 by Theodore LeSieg and A.S. Geisel, reprinted by permission of Random House, Inc.

Lines from "The Poem You Asked For" by Larry Levis, copyright ©1972 by University of Pittsburgh Press, reprinted by permission of the University of Pittsburgh Press.

Lines from "Trying to Surprise God" by Peter Meinke. Reprinted with permission from the August 1979 issue of *Yankee* Magazine, published by Yankee Publishing Incorporated, Dublin, NH 03444, copyright 1979.

Lines from "The Chipmunk" from *Verses From 1929 On* by Ogden Nash, copyright 1952 by Ogden Nash. First appeared in the *Saturday Evening Post*, reprinted by permission of Little, Brown and Company.

Lines from "Adoration" from *Sentences* by Howard Nemerov, copyright ©1980 by Howard Nemerov, reprinted by permission of Howard Nemerov and the University of Chicago Press.

Lines from "Chez Jane" from *The Collected Poems of Frank O'Hara*, edited by Donald Allen, copyright ©1950, 1951, 1952, 1954, 1955, 1956, 1958, 1959, 1960, 1961, 1962, 1964, 1965, 1966, 1967, 1968, 1969, 1970, 1971 by Maureen Granville-Smith, reprinted by permission of Alfred A. Knopf, Inc.

Lines from "Perseus: The Triumph of Wit over Suffering" from *The Collected Poems of Sylvia Plath*, edited by Ted Hughes, copyright ©1958 by the Estate of Sylvia Plath, reprinted by permission of Harper & Row, Publishers, Inc.

Lines from *The Collected Poems of Wallace Stevens*, copyright ©1923, 1931, 1935, 1936, 1937, 1942, 1943, 1944, 1945, 1946, 1947, 1948, 1949, 1950, 1951, 1952, 1954 by Wallace Stevens, reprinted by permission of Alfred A. Knopf, Inc.

Lines from *Opus Posthumous* by Wallace Stevens, edited by Samuel French Morse, copyright ©1957 by Elsie Stevens and Holly Stevens, reprinted by permission of Alfred A. Knopf, Inc.

Lines from "More Trouble with the Obvious" from *More Trouble with the Obvious* by Michael Van Walleghan, copyright 1981 by Michael Van Walleghan, reprinted by permission of the University of Illinois Press.

Lines from "To a Panhandler Who, for a Quarter, Said 'God Bless You'" from *In Broken Country* by David Wagoner, copyright ©1979 by David Wagoner. First appeared in *Poetry*, reprinted by permission of Little, Brown and Company in association with the Atlantic Monthly Press.

Lines from "Boy Jesus" by David Wagoner, first published by the *Times Literary Supplement* of 27 August 1976, reprinted by permission of the editor of the *Times Literary Supplement*.

Lines from *Leaves of Grass* by Walt Whitman, edited by Harold W. Blodgett and Sculley Bradley, copyright ©1965 by New York University, reprinted by permission of New York University Press.

Lines from "Carpenter of the Sun" from *Carpenter of the Sun* by Nancy Willard, copyright ©1974 by Nancy Willard, reprinted by permission of W.W. Norton & Co., Inc.

Lines from "Portrait of a Lady" from *Collected Earlier Poems of William Carlos Williams*, copyright 1938 by New Directions Publishing Corporation, reprinted by permission of New Directions Publishing Corporation.